Minding the Soul

D1384592

RELATED BOOKS FROM FORTRESS PRESS

The Caring Church: A Guide for Lay Pastoral Care
Howard W. Stone

Ethics in Ministry: A Guide for the Professional
Walter E. Wiest and Elwyn A. Smith

Faithful Companioning: How Pastoral Counseling Heals
Chris R. Schlauch

Good and Evil: Interpreting a Human Condition
Edward Farley

Healers—Harmed and Harmful
Conrad W. Weiser

Ministry and the American Legal System:
A Guide for Clergy, Lay Workers, and Congregations
Richard B. Couser

Pastoral Care and the Means of Grace
Ralph L. Underwood

Risk Management
Aaron Liberman and Michael J. Woodruff

The Skilled Pastor
Charles W. Taylor

MINDING
THE
SOUL

*Pastoral Counseling
as Remembering*

James B. Ashbrook

FORTRESS PRESS   MINNEAPOLIS

MINDING THE SOUL
Pastoral Counseling as Remembering

This publication is designed to provide accurate and authoritative information in regard to the subject matter covered. It is sold with the understanding that the publisher is not engaged in rendering legal, accounting, or other professional services. If legal advice or other expert assistance is required, the services of a competent professional person should be sought. From a Declaration of Principles jointly adopted by a Committee of the American Bar Association and a Committee of Publishers.

Scripture quotations unless otherwise noted are from the New Revised Standard Version Bible, copyright © 1989 by the Division of Christian Education of the National Council of the Churches of Christ in the United States.

Interior design: David Meyer
Cover design: Brad Norr
Cover art: *Ripple*, © 1995 M.C. Escher, Gordon Art, Baarn, Holland. All rights reserved.

Library of Congress Cataloging-in-Publication Data
Ashbrook, James B.
   Minding the soul : pastoral counseling as remembering / James B.
  Ashbrook.
      p.   cm.
   Includes bibliographical references and index.
   ISBN 0-8006-2673-7 (alk. paper)
   1. Pastoral counseling. 2. Pastoral counseling--Case studies
   3. Pastoral psychology. 4. Psychology, Religious. I. Title.
   BV4012.2.A83   1995
   253.5--dc20

The paper used in this publication meets the minimum requirements of American National Standard for Information Sciences—Permanence of Paper for Printed Library Materials, ANSI Z329.48-1984.

Manufactured in the U.S.A.   AF 1-2673
0 0   9 9   9 8   9 7   9 6   1   2   3   4   5   6   7   8   9   1 0

CONTENTS

PART TWO
Engaging the Soul: Focusing on the Task

PART THREE
Making Sense of Soul: Beginning with Oneself

FIGURES

Preface

■　■　■　■　■

The specialized ministry of pastoral counseling is part of a long and varied tradition. It stretches back three millennia in the care God calls forth in response to suffering and oppression. It moved from the confessional of the Roman church to the pastoral conversation of the Reformed churches. It shifted from a focus on personal salvation in the nineteenth century to concern with self-realization in the late twentieth century.

In the early 1890s Sigmund Freud and Joseph Breuer pioneered the technique that came to be known as "the talking cure." By sharing their inner experience with the physician analyst, patients improved. Under Anton Boisen and the early pioneers of clinical pastoral education (CPE) people in stress were studied as "living human documents." What ministered to them was attention to their "living human experience." CPE refined the relational aspects of ministerial practice, emphasizing the personhood of the pastor/chaplain and its impact on professional contacts. Carl Rogers' client-centered therapy became a widely applicable way of liberating people's organismic valuing process.

With the advent of psychotropic or psychoactive drugs in the mid-1950s psychiatry moved progressively from a dynamic orientation to a remedicalization of its contribution to psychic pain. At the same time pastoral counseling began to emerge as a specialty. In 1954, for instance, I was the first pastoral counselor intern at the American Foundation of Religion and Psychiatry in New York City, under the directorship of Frederick C. Kuether. This school is now known as the Blanton-Peale Graduate Program of the Institutes of Religion and Health. Despite the prominence of biological psychiatry and the positivism of behavioristic psychology, the relationship between the one seeking help and the one giving help has taken on increasing importance. Further, the meaning or impact of distress on the person has created a larger role for hermeneutics in the healing process. A persuasive relationship of care, according to psychiatrist Jerome Frank (1973), is basic in all healing.

Thus, as we approach the end of the twentieth century, pastoral counseling as a specialized form of ministry is heir to quite diverse traditions—religious, medical, psychological, humanistic. What is its place within the generic role of religious responsibility? How does it fit among the different and often competing disciplines in the marketplace of concerns with mental illness and mental health? What does it contribute to human beings becoming the human beings that we are?

In addition, the pervasive power of oppressive systems undermines, if not destroys, every approach to individual persons. People suffer as much, if not more, because of the violence of sexism, racism, homophobia, and ethnocentrism than because of wounded narcissism. The specter of global agony and ecological disaster makes attention to the counseling process almost absurd in its limitation.

Yet people continue to turn to ministers, rabbis, and priests in times of stress. They continue to seek out physicians and therapists in periods of panic. Their needs for supportive care, reflective exploration, and corrective emotional experience multiply. No system functions without individuals as part of that system; and no individual lives without functioning within systemic structures. The task of the pastoral counselor is to mediate between the "principalities and powers" of systemic injustice and the relational power of personal experience.

This book is an effort to understand the contribution of pastoral counseling as a specialized form of the ministry of the church. I place it in the cosmoscopic setting of minding the soul, which is a task built into the structure of every human being. I explore pastoral counseling in the macroscopic setting of human relationships. Its features operate in all that we are and do. And I examine it in the microscopic setting of the therapeutic process. What brings people for help and what helps people in that hope?

I urge the reader to be aware of my approach in the chapters that follow. I hold together religious conviction and scientific commitment. Neither is subsumed, for each illumines the other. The counseling task can be analyzed with the various lenses of theology, psychology, and the neurosciences, the primary disciplines upon which I draw. These perspectives highlight various aspects of this personal enterprise, but I resist efforts to isolate the disciplines. For me they are woven together in the seamless robe of reality itself. Thus, my style can be likened to the result of simmering the meat of science with the vegetables of psychology and the seasoning of theology. Pastoral counseling contributes to the nourishment of the human enterprise.

Pastoral counseling is one way people make life meaningful. It is not better than other forms, nor is it more limited than other forms. It simply is a calling in which some of us find ourselves investing our lives. It is a task, however, in which we want to be worthy practitioners. To that end we share what we learn. This book is my contribution to that sharing.

Acknowledgments

■ ■ ■ ■ ■

This book gathers up more than forty years of professional learning. I am the recipient of the trust and pain of parishioners, students, clients, colleagues, friends, and family. Without them I would have little to share. Because of them I have much to share.

Professional colleagues have influenced me in more ways than I can identify: John E. Hinkle Jr., Lallene Rector, Edward Wimberly, and Emma Justes in recent years; Forrest L. Vance, J. C. Wynn, Maxine (Walaskay) Glaz, and Robert Niedeffer in earlier years. Psychiatrist Richard Johnson and psychoanalyst Sidney Rubin served as mentors over the decades. John Karl and the staff of the Pastoral Counseling Center of Rochester, New York, were pivotal in my learning what a pastoral psychotherapist might be. Rollo May, Frederick Perls, and William Glasser have influenced me far beyond the limited contact we had. Participation in the American Association of Pastoral Counselors has formed my vision and honed my skills.

The focus on minding the soul emerged from an invitation to give the first memorial lecture (1989) for Leroy G. Kerney, who, for more than a quarter of a century, had guided the development of the Department of Spiritual Ministry in the Warren Grant Magnuson Clinical Center of the National Institute of Health in Bethesda, Maryland. Much of chapters 12 and 13 are taken from that lecture in revised form as it appeared in *The Journal of Pastoral Care*, Summer 1991, and in *Zygon: Journal of Religion and Science*, March 1992.

I owe the specific impetus for this book to editor Harold Twiss. Publisher David Meyer and editor John Eagleson nurtured it into being. Timothy G. Staveteig persisted in my restructuring the work for publication with Fortress Press, while J. Michael West and Lois Torvik added finishing touches. My association with the faculty and administration of Garrett-Evangelical Theological

School has made this venture possible, including sabbatical leaves in the fall of 1989 and 1991 and a reduced teaching load in the spring of 1990. Joan Svenningsen, administrative assistant of the Department of Pastoral Psychology and Counseling, continually encouraged me by transforming the scattered pieces of my work into meaningful text and insisting that I had something worth sharing.

Lallene Rector, J. C. Wynn, and Doralee Grindler Katonah read an earlier draft. Wolfgang Roth and Susan Ashbrook Harvey critiqued parts of the manuscript. Bonnie Niswander made a comprehensive and detailed critique of the manuscript. Barbara Stinchcombe helped as an editorial consultant for years in making my writing more understandable.

My marriage to Patricia Cober Ashbrook has given me life and shaped my understanding of life. With her we have raised four children—Peter, Susan, Martha, and Karen—and now enjoy adult relationships with them and their families. We have learned to share the joy of being together and to relish the satisfaction of being ourselves. Without Pat I would be a less real person and a less capable professional.

—Evanston, Illinois

Introduction

■ ■ ■ ■ ■

Pastoral care provides a way of remembering and attending to what is meaningful in life. That includes remembering and attending to meaningful aspects of ourselves. And what is meaningful in ourselves includes remembering and attending to what is meaningful in God.

The desire to help people in pain awakens many people to a pastoral care ministry and directs some into the more specialized ministry of pastoral counseling. Pastoral counseling brackets the pain of society in order to engage the pain of individuals. Counseling, a personalized way of helping people in pain, includes four features: (1) the resources of a person (2) who represents people of faith and (3) who has knowledge of individuals and (4) skills to enable them to make the most of who they are.

Traditionally pastoral counseling—and its more generic form of pastoral care—was called "the care of souls." I propose calling it "minding the soul." Pastoral counseling enables people to remember who they are. The word *minding*, as a transitive verb, conveys tending, taking care of, watching over, being careful about, feeling concern for. The word *soul* gathers up that task of remembering by directing attention to the core of our lives. In minding the soul we cultivate that which is genuinely human in ourselves and in each other. We connect with pain, and in so doing we come alive. When people remember and care about who they are, they once again move toward God.

This book shares a unique vision of the potential for this specialized form of care. It combines four sources of understanding: intuitions of faith, knowledge of the working brain, knowledge of human development and "the evolving self," as cognitive psychologist Robert Kegan (1982) calls it, and an understanding of the psychotherapeutic process. This convergence makes remembering who one is a sensible activity. To be sensible, however, does not eliminate its awesome quality. In minding the soul, the pastoral counselor enables people to come to themselves and find their way home. By *home*, I mean our origin and destiny in God.

I am writing for people who are learning and growing in the specialized ministry of pastoral counseling. Such people may have been helped in their own pain by the caring presence of a nonprofessional or, more likely, by a skilled specialist. Having been helped, they want to help others. They seek a competence that moves beyond a general acquaintance with caregiving to specialized competence in pastoral counseling.

I also have other assumptions about my readers. Both beginning and seasoned practitioners want to know about pastoral counseling from the inside. What is it? How does it come about? What enables us to engage in it? In the anxious presence of another human being, we ask: What are we about when we sit with that person in pain? How can that pain be healed? What do we need to know to meet that person at his or her point of need?

We discover that some attitudes and actions are more helpful than others, especially under stress. We wonder how we can open ourselves to the pain of others in spite of pain in ourselves. As we balance human grandeur and human misery, we seek to know how the powers of life can be reorganized to empower people to be who they are. What enables us to participate with God in the suffering of the world?

Every pastoral counselor brings to the therapeutic task a sense of awe at the mysterious movements of the human heart. Every pastoral counselor risks entering the hurting and hurtful places in the psyches of others by entering the hurting and hurtful places in his or her own psyche. Every pastoral counselor senses the wondrous power of God in human longing and human presence. In short, every pastoral counselor attends to the reality that we are copartners with God in creating meaning.

Cognitive psychologist Jerome Brunner once observed that any subject could be taught with integrity at any level. In pastoral counseling, the specialist and the generalist, the beginner and the practitioner all work with the same material, only at different levels of complexity. Hopefully, with each level of competence, practitioners increase in their knowledge and skill.

Effectiveness, however, does not inevitably follow experience. Some years ago psychotherapist Lawrence Kubie confessed that beginning therapists often do more effective work than seasoned therapists. The difference lies in the freshness with which the therapist encounters the client. Too much experience can lead us to believe that we know what is going on. Thus we can miss the uniqueness of the relationship. Only out of genuine encounter does creative meaning emerge. Wisdom consists in discovering the complex simplicity of pastoral counseling.

The resources of faith, knowledge of the brain and psyche, and expertise in interpersonal dynamics are languages of discourse. Each language minds the soul in a different way. Faith illumines an intuitive discernment of the whole; brain research describes the adaptive processes of evolution; the developing self portrays change and continuity in the psyche; and therapeutic skill identifies the dynamics of cultural and personal interaction. Together, these four languages enhance our understanding of God's ways with us and our ways with each other.

I focus on the interface between ourselves as helpers and those seeking help. This is the level of interpersonal relations. Each move can be viewed as an effort to maintain and enhance self-esteem. Each move integrates a relational dimension of closeness and distance with a power dimension of dominance and submission.

Another perspective includes exploring selfobject relations. These are the internalized meanings others have for us in our security and growth experiences. We use selfobjects to supply what we lack in our own self-organization. Much of intensive psychotherapy consists of exploring these influences in our functioning.

And most especially as pastoral counselors, we engage the intersubjective realities of ourselves and God as the source of life. This activity may be viewed as "beyond transference and countertransference." It expresses the transformative power within us and among us. That includes the spiritual longings and reaches of our psyches in relation to the cosmos.

Actually, the interpersonal, the selfobject, and the intersubjective dimensions are present at every moment of the therapeutic process. However, which one takes prominence depends upon what we are about at any given time. Counseling focuses more on interpersonal and immediate concerns, psychotherapy more on the selfobject and the reconstruction of the self. The intersubjective is the ground of both the immediate and the long-term. It contributes to our maintaining a genuinely human mutuality.

To mind the soul, then, helps people remember who they are. We attend to and are concerned about the core of others and ourselves. To mind the soul reconnects us with vulnerability—the pain of being exposed, abandoned, excluded. To mind the soul recovers vitality—the power of being affirmed, nurtured, being part of what matters. To use the imagery of the creation myth of Genesis (2:7), God breathes into us the breath of life, and we become living souls.

When we remember who we are, we are once again on the road to God. C. S. Lewis insisted that every point is a turning point, a point from which we can move directly to God. No point is so remote that we cannot remember and attend to who we are. That faith pervades all we do. We can find our destiny in God because our origin is in God.

As pastoral counselors we are bearers of God. For better or worse we represent and symbolize the transcendent dimension of human experience. Seward

Hiltner and Lowell Colston (1961) made that point in their classic study of *The Context of Pastoral Counseling*. People define what they are about, initially, by the place they seek help.

What follows suggests how pastoral counseling specializes in minding souls in pain.

Part One takes Isaiah's image of "a great rock in a weary land" (32:1–2) as a way of unfolding the task of pastoral counseling. Implications of that image are then explored by taking account of the struggle between survival and growth patterns. Survival behaviors may be thought of as basic emotional assumptions, while growth behaviors may be thought of as basic theological assumptions. Survival ultimately constricts the soul because of its "rockiness"; growth increasingly liberates the soul because of its "rocklikeness." If every point is capable of being a turning point to God, then every struggle bears the possibility of growth. Danger carries opportunity.

I link that transformation of threat into promise with biochemical processes— a shift from arousal to alertness, from vigilance to vitality, from anxiety to excitement. Technically, it shifts our autonomic nervous system from a runaway fight-flight sympathetic arousal to an adaptive parasympathetic relaxation. Being connected with others replaces being isolated from others. Only by remembering and attending to who we are do we transform being lost into being found. In this way we come to ourselves and find our way home.

The phrases "coming to ourselves" and "finding our way home" reflect a subtle complexity in minding the soul. While they apply to everyone, each phrase has its own origin and emphasis. Their origins and emphases mark explicit differences between male and female.

Feminist theologian Nelle Morton lifted up the second phrase in her 1987 book *The Journey Is Home*. Women have resonated with that sense of finding their way home. Home has meant discovering their own voice, becoming their own person, being at home in the universe as themselves. Home conveys a sense of belonging, caring, nurturing, mothering, mattering.

The phrase "coming to ourselves" is found in the parable of the prodigal son (Luke 15:11–32). The younger son asked for his share of his father's inheritance and took himself "to a distant country," where he squandered all that he had. To survive he took a job feeding pigs. In the midst of that menial chore and in the absence of any one caring about him, we read that "he came to himself" (v. 17). He felt the pain of isolation, the loss of relatedness with home. He ached to reconnect, even if it meant taking a marginal position in the household. Coming to oneself conveys a sense of knowing who one is, where one belongs, with whom one is connected, fathering, mattering.

Finding our way home and coming to ourselves apply to women and men in different ways. Neither phrase is exclusively feminine nor exclusively masculine. Neither reference is restricted to a mother relationship nor a father relationship. Neither metaphor cuts us off from our roots, our relatedness, our self-worth.

For females the focus is more a risking of their own voice. As they learn to speak "in a different voice," to use the compelling imagery of psychologist Carol Gilligan ([1982] 1983), women come to themselves and find their way home. They experience the validity of their own experience, gain confidence in their own intuition, and discover their own power.

For males the focus is more a risking of relatedness. As they learn to be vulnerable, men come to themselves and find their way home. They discover the abyss of their limitations, find the comfort of their intimacies, and experience the power of their connections with others.

This contrast between women's courage to be as themselves and men's courage to be related to others oversimplifies gender and sex differences. Women also want to relate, and men also want their own voice. From the beginning, however, these differences alert the reader to the gender relatedness of pastoral counseling.

We have too easily talked about humanity or human beings as though there were a generic *homo sapiens*. Sex and gender differences are noted at the very heart of creation. In Genesis 1:27 we read, "So God created humankind . . . male and female." Humanity is differentiated sexually. Only in our sexual differentness do we represent the image and likeness of God (Bird 1981; 1987; 1989). No individual man and no individual woman bears the full likeness of God. Implications of this will be explored later.

Now I take the point about differentness a step further. If there is one truth to which we have had to come in the late twentieth century, it is the truth of diversity. This is not a new discovery. The biblical images of the arrogance related to the Tower of Babel (Gen. 11:1–9) and the inclusiveness of Pentecost (Acts 2:5–13) have shaped our consciousness. We live in a pluralistic reality. That pluralism is a pluralism of races and classes, of ages and stages of development, of haves and have-nots. We have given the pain of pluralism names such as sexism, racism, classism, ethnocentrism, nationalism, ageism. For the most part, the naming of oppression has brought the undertow of our diversity to consciousness. The marginalized have reacted and acted to break the chains of privilege.

In minding souls, the pastoral counselor must attend to these principalities and powers (Eph. 6:12) with a hermeneutic of suspicion (Ricoeur 1974a, xvi). We all, in some form or other, are identified patients. We all bear the distortions of social dysfunctions. We all sacrifice our own future to maintain oppressive systems. And this sacrifice is acutely present in those who come to us for pastoral counseling. We must work with the differences—and the distortions—of sex and gender, of age and stage of development, of race and creed, of sameness and otherness.

Beyond these distinctions among people, however, there remains a basic fact. We are separate, unique, individual, idiosyncratic. No one has lived our lives for us, and no one can. We all bear the weight of our own particular existence. We may be similar culturally, yet we are biochemically specific. We live our own psychic autobiography. We have a soul of our own.

Part Two describes how we can engage the souls of those who have forgotten their place in God's world. Literally, they have lost their breath. Spiritually, they have lost the breath of God, the breath that makes them living souls. I identify how we can create a sanctuary, a place where they can catch their breath and regain their soul. I link the idea of people being able to get oxygen back into their blood with the holding environment of psychotherapy. By reminding people to remember their dwelling place in God, we enable them to turn again to life.

In the sanctuary of the office, people allow us into their lives. Together we find ways to connect, to enter into the depths of their experience. There, in the center of their psyches, we engage survival and growth. From such exploration their tales of pain turn into stories of promise. The process spirals between defense and transformation, hopefully, with an increasing shift in the direction of growth.

Part Three uses brain research as a way to make sense of soul. I link what faith has affirmed through the centuries in the concepts of soul and sabbath with the biochemical processes involved in meaningful memory. In attending to these integrative processes we help people remember who they are. By beginning with ourselves we can more fully empathize with others. Our stories of soul-making take us into the process of integrating our life with the lives of others and the ways of God.

What we are learning about the human brain makes more understandable the longings of the human heart. To speak of the heart and its longings is to think experientially. What we know of the heart comes from experience, action, reflection. We know what we know from the inside, all at once, in ever more significant ways. To speak of the brain and its mind is to think empirically. What we know of the brain comes from observation, experiment, research. We know what we know from the outside, little by little, with greater confidence.

The language of the heart is closest to that which is particularly congruent with pastoral counseling. On first impression the language of the brain seems irrelevant to our task. Yet the implicit and moving meanings of the heart can become more explicit and certain with knowledge of the brain. We can think about what we feel is true. We can reflect on what we know is real. We can join our subjectivity with the subjectivity of the other. In short, we can more responsibly mind the soul of those who seek us out.

What does brain research contribute to pastoral counseling? It relates the objective knowledge of neurocognitive processes with the subjective knowledge of experiential awareness. Psychological dynamics bridge that outside information with inside experience.

Whether you are a beginning pastoral counselor or a seasoned pastoral therapist, these foci of the empirical, the experiential, and the psychological are templates of one dynamic reality. Think of these foci as entrances into the home of humanity. Each brings us into the whole of the therapeutic encounter. Each engages the task of minding the soul. Each recalls us to who we are in God, in ourselves, and with those who come to us.

PART ONE

Rock-A the Soul
A Map for
Minding the Soul

Each will be like a hiding place from the wind,
a covert from the tempest,
like streams of water in a dry place,
like the shade of a great rock in a weary land.

Isaiah 32:2

CHAPTER ONE

The Rock That Gives Birth

A METAPHOR FOR MINDING THE SOUL

■ ■ ■ ■ ■

Pastoral counseling always takes place within the wider context of our relatedness with others. None of us is a person *until* we have been called forth by the responsiveness of others. This is true, beginning with parents and other caregivers.

An attending relationship also characterizes the therapeutic process. In fact, psychiatrist David E. Orlinsky and clinical psychologist Kenneth I. Howard believe that because of a positive cohesive bond, "therapy as experience" is more basic than "therapy as activity" or "dramatic interpretation" (cited by Gilbert 1980, 260). They contrast the sharing of experience "viewed internally" by the participants to the way in which interactions are framed or handled objectively.

To speak metaphorically, the bedrock of our lives consists of the emotional foundation others provide for us—"selfobject experiences," to use the technical language of self psychology. How we live with others rests upon how others have been with us. How we have been handled and held, cuddled and corrected, looked at and frowned at, affects how we interact with others. These include patterns of origin, development, and interaction. These experiences organize our living together as persons and our responsibilities as professionals.

In the Song of Moses, the writer of Deuteronomy juxtaposes two powerful images, which I suggest can symbolize the emotional foundation of our lives: "the Rock that bore you; . . . the God who gave you birth" (32:18). Second Isaiah continues the imagery:

> Listen to me, you that pursue righteousness,
>   you that seek the LORD.

> Look to the rock from which you were hewn,
>   and to the quarry from which you were dug.
>
>   (Isa. 51:1)

The thought of a rock giving birth startles the imagination. How can a rock have a womb? How can a womb be a rock? Yet rock and womb are brought together in a single image for the sake of calling the children of Israel to account for their being unmindful of their God. God gives life and God gives strength; God is strong and God is faithful; God follows us in our wanderings and comes to us as the Christ (1 Cor. 10:4; Anderson 1962, 412, 415). We are to remember—be mindful of—the Reality that creates and sustains us. We are to attend to who we are.

METAPHOR AND SYMBOL

The Bible abounds with such images and metaphors of God. In truth, formal beliefs—theological statements—are concepts abstracted from what we can see and hear and sense and smell—that is, from what is tangible and concrete. This applies to language and cognitive development in general. All language is metaphorical (Lakoff and Johnson 1980), based upon taking some perceived "part" of the world—objects and activities—and making them carry implications for some other part. This view of knowledge recognizes the physical and bodily basis of meaning, imagination, and reason itself (Lakoff 1987; Johnson 1987). We use physical surroundings as a way of making meaning.

Metaphor allows abstraction, linking one area of life with another. The association enlarges each area in turn. Life's human qualities always carry this overflow of meaning. Thus we may understand the metaphors of "the Rock that bore [us] . . . the God who gave [us] birth" as one of the building blocks of culture. Such metaphors refer to that which stabilizes society. As a basic ingredient of theology, a womblike rock reminds us of our dependence on God; as a primary strategy of pastoral counseling as well as pastoral care, a womblike rock helps us let go of the need to have everything under our control; as a metaphor that can make us whole, a womblike rock connects us with God.

A WOMBLIKE ROCK

I have become intrigued with the image of a womblike rock and a rocklike womb. The combination reflects much of what empirical research has identified as inclusive images people use to characterize God (Spilka 1990, 465, citing Gorsuch). One set of images relates God to humanity with concepts such as wisdom, divinity, power, and righteousness, or what is labeled a *benevolent* view of God. Another set of images includes more human qualities such as charity, fairness, faithfulness, love, support, mercy, and warmth, or what is called the *companionable* view of God. But, as concepts, benevolence and companionship lack the evocative power of images such as rock and womb.

Despite imaginative power, every metaphor has limits. There comes a point at which the implications of shared features or a concrete image become absurd. In a similar way, every concept is limited despite its focusing power. Concepts start at a point removed from the emotional anchoring of our lives. In short, metaphors can distort reality even as they disclose reality; concepts can disclose reality even as they distort reality. In minding the soul there is no way we can avoid drawing on metaphors and no way we can avoid using concepts. Together, metaphors and concepts provide evocative meaning and studied content.

In setting before you the image of the rock that gives birth, I adapt the phrase philosopher Paul Ricoeur used for symbols (quoted by Laughlin et al. 1990, 189): metaphors "invite thought." Each of us discovers and uses metaphors that speak to us and that voice our experience. So in using "rocklike womb" I am offering but one image for thinking about our role in minding the souls of those who come to us.

Pastoral psychotherapist John Patton (1983) develops the metaphors of parent and lover as ways of making sense of pastoral counselors being the bearer or symbol of "a religious person." Theologian Sallie McFague (1987) explores the possibilities of the metaphors of mother, lover, and friend as models of God. She contends that these are ecologically sensitive and ethically just. Pastoral theologian Donald Capps (1984) plays with the metaphors or models of wounded healer, good shepherd, and wise fool as ways of illuminating the task of pastoral actions. These images reflect accessible, responsible, and believable aspects of the caregiver, respectively.

Many people ignore the imaginative mode for a more simplistic focus on Jesus. A Jesusology takes Scripture too literally. It assumes we can "do as Jesus does" without critical reflection on the difference between first-century Christianity and twentieth-century modernity (Tolbert and Hunter 1990). Even so, I am ever informing my counseling by reference to the Jesus of history, as discerned with the eyes of faith in the Gospels, and to the Christ of faith, as proclaimed by the witnesses and traditions that followed.

In the Bible we are given narratives of understanding how God comes to us, most fully in Jesus as fullest discloser of the mind and heart of God. No single interpretive window preempts other interpretive windows. Jesus is the loving Teacher in Matthew, the prophetic Healer in Luke, the courageous Sufferer in Mark, the illuminating Light in John, and the cosmic Redeemer in the Pastoral Epistles. Instead of a simplistic reduction of complex cultural and interpersonal dynamics, we are given a fuller range of interpretive resources.

You will find and use your own images—and interpretive schemes—even as you will find help in reflecting on these and other metaphors of meaning.

Perhaps as we pool our images and metaphors—abstract them into operating principles and overarching generalizations—we will find ourselves manifesting a true and faithful image of the God who is our origin and our destiny, the God who is with us in the in-between of alpha and omega, the God who moves us to remember and become who we are.

THE LEADER AS A ROCK

In the early eighth century B.C.E., the prophet Isaiah used the rock image to symbolize the relationship between those in authority and those under authority. The importance of this dependent role emerges as we understand our experience of separation, being cut off from the source of our emotional well-being. Isaiah spoke of the desired—that is, the ideal—relationship between a leader and a people. Most pointedly, he laid down the basis for social life, thereby setting before us "the ideal for every person" (Smith 1908, 248–57):

> See, a king will reign in righteousness,
>   and princes will rule with justice.
> Each will be a *hiding place* from the wind,
>   a covert from the tempest,
> like streams of water in a dry place,
>   *like the shade of a great rock in a weary land.*
>   (Isa. 32:1–2, italics added)

The author poet points out that good government gives the governed security and protection. Then he goes on to sketch the positive results that come from such a secure structure:

> Then the eyes of those who have sight will not be closed,
>   and the ears of those who have hearing will listen.
> The minds [or the hearts] of the rash will have good judgment,
>   and the tongues of the stammerers will speak readily
>   and distinctly.
>   (Isa. 32:3–4)

From a narrow interpretive view the Isaiah formulation is probably speaking of an ideal, future king. From a broader interpretation, I use the metaphor of the leader as a rock to explore authority relationships, including the therapeutic relationship.

Strong support—shelter from the wind, refuge from the storm, shade from the sun, water in dry places—allows vegetation to take root. And with a good root system, which means good relatedness, comes good living—eyes that see, ears that hear, hearts that know, tongues that speak.

In Hebrew the word *leb* means "heart," the seat of a person's will, consciousness, and identity. Hence *leb* is equivalent to "mind." And "the rash" are those who speak and act hastily—that is, without thinking, or mindlessly. Without a sure foundation—a foundation of integrity with caregivers and those in authority—life gets shaky, rocky (to play with a possible meaning of the metaphor), dysfunctional. In the words of a children's book title, *"Everybody Needs a Rock,"* especially a secure relationship, a foundational rock that has integrity.

Only in the late 1970s did I discover "rocks." Until then I hardly knew they existed, and I definitely did not realize how basic they are to understanding our living together and our role in pastoral counseling.

If you are someone who zeros in on a concept or an idea, you may want to skip this account of how I arrived at the image of the rock that gives birth. For you what follows could be distracting. Stories that generate metaphors take time, and sometimes we only have time for the conclusion. If, however, you like the process as well as the conclusion, you may want to know how I have come to think of minding the soul as a matter of rocks and our rocky and rocklike relationships.

Rocks, it seems, have a way of helping us remember who we are in our relatedness. In contemplating rocks, therefore, many of us are attending to our souls. We are minding what matters most.

MY RELATIONSHIP WITH ROCKS

My relationship with rocks began rather innocently and certainly naively. When our backyard became wild and unkempt we decided to create an oriental rock garden. Since I didn't know much about finding rocks for such a garden, I asked my long-time friend Forrest Vance to teach me.

Rocks are like fish, he explained. You have to go after them early in the morning before they get away. So one morning around 6:30 we started looking for rocks. As we drove through the countryside, I became increasingly aware that the land was filled with rocks—all kinds and shapes—little, big, ordinary, extraordinary. Rocks were everywhere! How had I missed seeing them? With that first lesson I began looking for rocks on my own.

COUNTING THE COST

At a construction company I found a wonderful rock. It stood on a wide base and stretched upward with a rounded peak. The next day I took my wife, Pat, to see it. It was gone!

"What happened to your rock?" I asked the man in the office.

"The Food Store got it."

"What did it cost?"

"Two hundred dollars."

"How did you arrive at that price?"

Patiently he explained to me that rocks came in different kinds and different sizes. Some rocks were 15¢ a pound; some 17¢ a pound; some 20¢, and so on. The construction company was having a special sale—10¢ per pound for a ton. One ton for $200. That seemed expensive to me.

I sought help elsewhere. "Where can I get cheap rocks?" I ask another colleague. He suggested, "Where roads are being built." A highway was going in near our home, so I ventured out.

I found myself in the middle of a field with giant earthmovers roaring back and forth around me. I went up to a man in a yellow hat, and in the most help-seeking way I knew I got his attention.

"I need help . . . ."

He appeared puzzled, but since I had elicited his help-giving response, he was more attentive than annoyed. "What can I do for you?"

"I'm looking for rocks," I said sheepishly.

This request caught him by surprise. Being a company man he knew the hierarchy even if he did not know the answer. "See that man over there in the white hat? Talk to him. He'll help you."

I was beginning to learn the power structure of construction companies: green hats on the bottom, yellow hats next, white hats on top. I also was getting adept at eliciting help and building a support system. With newfound confidence I walked up to the man in the white hat and said, "The man in the yellow hat over there said you could help me." I paused long enough to be sure I had his attention and his invitation to continue. "I'm looking for rocks."

"Rocks!" he exclaimed. "We're trying to get rid of them! You can have all you want. Just bring your own truck."

With that my agenda was clear. I spent a couple of days scouting out the rocks around the site, identifying those with intriguing shapes and special coloring. I took Pat and my friend Vance to see them. I measured them, made sketches of them, and planned my garden with them in mind.

Next I got a truck. With six hearty friends I started out early Monday morning. The first rock was a beautiful black slab—like the one in which King Arthur's sword Excalibur had been inserted. It lay halfway up a hill, high enough, I thought, that we could easily drag it onto the truck.

We could not budge it. It must have weighed a ton or more. I was beginning to learn that rocks were harder to handle than I had imagined.

We crossed the bridge over the canal to another pile I had scouted. As we walked toward it, a car pulled up with two white hats in front. By now I knew that white hats meant both responsibility *and* authority.

"What are you doing?" the driver called out ominously.

"We're getting rocks," I answered confidently. "Ron, the head man on the site, gave me permission."

"That's another construction company—on the other side of the canal."

People have a way of getting reptilian about their territory, I thought to myself. But his rebuke had demolished my already shaky confidence. I was at a loss as to what to say.

Fortunately, without realizing it I had taken Jesus' admonition seriously. When he sent the disciples into the world, he sent them out two by two (Mark 6:7; Luke 10:1). I suspect that was so they could support each other when faced with difficulties. When we are joined with another, we can stay with a hard task in ways that seem impossible alone.

My friend Charlie stepped in. "We can pay for them," he stated firmly, although he had not consulted me, and it was my checkbook, not his, that was the source of supply.

The intervention alerted their "framing" of the situation. I can imagine their minds went something like this: "rocks . . . money . . . us . . . ." In any case, they looked at each other long and hard. Slowly, the driver turned and muttered, "Well, we could use beer money."

By now Charlie's brain was really racing. He knew that the truck was not enough. "But we need equipment," he added quickly. What had begun as a simple task rapidly was assuming unexpected proportions—for me, for my gang, for the white hats.

The white hats took us back to the site headquarters and told us to wait. They disappeared inside the trailer only to reemerge and point to a place on the highway where another bridge was being constructed.

"See that pile of rocks? Go down there, and we'll get the equipment for you."

The rocks were piled up on one side of a six-lane highway. I had never seen the rocks before, so I had not "pondered" them in my heart, a prerequisite for the coming of sacred life, as we know from Mary the mother of New Being (Luke 2:19). As I anxiously scrambled around the pile the traffic slowed and came to a halt. A fifty-foot crane lumbered across the road.

The driver leaned out of the cab, shouting above the roar, "Which one do you want?" I pointed "here"—and then "there" and "there" and "there" and "there!" I was greedy for more and more and more. With each gesture the operator delicately maneuvered the crane, scooping up the rock and placing it gently on the truck. Charlie quickly panicked about how much weight the truck could bear. We went for another truck.

But by the time we returned the crane was gone. Again traffic slowed and stopped. This time an enormous front-end loader chugged across the road. The driver's expertise with the wide scoop was as impressive as the other's expertise with the narrow bucket. The same scenario of frantic decisions about specific rocks followed. Again Charlie grew concerned about how much weight the truck could carry.

With the rocks aboard we returned to headquarters to complete the deal. Meanwhile, back at the site a fire had broken out. Engines roared up; hoses spewed water; people ran frantically back and forth. And Charlie asked how much we owed.

"Twenty-five dollars."

Later I learned that equipment like that came at $500 per hour per piece. We had lucked onto a bargain.

SECURING THE FOUNDATION

We got the trucks home only to be faced with a new obstacle. I had forgotten Jesus' parable about long-range planning:

> For which of you, intending to build a tower [or garden], does not first sit down and estimate the cost, to see whether he has enough to complete it? Otherwise, when he has laid a foundation and is not able to finish, all who see it begin to ridicule him, saying, "This fellow began to build and was not able to finish" (Luke 14:28–30).

Have you ever tried to get a rock *off* a truck? It is almost as hard as getting a rock on a truck. But despite the lack of equipment, we did manage to drop the rocks in various places around the yard. We placed the biggest one in the middle of the front yard. But a rock needs special attention. One does not simply "drop" a rock or "place" a rock without "minding" what one is doing. Rocks require planting, attending to. And without equipment it is no easy task to plant a rock, especially one that resembles a small walrus. The six of us worked a couple of hours to plant that one, but we did it.

About three weeks later I noticed that the rock had sunk about ten inches. Again I was chagrined to realize that I had forgotten Jesus' wisdom that if you build your "house [of life] on sand," it will sink. And that fall will be the destruction of your life (Matt. 7:24–27). We had simply planted the rock in the dirt, failing to set it on a firm foundation. No wonder it sank. We had neglected its soul.

I do not know whether you have ever see a rock that's "down," but a "depressed" rock is very hard to get up. Fortunately, my preaching colleague Thomas Troeger had taken physics in college. He knew that if you had a long enough lever, supported by a fulcrum, and placed it at what is called "the moment of truth," you can lift a lot of weight with very little effort. Within two hours the two of us had raised the "walrus," laid a firm foundation, and replanted the rock as Jesus intended us to do in the first place.

THE RELATIONSHIP BETWEEN ROCKS

Now a new difficulty confronted us. I had forgotten another admonition of the Lord. After creating the universe Yahweh God[1] looked out on all that the Rock had given birth to and saw that "it was very good"—except for one thing: "it is not good" for a rock to be alone (Gen. 2:18)! Physical pain can be managed, but social and spiritual pain are excruciating. Loneliness and isolation hurt more than anything else.

Have you ever tried to put two rocks together? It isn't easy. In fact, it is very, very difficult. If they get too close, they bruise each other; if they get too far apart, nothing happens between them. Tom and I spent another afternoon just working out the problem of putting two rocks together.

ROCKING ALONG ALONE

I could survey the garden from our bedroom window. One particularly heavy rock—like the one the Food Store got—had been hard to plant. The difficulty came with its unbecoming appearance. With much effort, however, we finally managed to situate it with a good profile. But the next spring I noticed that it had shifted about 90 degrees. It looked terrible. I thought to myself, *You try to help a rock be the best it can be, and look what happens. It just goes its own way. It doesn't help to help. Rocks are so unappreciative.* During the next few weeks I gave it an occasional glare of resentment.

Then one day I noticed that the rock had kept on rotating. It looked elegant, better than anything I had been able to imagine. I thought to myself, *If you just let rocks have space to move, they will find their own best place. I must stop trying to interfere.*

A few weeks later, however, I noticed that the rock had continued to rotate. It looked worse than before. Now I thought, *Rocks don't know enough to be left to themselves. They just keep going and go too far. I guess there is a place for collaboration after all.*

My encounters with rocks continue. People bring me special rocks to the point that Pat worries about our space and my sanity. People show me their rocks so often that I believe there are "closet" rock collectors everywhere.

---

1. The term "Yahweh God" is equivalent to "the Lord God." The Hebrew word *Yahweh*, or Lord, is found in the second story of creation (Gen. 2–3) and connotes a personal relationship between humanity and our Creator. The Hebrew word for God—*Elohim*—is found in the first story of creation (Gen. 1) and connotes the cosmic source of our appearance. As a single naming of the origin and destiny of our being, therefore, Yahweh God integrates intimacy and transcendence.

Rock sharing is a metaphor of our intentions with each other. In the implicit give and take there is an explicit message: Are you a rock for me?

People share their rocky lives—with us as pastoral counselors and pastors— in hopes of our being "a rock," even as God is the Rock of our salvation (Ps. 89:26), the Rock that gives birth to being (Deut. 32:18).

METAPHOR AND MEANING

My discovery of rocks came at a time when I was reengaging my own psychic rockiness. The construction site lay about a half mile beyond my therapist's office. I could neither arrive for my session nor leave without remembering the source of my rocks and being reminded of their problems. I was, in truth, minding my soul.

I often wondered what he must have thought as I talked to him at seven o'-clock in the morning (remember: you have to go out early to catch them or they get away) about planting rocks in my garden. I write "I often wondered," but I know that he knew that I knew that I was attending to the foundation of my life. The outward task mirrored the inner process.

During that period of minding my soul by probing my psyche and be-friending my self, I visited Israel. I was amazed to see the land cluttered with rocks. In fact, I had never seen so many rocks in one place in my life.

I learned of the legend that God had gathered all the rocks in the world into two huge sacks, only to have one of them break over Palestine. Half the rocks in the world must be scattered across the landscape. No wonder the children of Israel kept referring to stones of stumbling and rocks of offense (Isa. 8:14; Rom. 9:32–33; 1 Peter 2:8). Rocks were everywhere and always in the way.

Yet in God's gracious work these rejected stones become cornerstones (Ps. 118:22–23; 144:12b; 1 Peter 2:4–6). The *dis*-traction was transformed into an *at*-traction. The rejected was not only accepted but made basic, central, crucial to life itself. I was finding that *metanoia*—that turn-about—true in my personal life. And it is true in the spiritual lives of pastoral counselors and possible in the lives of those who come to us in pain.

Isaiah provides us with an image of the pastoral counselor as "a great rock in a weary land" (Isa. 32:2b; Smith 1908, 253). A rock stops the drift of the sand, the endless shifting of unconnected and dysfunctional living. Its shade allows mois-ture to accumulate, the nurturing of fragile and vulnerable beginnings. Plant life can take root. Eventually more life flourishes in the very places where there had been no life.

Such is the pastoral counseling task of minding the soul. Our presence pro-vides refuge from the onslaught of others' demands. Psychotherapists call this a "holding environment." Our steadiness allows people to reexpose themselves to the harsh elements, to experiment with new life, to reengage in living with others. Even the rockiness we share with Cephas, the disciple Peter, in his grandiose bravado and panicked denial of Jesus (Mark 14:66–72) is paradoxically reframed by grace (John 1:42). Petros—Peter—rock becomes the foundation upon which true community is built (Matt. 16:18). God is the Rock that gives birth!

Translate the rock metaphor into the concept "foundation." In other words, think about possible meanings of the image. What are the foundations of our lives really like? Rocky or firm and steady? How *do* we get along with others? How *can* we live in ways that transform stones of stumbling into stepping stones and building blocks? Those are questions we ponder in minding the souls of those with whom we work as well as in minding our own souls.

The rock that gives birth serves as a metaphor for the pastoral counselor being "a rock in a weary land." Further, the conceptual focus of rock can denote that which is "foundational for the making of meaning." With rock as a metaphor for the God we represent and as a concept that shapes our professional work, I turn to the more systematic task of tightening the metaphor and concept into a model. A model enables us to tighten the implications and make the connections in the metaphor more specific.

In the following chapters I spell out a theoretical frame for pastoral counseling. If "rock" is foundational, then "rockiness" reflects unstable defensiveness and "rocklike" suggests stable growth. I identify defensive patterns as basic emotional assumptions and growth patterns as basic theological assumptions. The former constricts and oppresses life; the latter enhances and liberates life. Such a theoretical scheme helps orient us initially. Even more, such a scheme can lessen anxiety in the counselor when the going gets rough. We have something to cling to, even if it is modified or replaced at a future time.

CHAPTER TWO

Struggles of the Soul

ROCKINESS AND NEUROCOGNITIVE ACTIVITY

■ ■ ■ ■ ■

Most of us struggle to become who we are. This becomes most apparent in times of stress or transition. We balance being alive with becoming who we are.

As symbol-bearers of the rock that gives birth, pastoral counselors bear two burdens: the burden of caring for others and the burden of caring for ourselves. We are no different from those who come to us. We all engage the struggles of the soul.

The pastoral counseling task of ministry, then, reflects what goes on all the time in life, only it takes place under conditions that allow a more disciplined approach. Therapy intensifies the ongoing features of how we relate to each other. These features include working together, depending on someone special, and making it on our own. In counseling we bracket a mutual give and take for the sake of putting ourselves at the disposal of the well-being of others apart from our own needs. Such self-emptying is the core of *agape*, God-with-us (Phil. 2:4–8). Even though we therapists often find ourselves enlivened from such self-giving, that enlivening is not the intent of the counseling task.

In this chapter I identify the context of ultimate dependency in which we all live. I then describe those features of our relatedness that pervade our lives because of that dependency and become exaggerated under stress. Being aware of these foundation stones and their rocky aspects enables us to better mind the souls of those who come to us. A theoretical framework such as this helps us keep our balance when the course of therapy becomes uncertain. It provides a way of orienting ourselves as well as organizing what is going on. In effect, theory is a map of the territory to be traveled or a recipe of the meal to be prepared.

EVERYONE IS BORN DEPENDENT

As the Rock, Yahweh God gives birth to each of us. No one is *not* birthed. We all come from that reality we neither create nor control. We find ourselves in a universe not of our own making.

At the same time, we live in a world for which we are responsible—a world of people as well as a world of nature. The very image of the Rock that gives birth combines a physical environment—rock—and a human world—womb.

In the language of neurotheology, we are the recipients of three inheritances—one genetic with its biological givens, one cultural with its parochial constraints, and one purposeful with its aspirational possibilities. In the language of philosophy, we are made up of matter and spirit. In the language of the Bible, we are particles of dust into which God has breathed the breath of life (Gen. 2:7).

Each of these languages of discourse emphasizes that who we are depends on a context or universe of influences we do not create. We are part of communities that call us to become a part of humanity in a universe that makes meaning meaningful.

Because we are neither our own origin nor our own destiny, we are part of the great chain of Being. We refer to that in various ways as God, life, nature, humanity, universe, being itself, or—to use the Deuteronomic image—the rock that bears us. Augustine voiced that sense of how our literal dependence on the caregiver carries the reality of our ultimate dependence on God: "Thou didst sometime fashion me [O God]. Thus even though they sustained me by the consolation of woman's milk, neither my mother nor my nurses filled their own breasts but thou, through them, didst give me the food of infancy" (Augustine 1955, 1.VI.7). For good and ill, our experiences as infants influence our understanding as adults, which in turn influences our understanding of God (cf. Rizzuto 1979; Jones 1991).

We live only as we are connected to that which is other than ourselves. From the umbilical cord that connects the fetus at the navel with the mother's placenta, to the astronaut's lifeline supplying oxygen and communication while outside the spacecraft, to the spiritual "tie that binds our hearts in . . . love," we live only to the degree that our supply lines are working properly.

THE CRY OF SEPARATION

What connects the physical cord and the spiritual tie? The question is at once literal and metaphoric. So the answer must be at once literal and metaphoric.

The vocal cry. The cry from the heart on behalf of life together. The cry born of a sense of helplessness and hopelessness. That cry of separation connects the physical, the cultural, and the spiritual dimensions simultaneously.

The vocal cry is the basic response to the pain of being cut off from that which supplies and supports life. Its origin lies in the startle response. The startle response reflects the gap between an organism and its environment. Rocks do not jump at the crash of thunder or flash of lightning; only living organisms startle. That distance between "what is" and "what might be" is the basis for all learning.

Whether we are cut off from oxygen or from a significant other, the rift triggers a cry for help. Our world is threatened at its core. Life, in part, may be characterized as a search for that central reality on which we can depend and to which we must adapt. Ours is an interpersonal world from the beginning (see Stern 1985).

THE THEORY OF ATTACHMENT

The search for something on which to depend reflects the dependency and vulnerability of infancy. We have to learn how to cope. We have to choose to grow. *Attachment, Separation,* and *Loss*—the titles of John Bowlby's pioneering trilogy on personality development (1969, 1973, 1980)—neatly summarize three crucial features of our life together: (1) patterns of affectional bonds (with the mothering figure), (2) separation anxiety, and (3) the loss of relational support.

Without support we are undermined. Even a brief absence of mother can produce cries of panic in an infant. The loss of a loved one causes agony. In the presence of deathlike threats to the self, we are flooded with anxiety.

The trauma of separation can be soul-shaking. As Bowlby emphasizes, we tend to "underestimate how intensely distressing and disabling loss usually is and for how long the distress, and often the disablement, commonly lasts" (Bowlby 1980, 8). Because relatedness is key to pastoral counseling, I sketch its more formal aspects as developed in Attachment Theory (Bowlby 1980, 39–41):

- In contrast to dependent behavior, attachment behavior includes any activity that helps one remain close to a significant caregiver. As long as that person is accessible and responsive, the activity may be no more than a glance or a greeting. Under unusual circumstances, hanging on to the other person, as well as calling or crying, may be present.

- In healthy personality development attachment behavior leads to bonds of affection and relationship, at first between child and parent and later with other adults.

- The threat of loss arouses anxiety; actual loss results in sorrow.

- Whereas the bonds of relatedness persist, the behaviors that reflect the attachment appear only when needed to regain a sense of security. These stress-filled conditions include strange places and people, fatigue, anything frightening, and the absence of the available and responsive attachment figure. A familiar situation and the closeness of the attachment figure ends the attachment activity. Under intense conditions, the behavior persists until touching, clinging, and reassurance are received from the caregiver.

- Attachment activities serve the goal of maintaining a comfortable degree of closeness to the caregiver.

- Attachment behavior has the goal of calling forth from the caregiver a complementary response—namely, protecting one—especially in times of stress, confusion, conflict, ill health, old age, or death.

* Attachment activity is neither pathological nor regressive except when a person's psychological development includes unresolved disturbance in significant relationships.

In relation to significant others, attachment behaviors—such as seeking, glancing, calling, touching, crying, clinging—are intended to maintain the relationship. Whatever endangers that bond elicits behavior to preserve the bond; and the greater the threat of loss, the more intense the action to prevent it.

In sum, attachment behavior appears whenever we are threatened, whether that threat is physical, psychological, or spiritual. Personal anxiety is the subjective experience of threat; physiological stress is the objective evidence of threat.

Pastoral theologians Kenneth R. Mitchell and Herbert Anderson contend that loss and grief are everywhere in our experience. Even more, "[l]oss, not death, is the normative metaphor for understanding those experiences . . . that produce grief" (Mitchell and Anderson 1983, 19). Since life is made up of both attachment and loss, "there is no life without grief" (21) and no grief without life.

THE SEARCH FOR CONNECTION

In a lecture at Earlham College, anthropologist Richard Leakey tells of finding a circle of seven-hundred-pound stones in a small area seven miles from where they had been formed. What would have led a mammal—the human mammal, he speculated—to have dragged so much weight such a distance for no utilitarian purpose? A need other than immediate necessity was at work. In such activity we come upon the imaginative consciousness of human life.

The circle of stones reflects the meaning-making activity distinctive of *homo sapiens*. Its creation is a symbolic act suggestive of the separation call, a gesture of reaching out to make contact with the invisible power that holds us. It is an exercise in intentional behavior. This behavior depends on the maturation of the frontal lobes of the new brain in evolutionary development (Laughlin et al. 1990, 92-101). It is aligned with the basic urge to know—what has been called the "cognitive imperative" (xi). We consciously seek the Rock that bears us.

The human mind orders events into symbols and images. These, in turn, become ideas and words that lead to action. We give voice to our primary visceral and vascular processes—the guts and blood of life—as a way to cope with threats to the meaning of life. A purpose or meaning or order in events—(that phenomenon is described differently by different theoretical orientations)—enables us to regulate our emotional response to the experience of ambiguity, most especially to the threat to our sense of self in an immediate way and ultimately to life itself. Our nervous system is designed to give structure to what happens. Biogenetic structuralists Charles D. Laughlin Jr., John McManus, and Eugene G. d'Aquili (1990) refer to that meaning-making process as a neurocognitive system. By a neurocognitive system they mean the organization of the nervous system for the purpose of knowing what is necessary for adaptation and development.

The experience of loss is familiar to every living creature. The "separation call" between a mother and her offspring, according to neurophysiologist Paul D. MacLean (1985), "may be the most basic mammalian vocalization." It occurs when either the mother or the offspring becomes too far removed from the other. The separation call is a stress signal in the absence of that relatedness.

Bowlby's work involved studying the effects of the loss of mother on young children. Protest and an urgent effort to recover the lost mother tend to be the initial responses of children between one and three years of age. They often cry loudly, throw themselves about, and seek eagerly for any sight or sound that might be the missing mother (Bowlby 1980, 9). The separation call is always in relation to an "other," actual or imagined. Whether a frightened infant or a threatened adult, remembering who we are inevitably involves reconnecting with those who matter to us.

Because it is an attempt to reconnect, I think of the separation call as "the search for connection." In its deepest meaning, the separation call becomes "the cry to God." It is "simultaneously a cry of pain . . . and a cry for help" (Boyce 1988, 22, 71). The cry for help is the search for understanding, and it is always directed to some person or object which, ultimately, means to God or what one believes to be the Ultimate Power of life itself. Martin Luther voiced the experiential meaning of ultimate support: one's god is whatever one's heart clings to and relies on.

Think of "God" as the integrating of power and meaning, to use categories that theologian Paul Tillich (1951) systematizes. God—whether an image or an idea—shapes life and "frames" or patterns the emotional impact of what happens to us. The separation call—whether a soft sigh, an anguished cry, a sustaining belief, or a cognitive scheme—rises up in our heart and courses through our brain as a search for that which gives sense in the midst of nonsense and security in the face of uncertainty.

My editorial consultant, Barbara Stinchcomb, recalls a story told by a friend, a thoughtful and firm nonbeliever whose conclusions about existence have no place for the magic usually associated with the idea of God. One day his wife was in an accident. As he heard the news by phone, he suddenly burst out, "God, help me," and he prayed for his wife's safety.

Later, he remarked about the incident. His calling on God had come spontaneously, unlike his processed, thoughtful ideas. His outburst was an immediate and unaccountable cry for help. He admitted that in that moment he had no one to whom he could turn except this Reality who had not been part of his conscious life. Yet, when he called out, that Power was there. It came from some unknown place inside. Though he did not become a believer, the incident made an impact on his thinking.

Augustine's conclusion about experience rings true: "If anyone thinks of God as anything other than life itself, [that person] has an absurd idea of God" (*De doct. christ*, 1:8, quoted by Miles 1990, 229). God is "life itself"; and in the loss of life, our life cries out for life with life.

Contact with God frees us from the constraints of the past for the sake of that which is needed in the future. Minding the soul consists of finding an optimal way of putting life together given the facts of what has been and the possibilities of what might be. Whether acknowledged or not, God is our "Cosmic Ally," our "Source of Hope," because God brings to every experience "just that possibility most relevant to where we are" (Jackson 1990, 958).

COPING WITH ULTIMATE DEPENDENCY

The reality of this cosmic dependency may be identified in two experiences, the first of which is death. We come from dust, from the biochemical processes basic to life as we know them in the universe in general and on earth in particular, and we return to dust. We have no say over our finitude. We only have a say over the quality of life as we live it. Death reminds us that in the final analysis we are not in control of our lives.

The second evidence of cosmic dependency is the recognition of the power of life's emotional meaning. That emotional influence has both a cultural and an evolutionary dimension.

In terms of the cultural component, Freud saw his discovery of unconscious processes as rendering a psychological wound to humanity's belief that it was "master in its own house." In his later years he revised his view that all that is unconscious is pathological, because in his clinical experience he had come on an "unconflicted unconscious" (Freud [1923] 1962, 7–8, 14). In truth, the pathological unconscious proved to be only the "superficial strata of the mental apparatus." Jung, Jungians, neo-Freudians, and transpersonal psychologists, especially, have explored the primacy of the creative unconscious. In relation to the brain itself this involves subcortical processes. I regard the primacy of the creative unconscious as the province of—or at least a basic access to—all that we take to be transcendent (see Theissen 1987).

Transcendent means that which goes beyond conscious control. We recoil against that which we cannot manage—either by how we act or by how we think. We reach the limit of what we can do rationally (Tracy 1975, 91–120; 1987, 86–87) and let go of the expectation that we can control life. In that experience we trust life's creating power—"however that Reality is named," as theologian David Tracy puts it, be it "God, Emptiness, Suchness, the One, Nature, the Many, the power that is the ultimate power with which we all must deal" (Tracy 1987, 85, 89, 90). We give up a self-conscious, deliberate, aroused sympathetic process for a more life-aware, receptive, relaxed parasympathetic process. We respond adaptively instead of reacting self-consciously. Safety replaces defense (Gilbert 1989). Quite simply, we "let be whatever is" (see Brewer 1975).

The creative unconscious links us to the milieu in which we live and move and have our being. In the language of emergent evolution, it is the empathic activity of the old mammalian brain that works to find the optimal environmental adaptation at any particular moment. That adaptation is based on the emotional meaning of the situation. And that emotional meaning serves the survival of the species. In the language of neuropsychology, the creative unconscious is the subsymbolic, subcortical processing of the whole brain, in parallel and distributed ways. That processing shapes conscious intention. We are given access to information both in the peripheral and in the central nervous systems. The peripheral system connects us with the outer environment; the central system connects us with the inner world. In the language of neurotheology, creative unconsciousness is the work of the Holy Spirit in its whole-making activity. That is why I call my approach to pastoral counseling a "minding of the soul" for the making of meaning.

Experiences of separation—whether literal, psychic, or spiritual—set off our survival alarm. The alarm may be in the service of survival or of adaptation. In the survival mode the biology of the body shifts from growth to defense, from adaptation to protection, from excitement to anxiety. In technical terms, the sympathetic adrenal arousal system takes over from the parasympathetic adaptation system. Optimal autonomic tuning is suspended. All systems are on alert to defend against attack.

The reverse is true in the adaptive mode. The biology of the body shifts from defense to growth, from protection to adaptation, from anxiety to excitement. In technical terms, the parasympathetic relaxation system takes over from the sympathetic survival system. Dysfunctional autonomic tuning is inhibited. All systems are in the service of enhancement.

Members of a small house church were asked what the word *transcendent* meant to them. Their responses reflect this adaptive quality of the unconscious (Jud 1975, 134):

- It's an experience beyond words.
- It's an overwhelming sense of the unity of things.
- It's getting out of your box—your normal limitations.
- It's ecstasy.
- It's standing back, taking a look at yourself, and laughing.
- It's an overwhelming experience of "Yes!"
- It's experiencing God!

The soul's challenge, therefore, is to turn rockiness into steadiness. The soul struggles to integrate that which is growth-producing and to sift out that which is growth-inhibiting. This is also the task of pastoral counseling. We are to so mind the soul that the struggle for survival is transformed into the sharing of the making of meaning for the whole human family.

While we all struggle with separation and connection, our struggles take different forms. Think of these forms as organized patterns designed to handle the stress of our ultimate or absolute dependency on the Rock that gives us birth. In short, the cry for connection discloses a shared responsibility for life as we know it.

These patterns can be either defensive or growth-enhancing, depending on how we assess the meaning of what is happening.

Rockiness and Defense. In survival these dynamics are "basic emotional assumptions." The term "basic emotional assumption" comes from British psychiatrist W. R. Bion, drawing on the work of Freud and Melanie Klein (Grinberg et al. 1977), and elaborated through the work of the Tavistock Institute on Human Relations in London and A. K. Rice Institutes of group relations training development in the United States (Bion [1959] 1974; Colman and Bexton 1975; Colman and Geller 1985). We experience survival assumptions in personal behavior as well as in group behavior.

Basic emotional assumptions refer to the intense emotions of early origin. These emotions are based on "a shared fantasy of an omnipotent or magic type." They are always unconscious and often contrary to what we intend consciously. These emotions are organized to avoid the frustration of learning from threatening experience (Grinberg et al. 1977, 8–10). In contrast to a public reality of shared responsibility, we fall back on an imagined reality that frees us of responsibility.

Basic emotional assumption is a psychological way of identifying the mythic experience of hearing Yahweh God in the garden. In the gap between ourselves and the world, we—as Adam and Eve—become self-conscious and afraid. We try to hide from the real symbolized by Yahweh God walking in the garden (Gen. 3:8–10). God asks, "Where are you?" Our defenses take over, and we react in survival mode. We act in order to negate the work of reality.

Rocklikeness and Growth. In their adaptive forms these organized patterns are "basic theological assumptions." The term "basic theological assumption" reflects belief in the activity of a caring and liberating God. It refers to the neurocognitive processes of alternating "pulling together" in adapting to outer reality and "coming alive" in adapting to inner reality (cf. Laughlin et al. 1990, 282–83). It reflects the transcendent power of our being created in the image of God. It is remembering and attending to who we are by minding our soul.

I associate the basic theological assumption, in part, with the mythic experience of the seventh day. The seventh day connects our embeddedness in the universe (Gen. 2:1–3) with the Ten Commandments, which declare our responsibility in history (Exod. 20:1–17; Deut. 5:6–21). The basic cycle of rest and activity, which I describe in chapter 13, integrates all the processes of life in the service of adaptation. God acts through the structures of life to open possibilities of more life.

Both Rocky and Rocklike. In the story of the apostle Peter the New Testament provides an example of the ambiguity of our assumptive reality—our acting "as if" the world is a certain way. Jesus changes the name of Simon, the son of John, to Cephas, which means Peter (the respective words for *rock* in both Aramaic and Greek; John 1:42). The irony of that steadfast identification comes with Peter's pattern of discipleship (Matt. 26:33–35; Mark 14:29–31; Luke 22:33–34; John 13:37–38). The foundational "rock" (Matt. 16:18) exhibited "rocky" reliability. At one moment he showed too much independence and the next too little independence, as in his refusing to let Jesus wash his feet and then insisting that Jesus wash his hands and his head as well (John 13:5–9). In the face of threat, the theological assumption of adaptation collapsed into the emotional assumption of survival.

The emotional assumption shows itself when we deal with reality in inappropriate and dysfunctional ways. The survival assumption prevents our being open to each other and inhibits our being open to our own clarity. This anxiousness keeps us living in a fantasy world sealed off from the real world of God's possibilities.

THE BASIC ASSUMPTIVE PATTERNS

Three basic patterns—emotional and theological assumptions—organize the rockiness and rocklikeness of our soul-making activity. They are anxious inclusion, anxious autonomy, and anxious attachment.[1] *Anxious*, as the qualifying word, refers to the defensiveness of the patterns. The nouns themselves—*inclusion, autonomy, attachment*—identify the adaptivity of the patterns. Defensiveness makes for dysfunction; adaptivity makes for life.

We all carry these assumptive patterns inside ourselves. When psychiatrist Harry Stack Sullivan observed that we are all more simply human than otherwise, he was emphasizing the commonality of our humanness. I assume he meant our dysfunction as well as our adaptation.

Which pattern is dominant and whether it is for survival or growth depend on a variety of conditions. We need to take into account such genetic predispositions as slow or rapid responses and early or late maturation of language. We need to consider such societal predispositions as socialization of gender as well as positive and negative views of race and ethnicity. We need to attend to familial predispositions of parenting, whether they were relaxed or tense, responsive or repressive, consistent or inconsistent.

These dynamics apply equally to the one receiving pastoral counseling and to the one giving pastoral counseling. The issue, therefore, is whether we together—as an interacting system of giving-and-receiving therapy—collude in avoiding the work of reality or collaborate in attending to the work of reality. Do we mind the soul or concentrate on surviving?

The next chapter sketches the concrete situation that helped me make sense of these assumptions. The situation involved my twelve-year consultation with a large, multilevel care facility for the elderly. My responsibility ranged from initial care conferences about hard-to-manage patients to a total institutional staff program of Quality of Life. Everything we did was based on prescribed staff attitudes determined by an assessment of emotional assumptions in residents and patients (Ashbrook 1975, 113–18; 1986). This anchoring of the soul's struggle in interpersonal interactions becomes the bridge to chapter 4 which describes the patterns of minding the soul more fully.

---

1. This analysis draws on the work of Bowlby (1969, 1973, 1980); Ainsworth (1979, 1982, 1989); Bion ([1959] 1974); A. K. Rice Institute (Colman and Bexton 1975; Colman and Geller 1985); Parks and Stevensen-Hinde (1982); and May (1980).

CHAPTER THREE

Stabilizing the Soul

A CLINICAL CASE STUDY

■ ■ ■ ■ ■

My understanding of the soul's struggles emerged from the experience of the staff of St. Ann's Home for the Elderly in handling hard-to-manage patients.[1] For twelve years we worked together to reduce stress and to enhance quality of life. Although the approach focused on the confused elderly, we quickly learned that it applied to us all. St. Ann's became the laboratory in which I developed an understanding of some of the forces that drive our lives and possible ways of coping with them. St. Ann's was a community in which we worked intentionally to remember who we were for the sake of our basic "personhood" (Ciaccia 1984), our souls.

I describe the program in the three phases of its development: initially, individual cases and basic attitudes; subsequently, attention to quality of life and two interpersonal styles; and finally, a revised attitude program that took account of a third style, perhaps the most basic of all. This last phase marked a major change in my understanding of emotional assumptions, interpersonal styles, and theological possibilities. An unexamined male bias surfaced, bringing new clarity to the ways men and women cope. Implications for minding the souls of our clients and ourselves are broad-ranging. I build on this background in the next chapter in elaborating patterns of the soul in its survival modes and in its growing possibilities.

1. I am appreciative of Sister Marie Michelle Peartree, president of St. Ann's; Jean Donato, R.N., who initiated the program; June Norter, R.N., director of nursing; Paul Duffy, M.D., medical director; William Hart, M.D., psychiatric consultant; especially Cecilia Ciaccia, R.N., coordinator of Mental Health Services; and the entire staff for their support and collaboration.

INDIVIDUAL CASES AND BASIC ATTITUDES

The approaches to the confused elderly were adapted from a program known as "attitude therapy" (Folsom 1968), which was first developed with brain-damaged patients in a Veterans Administration Hospital (Folsom 1965). The program prescribed specific attitudes for staff behavior in reaction to disruptive behavior by patients. Because the confused person does not cope well with inconsistency, the attitudes were to be maintained by all the staff who had contact with the patient, twenty-four hours a day.

The consultation process went as follows. When the staff identified a hard-to-manage patient, I interviewed that person in the presence of the head nurse. Then we held a case conference to be attended by anyone who had contact with the person—from housekeeping aides to recreational and occupational therapists to nurses and occasionally physicians.

After the head nurse reviewed the reasons for the referral, I invited everyone to share their experiences or impressions of the patient. I inquired about similar situations they might have encountered, either on a professional or a personal basis. At first, staff would pour out their feelings of frustration; eventually someone, often a nonprofessional, described the person differently— namely, as someone who was not hard to manage. I then related that staff person's experience to specific attitudes, along with a rationale for such an understanding. Finally, I prescribed the attitude that everyone was to maintain around the clock.

The attitudes seemed simple and self-evident, a common-sense understanding of the ways we all are (see figure 3.1), although prior to my consultation St. Ann's had been applying the approach with discouraging results. I brought a fuller view of interpersonal behavior (Leary 1957).

With shy people, those who felt they were unimportant, we used *active friendliness* (AF). Because the confidence of these people was low, staff gave them a lot of individual support, reaching out to them, touching them, and making comments like "Your hair ribbon looks so lovely today, Harriet," or "John, here's a shoelace. I noticed you needed one."

In contrast, with suspicious people, those who bristled at such friendliness, we relied on *passive friendliness* (PF). For them, the world was not to be trusted, so the staff waited for them to take initiative before engaging in more than a minimum of interaction. Staff restricted themselves to little more than a brief "Hello, Mrs. Birdwell."

I remember a Mrs. Foster (not her real name) who entered another nursing home on a late Friday afternoon. Because of a change in shift at the time, the staff did not realize she was there until Monday. They were horrified. She, however, raved, "What a wonderful place this is. No one bothers you!" Too much contact made her anxious.

Because suspicious persons were so baffling to the staff who wanted to be helpful, I used the analogy of being in the woods and wanting to find the wildlife. One does not run around yelling for it to show itself. Rather, one sits quietly by a tree, leans back, and waits for the natural curiosity of the creatures to cause them to poke their heads out to see what's there.

Besides active friendliness with shy persons and passive friendliness with suspicious persons, I prescribed an attitude for persons who manipulated or controlled the environment in disruptive ways. It was called *matter-of-fact* (MF). Staff could avoid power struggles with patients by maintaining clear limits. Regardless of patients' arguments, "Rules are rules. This is the way things are."

The results of this simple approach proved startling. Within two weeks of a case consultation, 60% of the patients improved as judged by the very staff who had despaired of them, 20% got worse, and 20% stayed the same. Over the year, the percentage of those continuing to be hard to manage stabilized around 15%. That meant that because of the consistency of staff attitude, 85% of the patients who had been difficult to handle were managing in more acceptable ways.

We dealt with patients who exhibited problems of depression, anger, agitation, hypochondria, demands for constant attention, overriding anxiety, sexual aggression, fear, isolation, regression, suspicion, physical abuse, grief, and bereavement (Ciaccia 1984). The change was awesome. Consistent attitudes, based on an assessment of how people coped with stress, and interpreted with a framework of interpersonal diagnosis (Sullivan 1953; Leary 1957; Ashbrook 1975, 86–92) had transformed staff morale and institutional quality of life.

An examination of the attitudes prescribed identified profiles of the most troublesome patients. Less than 25% needed active friendliness. About half required matter-of-fact. Many needed a combination. For instance, matter-of-fact would be used with impulsive or manipulative behavior, while *no demand* (ND) would be prescribed for uncontrollable rage. Staff simply backed off, acting only to prevent injury to others or to the patient. The most trouble came with those who required a combination of passive friendliness for their suspiciousness and no demand for their rage.

After four years of successful case conferences, we expanded the attitude approach. I had averaged nine one-and-a-half-hour case consultations per year. The mental health coordinator, Cecilia Ciaccia, and I began training head nurses to conduct case conferences on their own units. Although slower in developing than we had anticipated, within two years the number of case consultations, all led by head nurses, jumped to about thirty-six a year, three times what I had managed by myself. The approach does not depend on the esoteric knowledge of an expert. It is available for everyone, for the struggles of the soul in stress are not as mysterious as we have assumed.

With more experience we added a fifth attitude, *kind firmness* (KF). Originally, this attitude prescribed aggravating drudgery for the patient in a reactive depression. Since staff found that hard to apply, we redefined it to mean setting limits in a firm yet warm way. We prescribed it for shy, sociable patients who made endless demands to be exceptions to the rules. Staff took a positive approach that assumed patients could do what had to be done and ignored sympathizing with their misery. For example, "Bill, you know the craft program is only five days a week. This is one of those days. I'll stop by to get you at nine o'clock." The attitude expressed both the firmness of a fixed structure and the kindness of emotional support.

Matter-of-fact applied to those who were suspicious, negative, and demanding. Because the attitude was definite, the patient's underlying anxiety was contained. When Mr. Smith complained about the "sorry" food, staff would say, "This is the menu today"—no more explanation or justification than that.

We had taken a program designed for hard-to-manage veterans and modified it into a program for the confused elderly. By educating staff about interpersonal dynamics, they developed skill in modifying disruptive behavior in their patients. They had a way to think about what was going wrong and to intervene in a positive way.

The principles of interpersonal behavior—maintaining and enhancing one's sense of self-esteem (Sullivan 1953; Leary 1957)—applied to us all. Because of the limited and intense situation of the institutional setting, we could see clearly what goes on all the time. The attitudes simply focused a more comprehensive view of the ways we all cope with reality. This enlargement of the attitudes to more "normal" patterns moved us into a second phase.

QUALITY OF LIFE AND TWO INTERPERSONAL STYLES

After six years of working with hard-to-manage patients we turned to a broader issue. We projected a three-year program that included participation by all departments at St. Ann's—medical, social work, nursing, recreation, dietary, pastoral care, and mental health. Its purpose was "to identify the patterns that [would] give the individual resident optimum quality of life within the limitations of the institution." We focused on ways to encourage the positive aspects of people instead of dwelling on their deficits. We shifted from crisis intervention to crisis prevention. Thus we helped people remember who they were.

We agreed to concentrate on the transition event of admission to the institution. How could we make the move into St. Ann's less stressful and more comfortable? How could we organize what needed to take place in ways that would take into account the emotional needs of individuals? How could people continue to be themselves?

The attitudes were revised into two interpersonal styles—the people who preferred to be identified by their formal name, for instance, Mrs. Baker, and those who preferred an informal first-name relationship, for instance, Hank. We assumed that under stress formal types, most likely to be suspicious, would react with either fight or flight behaviors and depend on themselves; informal types, most likely to be shy, would react with dependent behaviors and depend on others.

This schema simplified and enlarged the attitude approach. Intake workers quickly distinguished those who needed formal procedures from those who responded to informal support. Depending on how stressful the admission process seemed to be, we would prescribe the attitudes of passive friendliness and matter-of-fact with the formal style and active friendliness and kind firmness with the informal style (see figure 3.2). Each of these reflected more autonomy or more attachment, respectively.

The simplified structure further clarified the nature of interpersonal dynamics, especially in relation to basic emotional assumptions (Bion [1959] 1974; Colman and Bexton 1975). These assumptions are reactive patterns we use under stress, in collusion with those in authority, to defend against the work of reality.

The formal type labors under an anxious autonomy. Feeling vulnerable, the person tries to survive by controlling what goes on. He or she defends against closeness by unconsciously eliciting distance from others, using the classic fight-flight pattern. The formality is expressed in a cautious attitude, the core of which is suspicion. To allow the person to feel in control, the staff would specifically spell out each procedure and reduce their amount of contact with the individual.

The informal type copes with an anxious attachment. Feeling deficient, the person tries to hold together by staying in contact with others. He or she exhibits a clinging/demanding pattern, a subtle way of getting contact by appearing to be helpless. The informality is expressed in a dependent attitude, the core of which is shyness. To provide the person with as much contact as possible, staff would be personal and available.

We analyzed the admission event more closely. Some people seemed to become troublesome around the tenth week, others during the first weeks. We identified the former as informal who needed support and felt abandoned after the initial flurry of activity, the latter as formal who needed control and felt put upon by the initial flurry of activity. We divided the event into five phases: preadmission; initial acute period, one to three weeks; latent adjustment period, four to ten weeks; secondary acute period, eleven to thirteen weeks; and normal institutional adjustment. In a master plan for each admission every department planned its contacts according to the prescribed type and attitudes.

As a result, the staff found itself dealing more with routine problems than with emergencies. Treatment team meetings kept attitude strategies appropriate. Most important, staff satisfaction increased. When difficulties arose, they had a way to rethink what was happening and to reengage the patient with more adaptive attitudes. The staff was learning how to help people live their unique lives in constructive ways.

REVISED STYLES AND ATTITUDES

The procedures were working well about 85% of the time, a tribute to the skill of the intake staff and the clarity of basic emotional assumptions. But what was happening with the remaining 15%? Staff labeled the group *mixed type*, meaning a patient was initially typed one way, but his or her subsequent behavior suggested the other style. With the reassessment and proper prescription of attitudes, disruptive behavior disappeared. That seemed straightforward.

Then came a special session with a frustrated dietary staff. "What can we do," they asked, at their wits' end, "with stragglers failing to get to meals on time? Nothing you have told us works. If we try the matter-of-fact attitude, they get upset. When that doesn't work, we switch to kind firmness, and they get even more upset. What can we do?"

I did not know what was happening, but I was convinced that the staff might know, even if they did not realize that they knew. So I asked, "What do you do when neither attitude works?"

Their response startled me. "We explain to them that this is the way the service has to be set up for the two shifts to be fed."

"What happens?" I asked, more curious than ever.

"They're satisfied."

"You mean to tell me," I responded, "that if you are reasonable, they are reasonable?"

"Yes, it works."

That exchange marked the revision—actually a revolution—in our understanding of the attitude approach. Basic emotional assumptions seem to reflect gender-related issues. I asked further about the 15% in the mixed type. The answers were always the same: the patient was first typed as formal and, after becoming upset with the passive friendly/matter-of-fact attitudes, was retyped as informal. The person quickly regained her psychic equilibrium. Without exception, every mixed type was a woman.

The problem quickly cleared up. Attitude therapy had originated in a Veterans Administration hospital that had mostly a male staff and an all-male population. St. Ann's had adapted the approach to its primarily female population and female staff. That it worked so well testified to the skill of the staff. As I pressed them about how they had applied the attitudes, I learned that they had been adapting them in their own way unconsciously and without letting me know their modifications. As women have done for centuries, they altered their experience to fit a male-constructed "reality."

The sharp division between shy and suspicious people, requiring kind firmness and matter-of-fact respectively, is more male-related. Formal and informal styles only reinforced the stereotypes. The mixed type was not mixed at all. Rather, it represented a type distinct in itself—a third pattern or, perhaps more accurately, a primary human pattern. We called this third type *reserved friendly*. Let me elaborate (see Ashbrook 1992b).

EFFECTS OF SEX AND GENDER

Once conception takes place the embryo is undifferentiated—that is, it is neither male nor female; it is simply "human potentiality." From this fact physician anthropologist Melvin Konner concludes that *"the basic plan of the mammalian organism is female* and stays that way unless told to be otherwise by masculine hormones" (Konner [1982] 1983, 122, italics added).

By the sixth week of pregnancy the hormonal activity begins to differentiate as either a female or a male neurological organization at three levels: internal sex structures, external genitals, and the brain (Fehlman 1990, 1152). Androgen plays a powerful role in "masculinizing" the brain—that is, in establishing and maintaining the asymmetry of the two hemispheres, with the right hemisphere tending to be thicker in males and the left thicker in females (Springer and Deutsch [1981, 1985] 1989, 218–20; Diamond 1984, 1988, 115–40). Also, females tend to exhibit more bilaterality, that is less specialized cerebral functioning— weak asymmetry, to use the technical term. However, the link between differences in the anatomy of the two halves and in analytical processing by the left brain and holistic processing by the right brain continues to be an untested but supportable assumption.

Although the data are mixed (Graber and Petersen 1991, 267–68, 272–73), as a group, girls tend to mature more rapidly than boys. This is especially true in relation to language (Waber 1976, 1979). By virtue of that rapid maturation, girls tend to use verbal strategies earlier and more easily. As adolescents, they do better on tests of verbal ability than spatial abilities. The reverse pattern appears in later maturers, most of whom are boys. This may be the neuropsychological basis for the fact that females are "specialized for understanding the social world" and males "for understanding the physical world" (Levy 1980, 369–70).

Early maturers are more likely to be sensitive to the situations in which they find themselves. They are more likely to understand interpersonal complexity or a web of relationships, thereby avoiding setting people against each other. Later maturers, when and if they are boys, are more likely to be less sensitive to the context. They are more likely to simplify the complexity of relationships, thereby making issues "right" or "wrong," "good" or "bad," "important" or "unimportant."

The early development of language facility has at least two consequences. One is the availability of verbal strategies for coping. Girls tend to think in words about what is happening; boys tend to move around physically in order to find out what's what. This may be the origin of the frustration women express about men being unable to talk about their feelings and the bewilderment men express about women always wanting to talk (Tannen 1990).

A second consequence is that both hemispheres in women tend to perform the same verbal/visual-nonverbal tasks. In men the hemispheres divide the work by specializing (Kolb and Whishaw [1980] 1985, 363–72; McGlone 1980). Furthermore, the male of the species is simply more violent than the female (Konner [1982] 1983, 106–26).

Biopsychologist Jerre Levy (1980, 367–71) summarized the implications of the mixture of verbal and nonverbal information in cerebral organization. Individuals with weak asymmetry, usually female, are more connected with the actual situations in which they find themselves—field dependent, to use a technical phrase—and more sensitive to the context, especially in its interpersonal nuances. Instead of responding to formal and abstract aspects of the environment, they respond to the more subtle experiential clues that interfere with the abstracting process.

This bilateral quality of brain function expedites integrating details and nuances. Perhaps that explains, in part, why a right brain quality like intuition is more prevalent in women (Benderly 1987, 256). The liability in that sensitivity to the context comes in a person's being less able to hone in on a few details relevant to a particular issue. Levy draws a crucial implication from such data:

> An understanding by women that most males are simply not so capable as they would wish at reaching the emotional and psychological states of others accurately, and an understanding and acceptance by men that women may not be able to provide a satisfactory "justification" for their conclusions because of the inferential complexity on which those conclusions are based, might go a long way toward decreasing the frustrating miscommunication that often mark male-female interactions. (Levy 1980, 370–71)

Additional qualities are associated with these genetic differences. Females are more able to tolerate ambiguity and mystery, while males tend to focus more on clarity and decisiveness. Women exhibit more appreciation for nonrational contrasts, whereas men demand logical reasons. Women trust the intuitive more, while men look to authority. Females exhibit a broader range of interests, whereas males tend toward specialized activities. In contrast to a more structured reality for men, women tend to experience life more flexibly.

Female tolerance for frustration is greater than male, it seems. This enables women to "hang in" with situations longer. They tend to exhibit a composed and contained pattern or, to put it more cautiously, a less volatile one. Men, in contrast, have more difficulty coping with frustrating situations and feel a need to resolve them in some decisive way, either by fighting and taking over or by fleeing and getting out.

Brain researcher Doreen Kimura (1985) has compared brain organization in men and women by showing that they define words differently. Women define words by using both hemispheres—in fact, the front and back parts of both hemispheres. The effect is evident in the fact that the source for women's understanding is more global, less conceptual, less dependent upon exact dictionary definitions, and more dependent on what they experience. Men, in contrast, define words by a process confined to their whole left hemisphere in its observational and analytic activity. This makes the meaning of words more precise and, to generalize, more conceptual than experiential. These differences underscore the importance of "experience" in "women's ways of knowing" (Belenky et al. 1986), in contrast to the male tendency to be suspicious of experience as being "too subjective."

In light of this gender-related evidence, the staff at St. Ann's called this third type of patient *reserved friendly*. Women's basic emotional assumption seemed to be uncertain inclusion. Not wanting to exclude anyone, under stress they try to survive by hesitating. Because they see themselves in relationship with others, they defend against standing alone. To that end they use strategies that allow alternatives, explain things in reasonable terms, and take a pragmatic approach to problem-solving, such as a schedule for meals at St. Ann's.

Ordinarily, women are composed, emotionally accessible without being dependent or distant. They are polite, even gracious. They organize what needs doing and take others into account. Under stress they tend to be more constricted and self-effacing than their male counterparts.

Based on this revised understanding the staff then identified all women as reserved friendly instead of mixed type. Two attitudes are associated with this basic interpersonal style: a *respectful friendliness* (RF), which is neither patronizing as active friendliness can be nor distant as passive friendliness is; and *explained order* (EO), a rationale for why things are the way they are. Explained order is used under conditions of stress. In contrast to the arbitrariness of matter-of-fact or the benevolent protection of kind firmness, rules and procedures are explained. A "reasonable" structure gives order to what is happening.

The attitudes of respectful friendliness and explained order proved to be a more humane approach than the previously prescribed attitudes and thus were prescribed for every person admitted to St. Ann's, whether woman or man. Only when the verbal strategy of explained order failed did the staff turn to the other attitudes of passive friendliness and matter-of-fact for the formal type and active friendliness and kind firmness for the informal type. Figure 3.3 shows the revised styles and attitudes.

With the revision of the attitude approach, much of the difficulty with people entering St. Ann's disappeared. The staff approached each newcomer as a person of worth who was capable of coping with new demands, rather than as someone who was either deficient or defiant.

CONCLUSION

This reconstruction of assumptions and attitudes marked a major revolution in my understanding of the ways we cope with being ourselves. It also signaled the various kinds of pastoral counseling needed to stabilize souls in pain, making possible more adaptive responses for us all. The approach applies not only to resident populations but to all relationships.

I have sketched the development of my understanding of the struggle to create conditions in which people can be themselves. Working in the environment of constraints and possibilities that the St. Ann's Home for the Elderly provided over a twelve-year period helped me reshape my view of others and of myself. In the next chapter I draw from my experiences in this working laboratory, as well as from my years of involvement in parish life and pastoral therapy, to spell out a more comprehensive pattern of the way the soul survives and grows.

CHAPTER FOUR

Empowering Souls

TRANSFORMING ROCKINESS INTO ROCKLIKENESS

■ ■ ■ ■ ■

The clinical experience at St. Ann's helps organize the broader patterns of soul-care. More important than organizing the patterns, however, is using that understanding in the therapeutic task. Based on a knowledge of how people cope under conditions of survival and growth, we as pastoral counselors have clues as to how we can engage others in their pain. We are about the task of transforming the rockiness of survival into the rocklikeness of growth.

Therapy accentuates transference. What we have experienced in earlier and significant relationships influences what we experience in the immediate give and take of therapy. That is true of those who come to us for counseling and of us as well. What goes on between us carries undertows of past ways we have handled the vicissitudes of life. As I have come to understand the attitude approach through my work with the confused elderly, I have discerned an approach applicable to all relationships regardless of the situations in which we find ourselves. It is simple in its basic focus on managing stress, yet it is sophisticated in its ramifications for minding the soul.

Pastoral counseling is a way of minding the soul, a remembering of and attending to who we are. Thus, the struggles of the soul are found in the assumptions we carry about the world and our relationship to it. Those assumptions are emotional and theological, constricting and liberating, depending on how we assess what is happening to us. They are the material with which we work in therapy; they are the dynamics with which we live. In brief, they express the transferential and transformative dimensions of who we are.

Because of their pervasive presence in our lives, I describe patterns of survival and growth in broad interactional terms. As we grasp this larger mapping, we will find that we can more effectively engage the more disciplined journey into the psyche.

In the Fourth Gospel, Jesus empowers us to love one another and to share with him his knowledge of God (John 15:12–15). This is the basic pattern of soul-care—namely, companionship with each other that reflects our connectedness with our Creator. Two patterns reflect and reinforce this relatedness. Think of one as the dependability of a mother hen gathering her brood under her wing (Matt. 23:37; Luke 13:34). This suggests our attachment to a protecting figure. Think of the other as the competence of a waiting father (Luke 15:11–32). This suggests our autonomy from enmeshed relationships.

From a neurophenomenological view, these implicit assumptions reflect the development of our nervous system (see Laughlin et al. 1990, 313–16, 336–38). The brain uses the symbols provided by the culture in both its perception of events and its interpretation of the meaning of those events. It takes experience and shapes it into a map of the way things are.

The pattern is our particular view of our own particular history. That view is based on the emotion or affect in the old brain. Affect reflects our assessment of the meaning of situations. We remember who we are by connecting our present with our past for the sake of our future.

What we perceive is shaped by what we intend (see Laughlin et al. 1990, 112–17). As the Letter to the Hebrews puts it, "faith is the assurance of things hoped for, the conviction of things not seen" (11:1). We live by faith, which means living in accordance with the assumptions we attribute to reality (Spilka et al. 1985). Who we are requires alternating and integrating, (1) our pulling things together in adapting to outer reality and (2) in our holding things together by differentiating inner reality. Cognitive psychologist Jean Piaget has labeled these processes *accommodation* and *assimilation* (Kegan 1982). We conform to the context with integrity. Such is the nature of soul-making.

The maturation of the brain requires interaction with other people. We learn to adapt in the community of others, and that adaptation helps us differentiate our own unique world. The voice within still carries the echo of the outer world (*What will people think?*), as the mind sorts out the personal from the impersonal in terms of the images we have of ourselves. Tension between the inner and the outer always exists. That tension can mar, upset, or confuse the idealized image we have of ourselves and of our relation to the world.

Sharing the outer world with others is a necessary condition for affirming our own reality. If done in a caring, loving context, such sharing transforms us. This context is envisioned in the new reality as portrayed in Christ's appearance—the gracious cosmos we neither create nor control.

Sometimes individuals or groups impose their reality on others. Cults from Jonestown to Waco are examples. Even in such an imposed reality of a single-minded, controlling leader, certain needs are met. In the end, however, getting one's needs met can be harmful, even deadly.

At bottom people do not wish to come out of this sharing of reality worsened or harmed or hated, although such violation is prevalent enough. We require a representation of reality that can confirm us in our own reality as part of a larger reality. That confirmation only happens with others.

At best, the match between our individual needs to be confirmed and the resources of others makes for adaptation, growth, and empowerment (Trevarthen 1986, 1990). At worst, the reciprocity makes for *collusion* as we avoid reality, behaving in dysfunctonal ways within the systems of which we are a part. Most of all, we lose all that is human in ourselves and with each other.

Psychiatrist Heinz Kohut has identified three needs basic to our development as persons: "first, the need to have our competence validated; second, the need to be protected in times of stress; and third, the need to be acknowledged by another as 'being like' the other." (Basch 1988, 140–41) The need to know we are alike in the partnership of being human reflects the assumption of connectedness, what I earlier have called inclusion and what pastoral theologian Henri Nouwen (1972) identifies as the wounded healer model. The other two needs—being protected and having our competence affirmed—reflect the assumptions of attachment and autonomy and what Donald Capps (1984) describes in terms of the models of the good shepherd and the wise fool.

CONNECTEDNESS AND COMPANIONSHIP

As noted in chapter 3, the initial form of the embryo is undifferentiated. Neither male nor female, it is "human potentiality." Only with the activation of male hormones do changes come. This is a structural issue, not a sexual or gender issue. Human potentiality underscores our commonality, our connectedness in all that is—genetically, psychosocially, theologically.

By combining the fact that "the basic human plan" is female (Konner [1982] 1983, 122) with evidence of more bilateral cortical processing in females, I speculate that a female-related pattern of emotional and theological assumptions is the primary human pattern. Initially it applies to all of us, men as well as women.

This does not mean that males are to become females or that females are better than males. Rather, the neurotheological givens of the human condition consist of its connecting features. These provide a norm from which the other two patterns are variants. As we learned at St. Ann's, to begin with an approach of respectful friendliness is more humane than starting with either the patronizing of active friendliness, which reflects an anxious attachment, or the managing of passive friendliness, which reflects an anxious autonomy. Like wounded healers, we are to be accessible to each other (Capps 1984). We are in this world together or not at all.

ANXIOUSNESS IN CONNECTION: SURVIVAL VIA RETICENCE

Two images connote the anxiousness in connection: Women are derided for being indecisive, and men are ridiculed for being wimpish. Each sex is criticized for failing to act in some decisive way. The person is perceived as unable to make up her or his mind.

This anxiety reflects a primitive merging of the self with its world. We minimize extreme responses by others and inhibit our own responses. What seems to matter is maintaining our composure. Stress undermines our ability to respond to others. Not wanting to exclude anyone or anything, we try to survive by holding back, by constraining ourselves. Because we see ourselves as necessarily in relationship with others, we defend against standing out and thereby standing alone. In short, we give the appearance of enmeshment.

Whether we are conscious of intending it, our reticence provokes others' involvement (Leary 1957). Becoming impatient with our hesitation, they jump in and take over. None of us tolerates others' confusion easily.

In theological language, the sin of anxious connection takes the form of *acedia*, a minimizing of our humanity in part or in whole. We feel helpless in the face of forces over which we have no power. In our holding back, others see us as helpless, lacking inner resources for coping and thus dependent on them.

How we act is shaped by a survival mind-set. Think of that survival-defensive mode as a neuropsychological correlate of Adam and Eve being confronted by God in the garden. Because we anticipate extreme behavior from others, we react with caution, hesitantly, with uncertainty and reticence. Others experience us as ambivalent and diffuse, and so we feel ourselves. We assume we cannot depend on others; we assume we cannot take initiative; we remain uncommitted. In the face of ambiguity we hide our identity. We camouflage who we are. Under extreme stress we freeze (Bowlby 1973, 90).

Thus we avoid responsibility in two ways: (1) we strengthen others while (2) we appear uncertain ourselves. Each way reinforces the other. Others' strength weakens us, our weakness strengthens others.

Because of the threat of dependency, we live in a fantasy world. We act as if the emotional assumption of anxious connection were true. That is, we feel powerless; we are unsure of our status; we see others as powerful and needing appeasement; so we create a self-possessed dependency. We keep our ideas to ourselves. I call the resulting behavior *survival via reticence*. To the powerful other we convey the attitude, *You have your way.* Inside we feel, *I know differently but there is nothing I can do to take charge. I'm on the margin, on the outside of power, unable to show my hand.*

We want to care for what is happening, to take responsibility for the situation. Yet we defend against taking initiative. We try too hard to take everyone into consideration. We neglect to take into account our own needs and insights.

This tactic of hesitation characterizes much of the behavior of marginalized people. Minorities keep their thoughts to themselves. Their feelings are veiled. They refrain from acting. Just as the female staff at St. Ann's failed to let me know ways in which the attitude approach did not fit their experience, so women and ethnic groups have accommodated their experience to what the dominant group has defined as the norm. So, too, do clients. They may tell us what they think is acceptable to us rather than disclose what they actually experience.

Further, when we are not in a position of power, we dilute intense feelings in others by rationalizing. We come up with face-saving explanations that may bear little relation to the facts. By intellectualizing we neutralize conflict (May 1980, 32). We may appeal to abstract principles. These diffuse individual blame. Alternatively we may blame ourselves for failing to act. At times the process is like one step forward, two steps back. We accommodate to the world and avoid being ourselves. However we act, we negate our presence.

The assumption of anxious connection shows itself in group life as well as in individual interactions. People say they get together because of their responsibility for the world (in acts of caring and love). But even in this connectedness tensions exist—a community of faith may still fail to do its work. The group does not develop cohesiveness. Instead people fall into pairings, as psychiatrist W. R. Bion describes (Bion [1959] 1974). Individuals pair up, taking over the discussion. The group silently allows them to distract it from the real work at hand. With the tacit assumption that people gather to preserve the group itself, discussions commonly

> become tiresome through preoccupation with absent members as a danger to the coherence of the group, and with present members as virtuous for being present. . . . There is no concern to make the group worth preserving and, indeed, protests about the way the group employs its time, or any proposed change of occupation, are regarded as irrelevant to the discussion of the feared disintegration of the group . . . adherence to the group is an end in itself. (Bion [1959] 1974, 53–54)

Whether with individuals or a group, here is the survival aspect of our connectedness—too much of others and not enough of ourselves (see figure 4.1).

A CONSTRUCTIVE RESPONSE TO ANXIOUS CONNECTION: GROWTH VIA COMPANIONSHIP

But this anxious connection has its adaptive core. That core is the theological assumption that everyone is part of God's creation. All of us have been created by God and in God "all things hold together" (Col. 1:16–17). What matters is the caring that connects the needs of everyone, including ourselves, as the second great commandment puts it (Mark 12:29–31). What matters is the making of meaning (Kegan 1982, 288). We are made to care about the whole of reality.

In giving his disciples the commandment to love one another as he loved them, Jesus gives us an image of positive connection: "I do not call you servants any longer, because the servant does not know what the master is doing; but *I have called you friends, because I have made known to you everything that I have heard from my Father*" (John 15:15, italics added). By sharing what he knows, Jesus transforms a hierarchy of dominant and submissive roles into a friendship. The responsibility of cocreation—giving birth and having care over the whole world—which God set before us in the beginning (Gen. 1:28), is reemphasized by the One whom we believe most fully discloses the heart and mind of God. We are in this world together, as partners, as friends.

At the personal level, the positive assumption of connection reflects one of Kohut's three developmental needs—namely, "the need to have [our] humanness, [our] kinship or sameness with others . . . quietly acknowledged" (Basch 1988, 142). In this alter ego, or twinship, transference, under stress we seek the comfort that comes from knowing that we are accepted (Tillich 1948, 153–63). In the presence of another, one who symbolizes shared humanity—a *selfobject* stabilizing our self system when that system is threatened, or a *representative symbol* of God's transforming power—we recover our connection with each other. Both the one under stress and the one giving care share a common humanity, a wounded reality as Capps (1984) and Nouwen (1972) describe it.

To that end, as companions—*partners*, to use feminist theologian Letty Russell's term (1979, 1981)—we use strategies that generate alternatives for everyone. There is no one right way, nor is there any one special person. The pragmatics of exercising care take precedence over abstract principles of what should be—that is, what is fair and right and the rule regardless of the people and circumstances involved (cf. Gilligan [1982] 1983; 1988). A rationale takes account of what has to be done based on the constraints of the situation itself. We are linked with others according to the tasks at hand. We know we are in this world together or not at all.

This emphasis on caring for the world pragmatically reflects theological convictions about prophetic action, as described by theologian David Tracy (1981, 390–98; see also Ashbrook 1988b, 202–4). The conviction identifies the holy with presence: "The cry of the Israelites has now come to me; I have also seen how the Egyptians oppress them. So come, I will send you to Pharaoh to bring my people, the Israelites, out of Egypt" (Exod. 3:9–10); and "[God] has scattered the proud in the thoughts of their hearts. He has brought down the powerful from their thrones, and lifted up the lowly" (Luke 1:51–52). We are instruments of transforming power. We are given responsibility to act in the service of justice and love. By being present to others, we make possible their transforming defense into engagement.

Prophetic action means pragmatic action—caring for others and caring with others in ways that make a difference to them where they live. Caring with others transforms what is given in the emotional assumption of survival to what God is about in the theological assumption of connection. In pastoral counseling we share responsibility for reality by being a companion to those who come to us. The genuine presence of the pastoral counselor can empower the reticent client to risk responsibility in caring for his or her life with others.

CLUES TO ANXIOUS CONNECTION

Clues that we are colluding in survival behavior are available. As individuals, we hesitate to act when we feel responsible. We deny that others fail to carry their share of the load. We take too much on ourselves, overfunctioning in ways that allow others to underfunction. We get frightened of the build-up of intense emotion. Fright triggers reticence, uncertainty, waiting for more time and clearer choices.

In our symbolic role as pastoral counselor, we may find ourselves reacting to clients' distraction by explaining more of what we are about. We may feel bewildered and then resentful at what we perceive as their hesitancy to do what we suggest. We may get frustrated at their not recognizing our authority. We may grow impatient at their vacillation, their withdrawal, or even at their acquiescence to our direction. In short, we experience a baffling sense of feeling accountable combined with an irritating sense of impatience.

When we experience in our symbolic-transference role these kinds of emotions—impatience, frustration, irritation—we are caught in a survival assumption. These feelings are being elicited by the other person's sense of responsibility for what is happening and their reacting with the tactic of hesitation. Our negative feelings are being provoked by their hesitating to take responsibility. As the authority, the alter ego selfobject, we are assuming that we should be all-sufficient—that is, steady as a rock. If we act on these feelings of impatience, then we collude in avoiding the work of reality.

The task is to become conscious of these dynamics—to mind the soul-making process of transforming reticence into engagement. By listening to our own impatience we gain access to the anxiousness in those with whom we are working. By remembering our basic similarity with them, we can aid them in their task of making meaning meaningful. By remembering and attending to who we each are, we become companions in God's work of reality.

AUTONOMY AND ATTACHMENT

We each carry all three basic needs in ourselves—the need to be like others, the need to be protected, and the need to have our competence recognized. At the same time the givens of our beginnings—our genetic predispositions and the constraints of cultural reinforcements—combine with the need to organize a basic or preferred pattern. This preferred pattern tends to characterize each of us, especially when we are under stress and lose the full range of adaptive behavior. Then we fall back on survival tactics. At such times the negative crowds out the positive.

These basic needs seem to have gender-related aspects, at least as viewed in our present culture. The assumption of connection tends to be more female-related. The assumptions of autonomy and attachment, which appear later in the development of the self, tend to be more male-related. Whether these patterns are confined to either sex—an ideological assertion which I view as sexism—is less crucial than the recognition that we all share the basic needs and patterns, and *the meeting of these needs is basic to our becoming the human beings we are capable of being*. In the dynamics of counseling, these needs become exaggerated. They provide a focus in our work together.

AUTONOMY AND COMPETENCE

The first variant, male-related assumption is autonomy and competence. Two images express the core of this pattern: one is the "rugged individualist," the other "the critical spectator." Capps's (1984) portrayal of the wise fool conveys something of the believability of such independence. While the profile is caricatured in the macho male, our culture also glorifies the self-made, self-sufficient, independent person, whether man or woman. Such people are viewed as able to stand on their own two feet.

ANXIOUSNESS IN AUTONOMY: SURVIVAL VIA CONTROL

Anxiety takes the form of a primitive narcissism, an intense protection of the self. We behave in ways designed to control situations. Stress undermines our ability to work with others and reinforces our working on our own. Not wanting to depend on anyone, we survive by taking charge. Because we feel vulnerable, we distance ourselves from others and so stand alone.

This controlled distancing provokes resentment and opposition (Leary 1957; Anchin and Kiesler 1982). Like begets like, and in this case, distance begets distance. Becoming aggravated with our control, others back away, letting us have our own way. Not easily tolerating closeness, we reject support. We are suspicious of the power others can exercise over us. Ordinarily, those with this pattern exhibit an assertive self-confidence. They appear to be formal and strong but are cautious about too much intimacy. Stress prompts either aloofness or anger.

In theological language, the sin of anxious autonomy takes the form of *hubris*, or pride. Pride implies unlimited self-elevation. This classic sin has been condemned by the church more than any other. We feel special, think we deserve to be special, and so do not take others into account. This exaggerated sense of our own importance tends to be a male sin more often than a female one.

In facing reality—Yahweh God in the garden—our behavior is survival driven. We anticipate danger. Suspicious of others, we move cautiously. We count on no one but ourselves. Here is the basic fight-flight syndrome. We avoid responsibility by attacking or avoiding others (see figure 4.1).

Under the threat of dependency, we live in a fantasy world. We act as if the emotional assumption of autonomy were a fact. That is, we feel vulnerable. Because of being hurt or let down we experience relationships as unreliable. We cannot depend on others to meet our need for self-esteem and self-worth. So we put distance between us. I call the resulting behavior *survival via control*.

On the outside we convey the attitude "I am everything." On the inside we feel lonely and vulnerable. We put up a big front, like the Wizard of Oz, only to turn out to be little people behind the curtains.

We want to be strong, invincible, the center of the universe, the whole show, as it were. Thus we defend against letting others know the real us. We are afraid of being hurt. We suspect that we are "neither lovable nor admirable" (Basch 1988, 239) and that we are unbelievable as a genuine person, to draw on Capps's analysis (1984). So we take charge, acting by ourselves, and then end up isolating and alienating ourselves from others.

Thus we give little thought to the concerns of others. Some of the time we act obsessively, endlessly mulling over what to do. Each moment is a struggle for survival. We behave—unconsciously, it seems—in ways to maintain an inflated or grandiose sense of self (Basch 1988, 239): "I am perfect and you admire me" (Greenberg and Mitchell 1983, 354). When disappointed we fight or flee.

The assumption of anxious autonomy shows itself in group life as well as in individual interactions. People come together out of a sense of danger whenever they are vulnerable. They expect the therapist or pastor to be all-powerful, invincible, omnipotent. And so too does the therapist or pastor. Both the group and the authority figure focus on the present as a struggle for survival. Both react to disappointment in nonadaptive ways. Members criticize the authority for not doing the job, and the authority feels angry at being attacked (Bion [1959] 1974). However we act, in the emotional assumption of autonomy we manage to negate others and their mirroring of our competence.

A CONSTRUCTIVE RESPONSE TO ANXIOUS AUTONOMY:
GROWTH IN CAPABILITY

The adaptive core of autonomy is the theological assumption that we are able, in the awesome words of Paul's Letter to the Philippians, to "work out [our] own salvation with fear and trembling" (2:12b). What matters is our ability to make whole that which includes the needs of all, including ourselves (cf. Mark 12:29–31). What matters is our capacity to make meaningful what is genuinely human in ourselves and others.

In telling the Philippian Christians to work out their own salvation, Paul speaks from the adaptive assumption of competence. Whether Paul is with them or absent from them, what counts is their being able to live according to what God is working in them (2:12–13). By acting in terms of their own life story, Paul shifts the potential for a power conflict between them and himself to an affirmation of their own capability.

In terms of Kohut's understanding of transference (1984), adaptive autonomy reflects the basic developmental need "to have one's competent performance validated and approved" (Basch 1988, 140). In this mirroring, the person under stress seeks to be understood and affirmed in his or her capability. In the presence of another human being who symbolizes appreciative encouragement—a selfobject stabilizing our self system when that system is threatened or a symbolic representative of God's transforming power—we recover our ability to be responsible. The dynamics of transference become transformative as we respond to the other as more than a selfobject.

I associate Tracy's (1981, 386–89; see also Ashbrook 1988b, 198–99) conviction about proclamation with this assumption of competence. The assumption specifies our ability to respond to the holistic imperative toward growth, the drive toward wholeness that is inherent in the bodily basis of our being (Laughlin et al. 1990, 150). For example, in calling Israel to be a responsible community under God, Moses declared, "Hear, O Israel . . . " (Deut. 5:1). And Jesus set forth the responsibility of a new relationship with God: "You have heard that it was said to those of ancient times . . . . But I say to you . . ." (Matt. 5:21–22a). And "Repent, and believe in the good news" (Mark 1:15).

Belief in proclamation means that we can face up to reality. We are capable of setting things straight and carrying things through. Because we are capable, we can transform what is given in the emotional assumption of control into what God is about in the theological assumption of competence. Soul-care emerges from what we find in ourselves as we take responsibility for life.

CLUES TO ANXIOUS COMPETENCE

Clues that we are colluding in survival behavior related to competence are present. On an individual basis, we perceive others acting to do us in. We think they are out to get us. Because we experience closeness as an assault, we panic. The fright triggers oppositional rage or hostile resignation. We have looked to others for validation. They let us down. The result is a narcissistic wounding.

In our symbolic role as pastoral counselors we may feel clients challenging our authority. They may seek to undermine and destroy our position, and we may resent their defiance. We may be angry at not being all-powerful and invincible. In short, we may find ourselves feeling attacked, held accountable without our competence being respected.

When we experience these kinds of emotions—resentment, anger, hostility—we are caught in a survival battle. These negative feelings are being provoked by others' drive to be competent. They react to our nonmirroring with attempts to control. As the selfobject of the other, we then are carrying the belief that we should be all-powerful, steady as a rock and wise as a serpent. If we act on these feelings, we collude in avoiding the work of reality.

The task is to become conscious of these dynamics—to mind the soul-making process of transforming survival into growth. By listening to our own anger—our need to be competent by controlling the situation—we gain access to the anxious autonomy in our clients. By mirroring their aspirations and capability, we aid them in their task of making meaning meaningful. Like the father in the parable of the prodigal son, who waited for his son to come to his senses (Luke 15:11–32), we wait for our clients to come to their senses. As a way for them to discover who they are, we mirror their aspirations. As with the attitude approach of passive friendliness in the nursing home, we wait for them to take initiative. We respond to their signals of concern and control.

ATTACHMENT AND DEPENDABILITY

In many ways the assumption of attachment is a mirror image of autonomy. That contrast, I believe, reflects the specialized developments in the two hemispheres of the brain—the dominant brain (usually left), which emphasizes differences in the world, and the nondominant brain (usually right), which discerns similarities. Differences reflect an assumption of autonomy; similarities reflect an assumption of attachment. This sharper division of cognitive activity comes with the later maturation of language and, according to some research, is more prevalent among males than females (Waber 1977, 1979; Levy 1980).

As with the other soul-care assumptions, two images express the core of this pattern of attachment and dependability—the *faithful follower* and the *dependent person*. The church tends to attract dependent people by its promise of being a nurturing community. In this milieu, attachment is viewed positively; we should look to others for support.

In our symbolic roles as selfobject and representative of God, we provide a prototype—an ideal—of how people are to be. People count on our being dependable sources of guidance, protection, and inspiration.

ANXIOUSNESS IN ATTACHMENT: SURVIVAL VIA CONTACT

Anxiety appears in a primitive identification with an idealized figure. We seek contact, especially with those we see as both strong and good. Stress undermines our own competence, driving us to cling to another. Unable to depend on ourselves, we survive by associating with power figures. Because we feel deficient, we find those who might fill our void and upon whom we can count.

This closeness provokes support and guidance (Leary 1957; Anchin and Kiesler 1982). In this case, a response of help elicits a response of support. Contact begets contact. The idealized other responds to our need to be protected by taking care of us. In idealizing someone, we minimize the pain of distance.

Ordinarily, those who rely on attachment are conscientious. They can be counted on. They are comfortable working with others. They accept others easily. They are eager for more contact. Under stress they may come across as either overly supportive or overly needy. A superficial view has associated this with female dependency when, in fact, that attribute is more a sensitivity to the context. That is, the person, in most instances a woman, takes others' needs and power into account, as I have described in the assumption of connection.

In theological language the sin of anxious attachment appears in the form of *concupiscence*, unlimited desiring in relation to others. This desiring may be the sin of lust, and it may express the drive to associate with those who can make up for one's deficiency. Someone who feels inadequate may find another, especially an authority figure, to serve as an all-knowing and all-loving selfobject.

In facing reality—Yahweh God in the garden—we behave in a survival mode. We anticipate dependability on the part of the other. Being shy about expressing our own needs, we hang back, interacting in compliant and appreciative ways. In intense form we cling to others as though our very life depended on them. We avoid responsibility by believing in their capacity to make up for our incapacity (see figure 4.1).

Under the threat of dependency, we live in a fantasy world, acting as if the assumption of attachment were a fact—that is, we feel inadequate. Because we cannot depend on ourselves to meet our need for self-esteem and self-worth, we create closeness with others, demanding that they care for us. I call this behavior *survival via contact*.

On the outside we convey the attitude "You are everything." On the inside we feel fallible: "You are perfect, and I am part of you" (Greenberg and Mitchell 1983, 354). So we put up a front. We build others up while defending against our own resourcefulness. We admire others, believe in them, and see them as strong and caring. Because of feeling inadequate, we fear being dependable, so we look up to others and depend on them to keep life together.

Anxious attachment shows itself in group life as well as in individual inter-actions. Because the group feels inadequate in the face of responsibility, it de-pends on the therapist or pastor. It expects the authority to be all-caring and all-wise, even omnipresent. It focuses on the security of the past and looks to possibility in the future while losing the reality of the present. When the need for protection goes unmet, the group becomes bored and depressed or else hos-tile and demanding. The accusation against Jesus that "he saved others; he can-not save himself" (Matt. 27:41–44) reflects that frustration. In short, the as-sumption drives the group to idolize the authority yet results in the group abandoning the authority when disappointed.

A CONSTRUCTIVE RESPONSE TO ANXIOUS ATTACHMENT: DEPENDABILITY

The adaptive core of attachment is the theological assumption that we can depend on one another as bearers of the gracious context of God. Jesus invites us to come to him with our burdens and cares, and he will give us rest. "Come to me, all you that are weary and are carrying heavy burdens, and I will give you rest. Take my yoke upon you, and learn from me; for I am gentle and humble in heart, and you will find rest for your souls. For my yoke is easy, and my bur-den is light" (Matt. 11:28–30). Like Peter we are to feed his sheep and to follow him (John 21:15–19). We can be dependable for others because we can depend on God as we know God in Christ Jesus. We are neighbors one to another (see Gen. 4:9; Matt. 25:31–46; Luke 10:29–37), priests one to another, as Martin Luther insisted. In this world of ultimate dependency (Ps. 55:22), we can be burden bearers for ourselves and for each other (Gal. 6:2, 5). In Capps's model (1984) we can be the good shepherd, the responsible person. In the model sug-gested by feminist pastoral theologians Glaz and Moessner (1991) we can be "good neighbors."

In terms of Kohutian transference (1984), adaptive attachment reflects the developmental need "to be protected and supported at times of stress or tension that are beyond the competence [of ourselves] to manage satisfactorily" (Basch 1988, 140–41). In this idealizing transference, we long to be supported by asso-ciating with an admired and powerful authority figure. In the presence of this figure, one who symbolizes protection and wisdom—a selfobject maintaining the stability of the self system when that system is uncertain, or a representative of God's transforming power—we regain our ability to function.

The assumption of dependability is similar to the belief pattern of mani-festation described by Tracy (1981, 376–86; see also Ashbrook 1988b, 199–202). With an emphasis on a grace-filled world, the assumption identifies God's ultimate dependability and ours. "There is no longer Jew or Greek, there is no longer slave or free, there is no longer male or female; for all of you are one in Christ Jesus" (Gal. 3:28).

Belief in manifestation means depending on the world as we experience it without elevating people and symbols into God. We can idealize without idolizing. We can turn to that which is outside of ourselves, trusting that these are bearers of being and not Being itself. Because we are dependable, we can transform contact for survival into "what God is about" in growth. What we can do in pastoral counseling emerges from what we find within ourselves.

CLUES TO ANXIOUS ATTACHMENT

Clues that we are reacting in the survival mode of contact are several. As individuals, we look too much to others for life. We believe they are the adequate ones. We feel we are undependable. We think too little of ourselves, underfunctioning in ways that allow others to overfunction. Because we experience distance as being abandonment, we may become depressed or demanding, sullen or hostile. Fright may trigger our trying to get others' undivided support or else our retreating into a fantasy of what might be if only others would do what we wanted.

In our symbolic role, we attend to what is going on inside of us. Here is a clue to what is going on with our clients or parishioners. We perceive them looking to us to take charge. We experience their expectations that we know what to do and can be counted on to do it. Flattery, homage, and hero or heroine worship are intimations of the transference (Basch 1988, 244, 245). We find ourselves on a pedestal.

In short, we feel others attaching themselves to us. They count on us. They expect us to be all and do all. If we feel guilty because we are not all-knowing and all-loving as they and we expect, we try harder, work longer, respond more quickly to "our" failure. When in our symbolic-transference role we experience guilt, failure, or expecting more from ourselves than from others, we are caught in a survival struggle. These feelings are provoked by others' sense of inadequacy and their reacting with contact. As the authority, the idealized selfobject, we too are assuming that we should be all-wise and all-loving—as dependable as a rock and reliable as a good shepherd (John 10:3–4, 11). If we act on these feelings of guilt, we collude in avoiding dependability.

The task is to become aware of these dynamics—to mind the soul-making process of transforming contact into dependability. By listening to our own guilt—our need to be dependable by being in contact with others—we gain access to the anxiousness in those with whom we work. By allowing ourselves to be idealized without being idolized, we help them in their task of making meaning meaningful. As a way for them to discover who they are, we protect them under conditions of stress. As with the attitude approach of active friendliness in the nursing home, we take initiative by being dependable, someone on whom they can count. We respond to their signals of concern and contact.

OVERVIEW

I have described the assumptions and needs with which we all organize the world. We need to be sustained by another's acceptance; we need to have our competence mirrored; and we need to discern the greater power of the ideal. These needs show themselves through the negative emotional assumptions of connection, autonomy, and attachment—assumptions that cause us to build a fantasy of reality that frees us of the anxiety of responsibility. We hide from Yahweh God in the garden by reacting in a survival mode.

In our role as symbol-bearer—representative of God or selfobject—we find these emotional assumptions projected on us. In response, we find their matching negative emotional assumptions in ourselves. Under stress we collude with others in avoiding the work of reality. We become aware of this collusion as we are mindful of our impatience with reticence, our anger at being criticized, and our guilt at not being perfect.

These assumptions have their adaptive sides as well. I think of them as positive theological assumptions—working with others as companions; encouraging competence and aspirations in others; and serving as a dependable, though fallible, ideal. As we become aware of avoiding reality, we transform survival into growth.

These patterns of soul-care are part of all relationships. They are present between a therapist and a client, between a teacher and a student, between a pastor and a parishioner, between a parent and a child, and between members of different groups. We cannot avoid them; neither do we live without them. They are ours. As we remember them as ours, we remember who we are at our best and in our limitations. They are our means of life and ministry, treasure in earthen vessels (2 Cor. 4:7).

PART TWO

Engaging the Soul
Focusing on the Task

Let the same mind be in you that was in Christ Jesus,
  who, though he was in the form of God,
  did not regard equality with God
  as something to be exploited,
but emptied himself,
  taking the form of a slave,
  being born in human likeness.
And being found in human form,
  he humbled himself
  and became obedient to the point of death—
  even death on a cross.

Philippians 2:5-8

For though I am free with respect to all, I have made myself a slave to all, so that I might win more of them. To the Jews I became as a Jew . . . To those under the law I became as one under the law (though I myself am not under the law) . . . To those outside the law I became as one outside the law (though I am not free from God's law but am under Christ's law) . . . To the weak I became weak . . . I have become all things to all people, that I might by all means save some. I do it all for the sake of the gospel, so that I may share in its blessings.

1 Corinthians 9:19-23

CHAPTER FIVE

Oxygen and the Breath of Life

CREATING A CONTEXT

■ ■ ■ ■ ■

Images of rocks help orient the task of pastoral counseling. Whether client or therapist, we all have rocky foundations and rocklike possibilities. We all struggle to live in the excitement of rocklike growth rather than in the oppression of rocky survival. A theoretical frame based on an interpersonal view of human functioning makes these images more explicit, enabling the counselor to more appropriately be with those seeking help, especially under conditions of stress and anxiety.

The pastoral counselor becomes "a rock in a weary land," stabilizing the uncertain world of clients, stopping the erosion of their lives caused by the blowing wind, and shading their psyches from the scorching sun. To shift the image, the counselor closes the door of the counseling room, enters into the closet of others' pain, and like Ezekiel with the exiles, sits "there among them, stunned" until a clear word of meaning emerges (Ezek. 3:15–16).

How can the helper sit with the one seeking help? How can that pain be lessened, even healed? What do we need to know to meet that person at his or her point of need, to use that very suggestive phrase of pastoral psychotherapist Carroll Wise ([1966] 1989)? What happens to the counselor in the anxious presence of another human being?

CHANGING PAIN INTO POSSIBILITY

When I shifted my ministry from the parish to the seminary, I invited various people with whom I had counseled to share with me what had gone on between us and within them. I was looking for clues to the means of meaning: What had

happened? What had been helpful? What had not been helpful? What change
had come? Was it good or bad? I was eager for anything that might inform as-
piring pastors and especially those considering the specialized ministry of
counseling.

One of the people with whom I talked was a woman in her mid-forties (Ashbrook 1970, 1971, 65–81), whom I will call Janet. Janet had come to me when
her marriage was collapsing. Her husband felt no need of help. After our initial
meeting I made a special visit to Janet's workplace and suggested to her that if
anything were to change, she herself would have to do the changing. Subsequently, she came to me for counseling. In a technical sense I was a counseling
pastor, a pastor engaged in a concentrated reflective exploration of a parishioner's pain. From her point of view, however, I was a pastoral counselor, a specialist who set aside general pastoral care for the sake of focal expertise. We met
once a week for four months. Nine months later we held two additional meetings. And, of course, we had regular contact through the various activities of the
church.

At the time of my work with Janet I had had several years of professional counseling activity and many hours of supervision from a variety of supervisors.
While not a novice, neither was I seasoned. Our work together, therefore, reflects
what often goes on early in one's specialization rather than later. However, she
reflected on our work together in a way that frames—narrates—the task of all
pastoral counseling.

I regarded what we had done as a failure. To the best of my knowledge little or nothing changed in the marriage. Janet and her husband eventually separated and divorced. So in asking Janet to talk with me about the possibilities and
difficulties of pastors counseling with parishioners I assumed I would learn more
about difficulties than possibilities.

Imagine how startled I was, then, to have her looking back over the period
of her pain and my ministry and declare without a moment's hesitation:

> Well, that would fill a book. When I heard the [Bach] *B Minor Mass*,
> the first three parts of that were extremely meaningful to me because
> it was the story of my therapy.

> The *Kyrie*, the cry for help from the bottom of my soul, and then the
> *Gloria*, when I had finally done something and proclaimed the fact
> that I was I and was never going to be anybody else—and devil take
> the hindmost, really—and then after that period of exaltation, there
> was a *Credo* when I could affirm what was real and true and deter-
> mine truth from ego. And that was a wonderful exalting experience
> with me.

I don't even know what the Catholic mass is supposed to be, but if that's it, it can have great meaning.

Janet had given her experience a lot of thought. I viewed our work as questionable; she regarded it as liberating. From the vantage of the late 1980s and early 1990s, the dynamics of her liberation are clear. Our counseling process had negated the power relationship between myself as a male authority and herself as a dependent female. She had found her own voice. Her growth came as she experienced a new connectedness to what was real (see Jordon et al. 1991; Saussy 1991). She experienced "public power," what Carolyn G. Heilbrun defines as "the ability to take one's place in whatever discourse is essential to action and the right to have one's part matter" (1988, 18).

Janet voiced her crying out in misery as a cry for help from the bottom of her soul. She made the first move by letting me know that things were "not well" in her marriage, and I followed that up in two ways: first, by suggesting she consider therapy, and second, by going to her at work and asking whether she had thought more about that possibility. Later she commented on the impact of my going to her in that way. "That's the kind of thing that's just priceless to anyone who's abjectly unhappy and seeing no possible way out."

Her response to my initiative reflects an idealizing selfobject relationship. In idealizing we desire to merge ourself with an idealized selfobject to recapture our earliest sense of perfection and omnipotence. Under stress we use such an idealized relationship to make up for the deficiency we feel within ourselves (Basch 1988, 140–41). In mature development we transform the idealized selfobject into ego-ideals and appropriate aspirations. In such idealizing relationships pastoral counselors become "good shepherds." We take initiative yet balance "the healing power of distance with the redeeming power of intimacy" (Oates 1990, 833).

Janet went on to spell out specifics of her move from the cry of the *kyrie* to the exaltation of the *gloria* to the truth of the *credo*.[1] I have always been moved by her story: her abject misery, my own sense of failure, her struggle with—and my blindness to—the dominance/submission dynamics in the male/female roles. Yet healing went on. Like Yahweh God with the Hebrews in Egypt (Exod. 3:7–10), I had heard her cry; I had seen her distress; I had come to her in her misery. In the end my sense of failure was proven naught.

Janet's imagery of the *B Minor Mass* gives us a sense of what is involved in moving from pain to possibility. Without specifying the steps in change, she

---

1. The first three parts of Bach's *Mass in B Minor* are: *Kyrie eleison*, "Lord, have mercy on us"; *Gloria in exclesis Deo*, "Glory be to God on high"; and *Credo in unum Deum*, "I believe in one God." The chorus introduces and ends each part, with the four vocal soloists singing duets and arias in the middle sections.

has used the *B Minor Mass* to indicate the phases of change. These phases describe therapy more as a process than as a finished product. In addition, Janet has provided glimpses of differences between women's and men's experiences in therapy. (I will say more about this later.)

I suggest that we take the chaotic and fragmented experiences people bring to us and transform them into a story, a song, a symphony. Their story has failed to come together or has "gone mad." The music of their lives is discordant or random. Through therapy their story may be repaired (Howard 1991) and their music be made joyous.

In the language of classical psychoanalysis that process is known as making the unconscious conscious, turning what is known yet isolated (because it is not named) into what is thought or named and thereby capable of being reflected upon and shared (Bollas 1987). In the language of biblical religion, it is the apostle Paul's admonition to be "transformed [*metanoia*] by the renewing of [our] minds, so that [we] may discern what is the will of God—what is good and acceptable and perfect" (Rom. 12:2).

With a story we can reconstruct the meaning of our lives. We can identify when and how that transformation begins to happen. Even though we can chart the phases, the creation of a new reality is always awesome to experience. It is truly a new birth of meaning.

As Janet tells us, therapy is precipitated by an experience of misery, a *kyrie*; it meanders in the wilderness of discovering the *gloria* of being uniquely one's own person; and it comes to fulfillment, a *credo*, in affirming what is real for oneself and true in reality. In minding the soul, the pastoral counselor enables people to come to themselves and find their way home. By coming to ourselves and finding our way home, I mean finding our origin and destiny in God.

Consider now the connection between Janet's *kyrie*, the cry from the bottom of her heart, and the initial phase of therapy.[2] What follows juxtaposes knowledge of the working brain and biblical imagery—that is, oxygen and the breath of life, sanctuary and ordering experience, and aspects of the holding environment of the counseling process. Together they make the remembering of and attending to who one is a sensible process.

OXYGEN AND THE BREATH OF LIFE

The Brain. The brain makes up about 2% of the body's weight yet consumes about 20% of the oxygen used by the entire body (Carpenter [1943] 1976, 600; see

2. The specific skills of the counseling process are widely known and readily available. This is true of counseling in general (e.g., Carkhuff 1969; Egan 1982; Truax and Carkhuff 1967) as well as of pastoral counseling in particular (Clinebell [1966] 1984; Patton 1983; Taylor 1991). Material on the more subtle and sophisticated aspects of various theoretical approaches is beyond the scope of this book (e.g., Greenberg and Mitchell 1983; Gustafson 1986; Basch 1988; Mahoney 1991).

figure 5.1). The frontal lobe, the area that has increased the most in size over the course of evolution, receives about 15% more blood than the mean for the entire cerebrum (Kolb and Whishaw [1980] 1985, 346–47). The importance of the frontal lobe in *humans* for processing information is suggested by the fact that the lobe occupies 25% of the larger human brain and only 3% of a cat brain (Diamond 1991, 172). Further, the right hemisphere, the locus of pattern-making, appears to receive "slightly more blood flow than the left" (Kolb and Whishaw [1980] 1985, 347). That which uses the most blood receives the most blood.

Without oxygen the brain dies within minutes. With the complete cessation of circulation in the brain, consciousness lasts less than ten seconds (Carpenter [1943] 1976, 600). The brain uses oxygen to maintain and enhance life. Both physiological stress and psychological anxiety reduce the amount of oxygen in the blood, thereby reducing the amount of information available for coping. The person is crippled in his or her capacity to respond constructively.

Lack of oxygen is the physiological basis for the experience of lack of trust. When a person mistrusts what is happening or those who impact his or her life, that person's bodily process shifts from engaging to defending. One fights to get one's breath. To survive one fights or flees or freezes (Bowlby 1973, 90; Gilbert 1989, 47–48, 84).

Biblical Imagery. In Hebrew thought our souls are located in the bloodstream. The Genesis portrayal of human creation emphasizes the centrality of breathing and life: God breathed into *Adam* and *Adam* became a living soul (Gen. 2:7).

In the early period of Hebrew religion, two words were used for "breath"— *ruach* and *nephesh*. Later in the Greek language *ruach* became synonymous with "spirit" or "word." *Nous* referred to that within us which related us to God. *Nephesh*, in contrast, became identified with "soul" or *psyche*. It designated the life principle (*vis vitalis*). For the Hebrew there was no separate term for "will" as we understand it. The soul acted in its entirety through the physical organism (Ashbrook 1958).

In the New Testament, soul, or *psyche*, and spirit, or *pneuma*, were differentiated in a way similar to that of the later Old Testament writings. *Pneuma*, or spirit, corresponded with *ruach*. They both characterized breath as the unity of power and mind—that is, "the power of life which is at the same time the bearer of the mind." Consequently, spirit was distinguished from soul but not regarded as separate from it. Spirit was taken as "the principle of soul" (Niebuhr 1951, 1:151). Basically, spirit meant our capacity for affinity with God. *Psyche*, or soul, on the other hand, corresponded to *nephesh*. It carried primarily the Old Testament usage of "vitality" or "life" itself.

Breath as Metaphor. The first task of a pastoral counselor is to provide a situation in which people can once again catch their breath. *Breath* is a metaphor that carries biological, psychological, and spiritual connotations. I have already sketched its physiological basis, its biological importance, and its biblical nuances. Turn now to a more cultural expression of breath, the mythico-religious view of sanctuary and the therapeutic idea of a holding environment. This represents a leap of association between levels of conceptual organization.

SANCTUARY AND ORDERING EXPERIENCE

In seeking to understand "persuasion and healing," psychiatrist Jerome Frank of Johns Hopkins University (1973) identifies *demoralization*—a loss of spirit, sense of failure, and feeling of powerlessness to affect oneself and one's world—as the basic problem with which healers are faced. Demoralized people have no power of being, no breath for life. Whether a helper is a traditional mental health professional, a clergyperson, or a parent, Frank believes certain features are basic to all healing: a special relationship, a special place, a rationale, and the trying of new behavior. For now I will comment only on the first two—the creating of a context through a special place and a special relationship.

Special Person and Place. The relationship between a sufferer and a healer is bedrock. As the loss of significant relatedness makes for demoralization, so the recovery of life requires meaningful contact with others. The pastoral counselor takes on the symbolic power of being a locus for help, a bearer of Being, a source of new life, a rock in a weary land.

The helper's symbolic role is closely linked with the place in which help is sought. In religious language, that special place is a *sanctuary*, a place to catch one's breath, literally and spiritually. It may take the form of a therapist's study, a teacher's desk, or a physician's office, but the reality is the same: in this space people can experience the loss of breath and explore the recovery of soul. Here they can deal with past experiences, feel "awful" feelings, try out untried behavior, or experiment with a modified or even a revolutionary lifestyle. Constraints are lifted; condemnation is eliminated; new birth is the task (John 3:3).

The special place—and the special relationship—has a numinous quality about it. It is sacred by virtue of being marked off and distinguished from other spaces. People enter reverently, like Moses, taking off their shoes because the place whereon they stand is "holy ground" (Exod. 3:5). Understandably, people approach the place and the person with quickening anticipation. Their hearts beat faster and their breath becomes shallower. Their mouth becomes dry and their palms sweaty. The hope of help arouses people physiologically, psychologically, spiritually.

The Symbolic Center of Reality. Mircea Eliade, who pioneered in the comparative study of religion, claims that the special place marks the realm of the real:

"[the] religious [person's] desire to live *in the sacred* is in fact equivalent to [one's] desire to take up [one's] abode in objective reality, not to let [oneself] be para-lyzed by the never-ceasing relativity of purely subjective experiences, to live in a real and effective world, and not in an illusion" (Eliade 1959a, 28). Eliade is uni-versalizing Janet's *credo*—namely, to "affirm what was real and true and deter-mine truth from ego." People long to live in a world larger than themselves, a world to which they can contribute because they are a part of the whole and not the whole itself.

The special place symbolizes the center. Because "the sanctuary reproduces the universe in its essence," it marks the symbolic meeting point of heaven, earth, and hell (Eliade 1959b, 17). Thus the sanctuary allows passage from one realm to another. When we catch our breath we move from the vibrant under-ground of felt-meaning, to the controlled ordinariness of the everyday, to the ecstatic transcendence of an eternal presence. Here is the realm of the real. But the way leading to the sacred is always fraught with difficulty. A sense of anx-iousness fills every transition from the profane to the sacred, from illusion to re-ality, from death to life, yes, from time to eternity.

In the special place with the special person—the space of the center—peo-ple begin to experience order. The entrance constitutes the boundary between inner and outer realities, between the ongoingness of time and the making of meaning. The place sets limits on space and time and allows people to transform a deadening present into a living future.

Yet the entrance, paradoxically, reveals the coincidence of opposites. It is the place where pain and healing meet. People begin to befriend the frightening; they start to inhabit the unfamiliar. By dwelling in that which they have avoided they find a new world, a new life (Eliade 1959b, 12–21), a new creation. God breathes into them the breath of life. They become living souls.

From the point of view of myth, "it is by virtue of the temple that the world is resanctified in every part" (Eliade 1959a, 59). Because of the special place the arbitrary distinction between a safe sanctuary and an unsafe world is reduced. Eventually there is no distinction. As the Book of Revelation declares, in the new reality, the new Jerusalem, there is no temple, for God has become all-in-all (Rev. 21:22–25). Once again the world reveals itself as cosmos, as ordered and sacred, as ultimately real. Once again the public square becomes as life-giving as the therapist's office.

Expectations of Those in Pain. A less mythical understanding of context comes in identifying the meaning of *pastoral* for those who come to pastoral counselors. What people expect affects what transpires. That is part of the power of persuasion, the expectation of being in a special place with a special person.

Recent (1992) Gallup research underscores this point. Seventy percent of women and sixty-two percent of men reported that if they had a serious problem requiring counseling, they would "prefer to see a professional counselor who represents spiritual values and beliefs." Further, 79% of the men and 81% of the women would want their values and beliefs integrated into the counseling process. While a basic trust is present in all healing relationships, the special feelings people have about a pastoral counselor shape the focus of concern and the resources of healing (Hiltner and Colston 1961).

A HOLDING ENVIRONMENT

Oxygen and sanctuary have their psychological equivalent in what British psychiatrist D. W. Winnicott describes as the holding environment (1965). By the way a mother handles and holds her infant, she creates an environment that facilitates growth by reducing threat and fostering well-being (Davis and Wallbridge 1981, 46). In a holding environment threat is contained—whether it comes from the outer world or the inner world. The person is sheltered from being overwhelmed.

Breath, trust, sanctuary, a holding environment—these are different ways of identifying a firm foundation. Without these we have little life and little hope of life. Only in breathing are we living souls.

The last forty years of experience and research in counseling and psychotherapy by psychologists such as Carl Rogers (1951; 1961) and Robert Carkhuff (Truax and Carkhuff 1967; Carkhuff 1969) have identified basic features of therapeutic facilitation. These are variously known as the therapist's openness, unconditional positive regard, genuineness, congruence between experience and expression, and capacity for empathy. These are relational and, thereby, foundational. Pastoral theologian Charles W. Taylor combines them into the single idea of *presence* (1991, 15ff.).

What goes into creating an environment that facilitates growth by a pastoral counselor or a pastoral psychotherapist?

Time Limits and Finitude. Finitude is basic to being human (see Hunter 1990b), for it is present in all limits and endings. Finitude applies to how much time we have to talk, how much energy we have to expend, and how much life we are able to live. When the Greeks counseled, "Know yourself," they meant "Know your mortality; remember that you will die" (Moltmann 1990, 361). In short, we are to recognize the reality of finitude. In realizing that life is limited, we liberate ourselves.

The counselor, therefore, frames the therapeutic task in terms of time. He or she may begin by saying, "We have about fifty minutes to talk. Why don't you take about thirty-five minutes to let me know why you've come. That will leave us about fifteen minutes to explore next steps." Deliberately using the word *about* frees the counselor from having to rigidly adhere to time limits. *About* is accurate, however, and it suggests that counseling is more a natural process than a mechanical one. The time cannot be packaged, though it can be predicted and ought to be used.

A modified form of time-limited therapy activates what I think of as a form of eschatological urgency (see Moltmann 1990). We must not put off until tomorrow that which demands attention today, for "Today is the day of salvation" (Mark 1:1–5). The counselor can bring the future closer by suggesting that the future is already present. The anticipated future works on our behalf if we allow it to be part of our present. By speaking of the *chronos*, or clock, nature of the counseling context, the pastoral counselor invokes the *kairos*, or meaningful character of time, which is God's time.

The limits of space and time are pivotal in the care of souls. Without limits and endings, the basic activity-rest-renewal process of sabbathing is hampered. Meaningful memory is muffled, and minding the soul is compromised (see chapter 13 for more on sabbathing and memory).

A Personalized Relatedness. Although the contract with someone seeking help is professional, the contact is personal. Therefore, it is important to call the person by name—whether first or formal name depends on how we handle our security needs.

The use of a person's name must also take account of cultural differences. I used to be puzzled by the formal way in which African-Americans would address each other. I was particularly puzzled when I overheard close women friends calling each other "Mrs. Roosevelt" or "Mrs. Johnson." Then I learned the significance of role and status. For those who had been slaves, stripped of dignity and status, the formal designation gave backbone to a real relationship. It was evidence of their being somebody, a bearer of a title and worthy of recognition.

Failure to recognize such expressions of dignity perpetuates the power imbalance between someone seeking help and someone providing help. In our pluralistic, multicultural world we of the dominant culture(s) are only now becoming aware of what pastoral theologian Benoni Reyes (Silva)-Netto identifies as the "hidden agenda in cross-cultural pastoral counseling" (1985). In the past, anthropological exploration has been carried on in a way that characterizes one's own culture as advanced and other cultures as primitive.

A parallel may exist in psychological and religious counseling. The person sought is viewed by both the counselor and the counselee as "better than" the one seeking help. Thus the counselor can be referred to with a title and the counselee with an informal name. From such a stance, contact may result in exploitation. Diagnosticism or the labeling of others with pejorative psychological categories constitutes one danger. As counselors we must not chain our clients with our own mistaken sense of absolute certainty and value.

In using the person's name, whether formal or informal, the counselor transforms the professional contact into a personal encounter. If the person is younger, we more easily use his or her first name. If older, we more likely use the formal title of Mr. or Mrs. or Ms. This applies especially to someone from a different ethnic background. Because of the imbalance in status between the seekers of help and ourselves as the source of help, we can too easily assume a pseudo-intimacy.

Sometimes I ask, "How do you prefer to be called?" And I, in turn, may indicate that "I'm comfortable with 'Jim' or 'Mr. Ashbrook' or 'Dr. Ashbrook' or 'Rev. Ashbrook.'" This is crucial if the issue carries the overlay of classism, sexism, ethnocentricism, or ageism.

The initial intent of structuring a *functional* relationship in contrast to a *hierarchical* one is basic to the counseling process. We are equals in our humanity, yet we have different responsibilities in our work together. As therapists, we are to put ourselves at the service of others, and others are to put themselves at the focus of our concern.

Pastoral counseling requires a relational reality, a named world. A person with a name is more than a person with a problem. She or he has an identity. She or he is a *somebody* just as we are *somebodies*. To know and use a person's name is to reflect the biblical understanding of the power of naming and being named (Abba 1962). Our names call forth the living soul of each of us.

Authenticity and Authority. Our authority to engage in pastoral counseling comes from our being part of a larger structure of accountability (see Williams 1961, 30–51; Southard 1990a; Patton 1990a). The American Association of Pastoral Counselors (AAPC) has standards of training and membership that attempt to legitimize what pastoral counselors do. A group of peers reviews one's formal education, one's recognition by one's faith community that one is engaging in what it regards as a legitimate expression of its ministry, one's specialized training and supervised experience in formal pastoral therapy, one's own psychotherapeutic exploration, one's identity as a *pastoral* therapist, and one's ability to utilize the resources of both the religious and psychological traditions. All this is a recognition of formal authority. It is a way of invoking a socially understood role responsibility. While it does not guarantee that pastoral counselors will not make mistakes or misuse this authority, it does provide standards of professional functioning. It involves a code of ethics and makes public the procedures for monitoring how pastoral counselors are to act in their professional role.

Much of the shift in cultural values involves suspicion of formal roles and rules. Unconsciously, cultural values and societal roles have reinforced dominant group(s) and undermined nondominant groups. Increasingly people are learning that "expertise" comes from lived experience more than from formal credentials.

The authority of one's personhood qualifies formal authority. Who one is in other areas of life affects one's effectiveness in role responsibility. Think of this personal authority as *authenticity*. It reflects the genuineness of the counselor being human like everyone else. Counselors are vulnerable, inadequate, dependent, and needy just like their clients. Their life experiences beyond their professional education and narrow professional role enhance their ability to help and to heal.

Usually this more personal part of the counselor's life does not belong in the counseling process. There have been times, however, when my being a husband, a father, a grandfather, a church member, or a cancer patient have been relevant. Self-disclosure is a complicated issue and requires integrating into the ongoing therapeutic task. For the most part, such authenticity heightens one's authority.

Identifying the Distracting and Disruptive. What cannot be ignored needs to be named. For the counselor being supervised, a tape or video recorder is useful. So also is a two-way mirror in which the helper-and-helpee can be observed without their knowing. Outside noise, schedule changes, interruptions, physical difficulties, sickness, and encounters outside the counseling session intrude on the working relationship. Dealing with the unwelcome opens up the issue of change itself: How do we transform something that is working negatively into something that facilitates growth?

Whatever commands our attention takes up neuropsychological space. If we expend energy in trying to eliminate it from consciousness, we end up struggling with a divided mind. And a divided mind makes for inefficiency. The many facets of a context can work against us or can be baptized to work for us. To name the unavoidable given is to remember to forget it at the very least and to use it in a facilitating way at the very most. Only as we connect with what distracts us can we attend to the therapeutic task at hand.

When I first became a pastor, I began to learn about reframing the annoying into the facilitating. My office was situated next to a busy thoroughfare, and the noise of traffic continuously polluted the silence of my study. Contemplative Douglas Steere wrote about the noise that often intrudes on prayer, and I followed his lead in trying to weave the world of traffic into the realm of prayer. I might pray: "O God, the world rushes by and I am given the space to stop. May my resting be for the renewal of others." Or again, I might pray: "Others go their ways, O Lord. Help me to know my way that I may go in your way." Or still again, "I am as busy as the world rushing by. Quiet my mind that I may know my heart. And in knowing my heart may I know your will."

In thinking back on those times, I now realize that it takes psychic energy to ignore intrusive stimuli. The harder I "try *not* to think of something, like a pink elephant," the more I think of it. At the very least, to name the distraction—

"traffic," "tape recorder," "supervision," "being late"—allows it *to be*, to be as it is in relation to what I am about. It is part of the context. Having recognized its presence, my mind is freer to attend to the agenda.

Sometimes in leading a workshop or conducting a class or starting a supervisory process—when there is a lot of initial confusion and rush—I begin with this exercise. I invite the group to put down their coffee cups, pencils, and papers and to close their eyes and get as physically comfortable as they can. I suggest that we slowly take three or four deep breaths—drawing the air in through our nostrils and feeling it expanding our abdomens like a balloon. We are to let the air slide out, helping it a bit by pulling our abdomens in. Then, with their eyes closed, I invite them, in their imagination, to leave the room and go somewhere—wherever their heart takes them or their mind insists they go. I tell them we have two minutes by the clock to be there, and I will give them a thirty-second warning before it is time to return.

After a minute and a half I say, "Thirty seconds more." Then after two minutes I say, "Keeping your eyes closed, begin to finish up what you are doing where you are. When you are ready, return to this room and begin to be here again. Open your eyes slowly, look around, move in your chair, and be here in this room."

I invite people to share their experience. Some report returning to complete an unfinished project. Most describe going to a peaceful place by the ocean or a lake or in the woods or on a mountain—sometimes alone, often with a loved one. They resent my calling them back because the relaxation and excitement are deeply satisfying. But having gone, they find themselves able to return and to attend to the task at hand. Because we can leave—in our imagination—we are able to be where we are.

The task with distraction is to get the feeling right brain communicating with the observing left brain. The weather often proves useful in this respect. A stormy day or trouble with traffic becomes the bridge from an annoying distraction to a facilitating attraction. One might observe, "It seems as though the weather reflects your stormy feeling . . ."; or "The pile-up on the road feels very similar to what is piling up inside of you . . ."; or "The road's icy conditions suggest you need to slow down in order to prevent trouble. . . ." The counselor shifts the other's attention from objective left-brain processing to symbolic right-brain processing. In this mode of meaning making everything is capable of bearing the meaning of life.

A process of meaning making goes on much of the time on the edges of our consciousness. This metaphoric potential breaks out spontaneously and transforms objects in the environment into symbolic expressions of our lives. Because we are meaning-making creatures, our right brain creates patterns and our left brain interprets them.

If a client rearranges a chair, one might wonder if he or she is having trouble settling down. One might ask if he or she is feeling a need for distance today? Or, one might note the behavior mentally and use it by being especially attentive to avoidant interactions.

Every aspect of the world is capable of bearing symbolic meaning, whether it is distracting or not. We can find in the world that which is in our souls. So in minding the souls of those who come to us for counseling, our task is to connect the emotional meaning of what they experience with the conscious intention of what they seek. And there is nothing that cannot serve that purpose. The stumbling stone becomes a stepping stone. To use the powerful imagery of the Bible, the stone the builder rejects turns into the chief cornerstone (1 Peter 2:7–8).

Focusing Expectations and Context. As a subtle expression of the collaborative nature of minding the soul, I may ask near the beginning of a client's first session, "Is there anything you want or need to know before we start or as we start?"

This is an ambiguous statement, for it could refer to the process itself or to something the person might want to know about me. I do not tell very much about myself, because we are getting together for the client's sake, not mine. What the person knows about me must be relevant to our working relationship. That is why I invite the person to ask what he or she needs or wants to know as we start.

My own office is filled with objects suggesting who I am. Many of my interests and values are readily apparent—plants and rocks of various shapes and sizes; a figure of a monk praying and another of a peasant riding a water buffalo; books on history, Bible, psychology, theology, mysticism; pictures of quiet settings. I am not content to be an ambiguous object that invites others' unfocused projections.

Sometimes clients comment on one of the objects. When they do, I engage in a brief exploration of what the objects mean to me. Sometimes I inquire how these connect with them. Often people get right down to business.

I invite orienting questions for two reasons. First, I want to know what they are wondering about as part of the dynamics with which we begin. Second, I want to activate their awareness of the nuances of the context in which we work. The context of expectations is the basis of all therapeutic work. I want them to be as aware as possible of what I represent and symbolize, and so I want some clue as to what I might mean to them.

Beyond professional and religious expectations I want my space to convey a sense of my being a human being in my own right. Even though pastoral counselors are in the role of "expert," we are real people in relation to those who come to us. We are not blank tablets upon which others can project their reality apart from our reality. Beyond transference and counter-transference lies the realm of our intersubjectivity (Natterson 1991), the realm of our realness with one another. We are in the room together as real people, each with his or her own uniqueness. That uniqueness is both our authenticity and our particularity, the resource we bring to each other.

No matter how much I know I never know enough to know the fullness of the life of another. In psychological terms this is the issue of whether I am humble enough to help (Keith-Lucas 1972). In christological language it is the self-emptying of God in becoming human, even to being rejected and crucified (Phil. 2:5–8). In our counseling it entails our being a servant to others without allowing ourselves to be mastered by them.

THE FEATURES OF THE HOLDING ENVIRONMENT

As pastoral counselors, we assist people who come to us to move from the pain of their present to the promise of God's future. We do that by creating a holding environment in which hope and hurt work together.

From a religious view we are instruments of God's breath of life. From a neurophysiological view we enable others to regain their breath by a recovery of oxygen in the blood. From a mythic view our place and our person provide a sanctuary, a center in which the bodily, the psychic, the social, and the spiritual interact in the reordering of what is real and true and right.

That holding environment includes the following features:

- structured time and peopled space;
- personal relatedness;
- an implicit, and sometimes explicit, recognition of our mutual humanity;
- an intention to put ourself at the service of the person coming for help;
- identifying and using the distracting and disruptive; and
- an explicit expectation that the client wonders about the kind of persons we are as well as carries assumptions about how we will work together.

The chapters that follow describe the counseling process of minding the soul in more detail. That process manifests a spiraling movement of connecting with the other, responding to his or her meanings, exploring their ramifications, and his or her reengaging life in a more satisfying way.

CHAPTER SIX

Surviving and Being Known

CONNECTING

■ ■ ■ ■ ■

The initial phase of the process of pastoral counseling involves connecting with the psychic reality of those seeking help. Clients invite us into their house (of life), and we are privileged to know as much as they intend for us to know. We are allowed to be a collaborator in how they are living. This basic step of connecting requires that we be *respectful* of who they are, *attentive* to what goes on—in them, in us, and between us—and *receptive* to different styles of coping and growing.

RESPECTFUL OF THOSE SEEKING HELP

Those who seek us out come with a variety of stories. Pastoral counselor Susan B. Montz, in describing some clients and their stories, gives us a glimpse of what pastoral counselors face in their initial contacts:

> A young, single daughter of a physician comes seeking peace and freedom from her memories of an abusive relationship as she tries to integrate two parts of herself that struggle with issues of sexual expression.

> A young homosexual man comes searching for meaning in his journey home from a distant city where he has been confronted by the betrayal of his lover whom he discovered is in a new relationship.

> A young married woman with a newly found faith in Christianity comes seeking God's answer to whether she should leave her abusive husband who adheres to another religion and wants her to return with him to the Middle East.

A man with a history of schizophrenia comes wanting someone to help him sort out the negative parental, Calvinist messages of a "punishing God" that he received from a "punishing father" and to address issues of childhood sexual abuse.

A depressed young man with a pattern of destructive living comes having failed in two recent suicide attempts. He says he is beginning to think there must be some reason he is alive, and he wants to discover a sense of meaning and purpose for his life.

Montz points out:

Christian and non-Christian, religious and non-religious, come to us, and I listen to their stories as they sit across from me in initial counseling sessions. In many cases, the questions they ask about meaning and purpose are the same questions I have asked, particularly in facing the crisis experiences of my own life. . . . My question becomes: How can I be most helpful to these clients as I work with them in their journeys? How can I most effectively function in the role of "pastor" with them?

Montz's experience reflects that of every pastoral counselor: How can I be most helpful? How can I function more effectively? What does it mean for me to be in the role of "pastoral" counselor?

Janet's story, in chapter 5, of transforming misery (*kyrie*) into new action (*credo*) by the experience of exaltation (*gloria*) was a prototype of the therapeutic process. She came to me out of a sense of misery. People rarely seek help unless pushed to the wall; they do not often come to ask how to prevent pain. When pain becomes unbearable people mobilize themselves to make their vulnerability known. Janet said of this initial move, it is "a cry for help from the bottom of your soul."

How does the pastoral counselor relate to such a cry?

AN INVITING PRESENCE

Some years ago Carl Rogers conducted a classic teaching interview for The American Academy of Psychotherapists.[1] He was researching the physiological reactions of hospital patients to being interviewed. After explaining the research situation to one particular patient, P.S., a seventeen-year-old girl, he said:

---

1. "The Case of P.S.—A Young Woman." Comments by Carl R. Rogers, Ph.D. Available from The American Academy of Psychotherapists, Tape Library, 409 Prospect Street, New Haven, Conn.

Now . . . what I would like would be for you to tell me anything you're willing to tell me about yourself and your situation, how you feel about yourself, or I guess another way of putting it is that anything you are willing to tell me that would help me to know you better, I'd be very glad to hear.

She responded immediately by asking, "Where do you want me to start?" In effect, she was saying, "I'm ready. Just tell me what you're wanting." And Rogers replied, "Wherever you would like to." Notice the open-endedness of Rogers' invitation and the proposed mutuality of the project. P.S.'s response suggests at least an acquiescing response and more likely a collaborative one.

An invitation of this kind ought to characterize every pastoral contact. We ask others to tell us about themselves—how they feel about themselves, what they think and imagine—such things that we, as bearers of God and representatives of the community, would "be very glad to hear." We want to enter into their lives because we care about their souls.

At this point in Rogers' interview we do not know whether P.S. is being cooperative or cautious. Such an assessment requires a discernment of the security operations in their relationship (Leary 1957; Anchin and Kiesler 1982) and an awareness of the impact of different interpersonal attitudes. By not focusing on a specific agenda, Rogers avoids setting up a regressive relationship, one that could reflect fixation on possible childhood deprivation. Her initial question, "Where do you want me to start?" seems more like conventional deferral to an authority figure. If she had been wary, he may have restructured the interview to say again what he was interested in.

Every therapist, secular or pastoral, begins with an inviting presence. Since we care very much about knowing clients on their terms, we make ourselves available for their soul's sake. But our presence includes more than invitation; it involves initiative.

AN INITIATING PRESENCE

In Revelation 3:20 we see Jesus standing at the door and knocking. For those who hear his voice and open the door, he will go in to them and be with them. That image illustrates how the therapist can be an initiating presence for those seeking help without violating their personhood. Jesus does not break down the door, nor does he sneak in the back way. He does not misrepresent his intent. Rather, Jesus intends to be with others in ways that are genuinely appropriate. He insists upon his right to knock, and he respects others' right to ignore.

How can the counselor proceed in a way that is both inviting and initiating?

If the client has reservations, the counselor might ask, as I suggested in chapter 5, "Is there anything you want to know about me as we begin working together?" The task, however, is to focus on what the client wants and needs. Questions such as "What brings you?" "What do you want me to know?" "Where would you like to start?" or "What are you hoping for in our meeting together today?" can help us begin to discover the person's needs.

Rather than directing these questions in the manner of a prosecuting attorney, the counselor's therapeutic presence must convey an attitude of mutual exploration. Thus, the counselor moves from a vague assumption about the person's wanting help to a disclosure of what matters to him or her in the here and now: "What is it—you're wanting—in our meeting together—today?" By separating each phrase, we emphasize the importance of this seemingly mild request.

In short, an inviting presence initiates the focus of interaction even as it is respectful of the other person. "*What brings you to me?*" "*What brings you here?*" "*What brings you now?*" The focus is on what the other wants, what the other intends, what the other expects, not on what the counselor wants or intends or expects. In respecting those who come for counseling, we take their presence seriously.

ATTENTIVE TO WHAT GOES ON

Connecting with the person in pain is seldom easy. It requires attending to the subtleties of what goes on between the person seeking help and the counselor. Each of us brings our own history, our own struggle between surviving and being known.

INITIAL WARINESS

Few, if any, enter counseling without some apprehension about what will happen. Even the most motivated individuals approach the threshold of therapy holding their breath. Their survival as a person is under siege. Their way of life is missing beats. Their life story has gone awry.

I write from personal experience. The night I made an appointment to reenter therapy (when I was in my early fifties) I had a disturbing dream. I was a prisoner on a train that was carrying me across the Siberian wasteland to a slave labor camp. We stopped at a deserted spot. It looked like one of those God-forsaken scenes from the movie *Doctor Zhivago*. As we prisoners were allowed to stand outside the train, I started to escape, sneaking across the landscape. I had not gone far before I saw one of the burly soldiers coming after me with a fierce guard dog on a leash. The guard looked like my therapist!

The emotional message was clear. Part of me was not looking forward to therapy even though I was seeking it. I experienced the prospect of liberation from pain more like becoming a prisoner of an oppressive system. Hurt loomed larger than hope—despite my conscious intent.

Getting into another's world is more difficult than we imagine. People want help—that is why they come—yet part of them fears help. Surviving feels safer than being known, and being known is what help requires. That is why I remember my own experience of anxious anticipation. It takes courage to put oneself in an exposed position. I do not want to forget that fact.

I think of such anxious moments as being confronted by Yahweh God in the garden. Adam and Eve "heard the sound of the LORD God walking in the garden . . . and . . . hid themselves from the presence of the LORD God. . . . But the LORD God called to [them] and said . . . , 'Where are you?' . . . [They] said, '[We] heard the sound of you in the garden, and [we were] afraid, because [we were] naked; and [we] hid" (Gen. 3:8–10).

All is going well. We are tending to the responsibility of being cocarers with God of God's creation. For all of us—therapists and clients alike—suddenly the harmony, the adaptive coping, between outer work and inner reality trembles. From a steady emotional state, the pain of self-consciousness sends our nervous system into overdrive. Threat to our psychic existence—our sense of well-being and self-worth—disrupts the unfolding drama of life. Whether the pain is physical, psychosocial, or spiritual is irrelevant. What matters is that we experience anxiety, the threat of nonbeing (May 1950).

The arousal of our survival instinct comes as we become aware of our vulnerability—our nakedness. Unconsciously we defend ourselves—hiding—against the threat we perceive in and from the other (Sullivan 1953). In such moments the old mammalian brain—the emotional mind—shifts from adaptation to defense. A predator is after us, or so we feel. Our psychic territory is under siege (see Gilbert 1989, 42–45).

The limbic system (figure 6.1) coordinates care-eliciting and caregiving activity, cooperation and competition (Gilbert 1989). Such activity involves survival of the self and continuity of the species, empathy and the nurture of others. It also includes learning and memory as the making of soul. Here in the center of the brain we find the delicate balancing between fight and flight, between rage and fear, between pleasure and pain, between expectation and actuality, between tension and relaxation, between avoidance and approach. Under threat of nonbeing, psychic life and life itself hang in the balance (Tillich 1952; Hampden-Turner 1981, 84–85; Basch 1988, 65–99).

ATTENDING TO WARINESS IN THE SEEKER

It is important to assume wariness and ambivalence on the part of those seeking help. No matter how much the pain and how strong the motivation, no one puts him- or herself at the disposal of the counselor's competence without being apprehensive. Early exchanges are clues or work samples of what is likely to follow. For example, William J. Collins, first-year fellow in Pastoral Care and Counseling at the Menninger Foundation, describes a woman, Mrs. White, needing to see him "for a few sessions to wrap up some minor issues which were left over from a very successful pastoral counseling experience" elsewhere.

> She began by speaking of how difficult it was for her to seek help again because it meant that she was going to have to open up some things that she wanted to put the lid on. She spoke of the terrible idea that she had that her skin looked awful and unattractive. I told her that I could understand how it would be a serious difficulty for her.
>
> It quickly became apparent that Mrs. White had some serious problems and that the issues she was dealing with were anything but minor. She had been unable to pursue her profession as a teacher for years because it was too stressful for her. She was very angry toward her family because she felt that they had done nothing but reject her, and she was presently feeling rejected by her husband. With some hesitation she told of some plastic surgery she had undergone a few months previously and her subsequent let-down when her mother could not notice the difference.
>
> When she asked me whether she should resume counseling or "put the lid on things again," I encouraged her to continue by telling her that she had raised several issues that she needed to work on. She appeared relieved to be told this. I encouraged her to focus on some objectives that she could work towards, and in the following session she produced a list of goals centering on coming to terms with her fears of rejection and the effects of previous family rejections. I told her that I thought she was much too ambitious and, following some discussion, I agreed to help her work toward feeling accepted by me at the end of the counseling relationship.
>
> In the third session she spoke of feeling trapped in a corner without being able to come out because of her fear of further rejection. She then told me that following the previous session she suddenly sensed a feeling of intense hatred for me because I had looked at my watch prior to the end of the session. I found the force and intensity of this expression of hatred to be something very different from her otherwise calm and reserved presentation of herself.
>
> Upon reviewing this interaction, I recalled that, immediately prior to Mrs. White's sudden outburst of hatred, I had begun to withdraw from her in the session. We had been exploring her feelings of being constantly rejected, and I had been unable to get her to examine her feelings or reactions. When I ceased this exploration, she intuitively sensed that I had done so, and experienced me as rejecting her.

This led her to lash out in anger and frustration at being abandoned once more. (Collins 1982, 131–32)

Collins emotionally withdrew from Mrs. White when she seemed unable to deal with her fears of rejection. He notes, "Her angry reaction invited me to reject her, as she felt that everyone else had done." He failed to realize that she had been telling him this in a metamessage as she related her feeling of rejection by her family, her husband, and her mother. It took her overt angry reaction to him in their third session to get him "to reject her, as she felt that everyone else had done."

The incident helped Collins realize that he "would continue to be tested and challenged by Mrs. White." Her pattern was to "maneuver people into situations whereby they would abandon her." She provoked rejection by being unable to deal with her feelings of rejection. With the help of supervision Collins was able "to explore with her how both of us interacted, and how we both contributed to what had transpired, in the hope of helping her realize that she herself contributes to the manner in which people react to her" (Collins 1982, 133, 134). By attending to the wariness in Mrs. White's protective pattern, Collins might have become aware of his empathic failure earlier in their counseling relationship.

Early exchanges express what may be involved in minding the souls of those seeking help. On the front porch of the seeker's psychic house, to use the metaphor of the dwelling place of the self, we are relating as we will be relating in the work ahead. We need not scurry around in closets and basements and attics to find what is crucial. We need not look in the living room, the dining room, and the kitchen. The care of soul is present in the beginning as well as in what is to come. Patterns of defense and growth are remarkably consistent.

How will the seeker respond to our knock—our presence—our inquiry? Will the person, to speak metaphorically, talk to us through the door that separates us? How much space will be between us? The early responses offer a clue—especially in what comes up in us—as to how we will be attending to the other's soul.

Every response matters, yet no particular response matters decisively. That is why we can be relaxed in connecting. More goes on between the seeker and the sought than either can calculate. "Good enough connecting" would be a psychoanalytic way of framing the therapeutic interactions. "All things" are usable, and "Nothing can separate us" would be Pauline ways of describing therapy (Rom. 8:28, 38–39). These early exchanges, in the language of ritual process, are betwixt and between the ordinary realm of conventionality and the extraordinary realm of creativity, between structure and antistructure (Turner 1969).

ATTENDING TO WARINESS IN ONESELF

Just as an initial dream presents core issues, so early interactions present the counselor with clues to what lies ahead. The counselor attends to what comes up in him- or herself: Am I being protective (because the person feels deficient)? Am I getting angry (because the person feels suspicious)? Am I feeling impatient (because the person is reticent to act)? By identifying such reactions the counselor experiences a work sample of what the course of the therapeutic work will be about.

Thus, at first the counselor does as little structuring as possible. The intent is to receive the way(s) in which the seeker organizes the story for her- or himself. The issue is being flexible enough to allow various parts of oneself to be activated by what the seeker presents. This requires a silent scanning of our own associations. What lurks at the margins of our initial impressions? What thoughts and images and feelings flit across the stage of our awareness?

This is a more subtle way of connecting with those seeking help than simply attending to what they are like. I became aware of the potential of attending to oneself when I served as the theological consultant for the Pastoral Counseling Center of Rochester, New York. The counseling center director, John C. Karl, and I evolved a way for the staff to combine their own religious or spiritual resources with their clinical activity (Karl and Ashbrook 1983; Karl 1989). What is relevant at this point is the process of immersing ourselves in the psychic reality the seeker presents to us.

We inhibit left-brain interpretation in order to activate right-brain immediacy. Rather than gathering a lot of information about the client, we respond to our initial impressions. We attend to the feelings, images, and thoughts swirling on the edge of our own consciousness, for these offer clues to the pain and predicament of the person coming to us.

At a typical staff consultation (Karl 1989, 144–50) the pastoral counselor read the following description of her client: "Jennifer, 32 years old, is a tired-looking woman who looks younger than her years. She speaks softly, slowly, and thoughtfully. She lives with her husband, Gene, 35 years old, a potter, and her 3-month-old son."

As consultant, I orchestrated the staff's responses in a predictable way. I interrupted the presentation at that point to maximize the associative process and minimize the interpretive process. The group initially identified what caught their attention.

Mary, a staff member, responded:

> The way she was dressed . . . tired and small. . . . I associate that with the poor. She was dressed in jeans . . . with a jeans jacket . . . and sneakers. She could easily be overlooked in a crowd. Someone without much social status. . . . Her hair is black and stringy. Her face is pale . . . more than a winter pale, sort of unhealthy. Pallor that people

have who don't have a well-balanced diet . . . not a lot of expression on her face. . . . Defeated—like the expression has been defeated out of her.

Because Mary experienced a sad pity for her, she felt drawn toward Jennifer. She felt "protective in a way." Jennifer's "small size emphasizes my greater size. [I] feel larger than her. It's a protecting almost enclosing movement." Jennifer's shyness is eliciting Mary's protectiveness—an idealizing transference.

Bill's experience was different. He found it "[h]ard to be in touch. She looks younger than her years. [Her husband's] name, occupation, 3-month-old baby—all that went by too fast. There's a lot of quiet . . . about him and her. Then only quiet."

Bill expanded about the quiet he experienced with her.

> There's a hush about it. It's her. A pervading stillness. [Her husband is] barely there. I missed his name. Hard to get in touch. . . . It will take a lot of work just to be in touch. A lot of patience. . . . I must listen very carefully . . . notice everything. I must tune-up my microphone. Get a new battery. Maybe there's a lot there, but it's very still, very hidden and cannot be gotten at easily. I must tune up inside to be in touch.

Bill experienced mixed signals from Jennifer—a vulnerable presence with an elusive reticence. She elicited from him less protectiveness and more a need for patience—a twinship transference.

Jim, a third staff person, spoke of a "breathlessness" about Jennifer. He noticed her "stooped shoulders" and her needing "a change." In sensing an "unhappy depression," he wondered about a postpartum depression. He found his own shoulders pulling in and felt a fear about how to mother the child. He expressed concern "not to rush because she could be easily bowled over." The need for a protective presence from Jim as an idealized selfobject was modified by the need for a cautious presence who would mirror Jennifer's fragile self.

In this sort of staff consultation, after the staff has shared its fleeting impressions, the presenter comments on them. Usually there is amazement at the accuracy and intimacy of the responses. In this instance, the presenter was startled at the precision of Mary's description of Jennifer's appearance—"jeans with stringy dark hair." Her face did look "defeated." She did present herself in a way to be "easily overlooked." This contrasted with Mary's own professional accomplishments.

Bill's difficulty in "getting in touch" was a clue to the presenter's misunderstanding of the client. She had tried to correct one misunderstanding by asking further questions. These resulted in Jennifer's withdrawing in confused silence. She would "startle, like a scared kitten," as Jim had sensed. They all discerned a "fearful, brittle, small person who could be 'easily bowled over.'" The configuration of marginal associations by the staff emphasized the importance of the therapist being an idealized selfobject who would protect without patronizing, mirror without undermining, and hold off collaborating until Jennifer's sense of self had developed more fully.

The process of accessing these marginal signals demonstrates how much information is available in condensed form—*if only we attend to it!* The unvoiced patterns of a person's struggle with surviving and being known are present from the beginning. Time confirms and modifies the early picture, yet the basic organization of the self in its relations with the world is ever present.

In being respectful of those seeking help and being attentive to what goes on, the pastoral counselor is basically being receptive to differences among people.

RECEPTIVE TO DIFFERENCES

Ours is a world of pluralism and difference. There is no one pattern of how a person is to be, no ideal of what it means to be human. The pastoral counselor confronts ambiguity and relativism with every client.

A MULTICULTURAL WORLD

Issues of race and gender, age and class, ethnic diversity and national loyalty challenge the flexibility of the pastoral counselor (Ashbrook 1982; McGoldrick et al. 1982; Augsburger 1986; Hinkle 1989; Hinkle and Hinkle 1992; Ramirez 1991; Silva-Netto 1992). Freud's Vienna of 1890 is not the norm. The YAVIS client—young, attractive, verbal, intelligent, successful (Schofield 1964, 133)—is not the criterion. Nor is the white-Anglo-Saxon-middle-class-male the standard.

In a monocultural world the therapist chooses between two basic approaches. Either one seeks a characterological reconstruction of a dysfunctional self, a long-term process at best, or one focuses on the relief of a specific symptom, which can be very time-limited. But, because pastoral counselors represent God as the reality that transcends every cultural expression, our task is more complicated than a simple "either self or symptom" responsibility.

We hold together the dynamic dialectic between the person in pain and the setting in which that person lives and moves and has her or his being (Ashbrook 1982, 123). In a formal sense we ask ourselves: What aspects of this situation are cultural and ethnic, and which are personal and individual? What changes are necessary in the person, and which must come in the environment? And beyond these contextual concerns looms the spiritual concern: How can people fulfill who they are in God? Beyond the self of culture lies the soul in God, the core of each person's being.

In sorting out what is personal, what is cultural, and what is spiritual, pastoral counselors can take themselves more seriously than they ought. We must avoid a messianic consciousness that we can work with everyone who comes or with every situation with which we are presented. Although we represent extraordinary power, we are quite ordinary persons.

As a group, psychiatric consultants are concerned about the ability of pastoral counselors to spot and work with those who are severely disturbed (Ashbrook 1990c, 295). Too often, they believe, we get in over our heads in the deadly undertow of psychodynamic conflict or get lost in the biological determinants of schizophrenic and affective disorders. As psychiatrist-psychoanalyst Mary Giffin says, "Good intentions and a kind heart are simply ineffective and in certain mental difficulties only increase the disturbance" (personal conversation). Supervision and referral to another professional are two of the best strategies available when we are in over our head.

Concerning differences, we can no longer assume that our images of the optimum person and the normative setting are appropriate. In recent years the inherent defects of a monocultural, ethnocentric view of reality have become obvious.

A hermeneutic of suspicion about dominant cultures and majority groups has exposed these oppressive and limiting forces. In contrast, the Christian tradition, especially in the event of Pentecost, provides a paradigm of a multicultural and inclusive reality (Ashbrook 1982; Hinkle 1989)—different people, different tongues; different cultures, different values; different genes, different voices (Ashbrook 1992b). Each hears about God and understands in his and her own language (Acts 2:8–11).

The human brain contains more noninstinctual cortical cells than other mammals (Penfield 1975; see figure 6.2), which makes for human idiosyncrasies. Experience and learning contribute to who we are as much as genes and instincts. Culture and nurture influence neuronal and endocrine developments. The sequence of early development, such as the wired-in ritual of emotional smiling and sociability, is transcultural and universal (Konner 1991). Yet the style and content of cognitive processing depend on culture. Each culture authors a distinctive story.

The pastoral counselor needs to be receptive to the richness and power of these cultural and individual differences. These differences include biological and cognitive features as well as cultural and ethnic features. And, finally, while we are more alike than different, every individual is unique, a reality in oneself, a profile with a particular biography.

CULTURAL AND ETHNIC DIFFERENCES

Today we are becoming increasingly conscious of differences in cultural and ethnic styles (McGoldrick et al. 1982; Augsburger 1986; Ramirez 1991). Despite being an individual, every person bears the imprint of the group of which she or he is a part. The pastoral counselor must be receptive to these different cultural contexts.

Cultural style includes a sense of common origin and a definable identity. It reveals shared standards of expectations and interpersonal behaviors (Harwood 1981). These ethnic identities include African-Americans, Hispanic Americans, Italian Americans, Native Americans, Chinese Americans, Filipino Americans, Korean Americans, and Japanese Americans. Caucasian Americans is a broad category embracing English, Irish, French, Dutch, Italian, German, Danish, Norwegian, Swedish, and Eastern European peoples. And so the list goes on, not only among groups but within groups.

These differences in cultural styles are associated with underlying neurocognitive processes (TenHouten 1985; Laughlin et al. 1990; Gibson and Petersen 1991). For instance, fewer left-handers exist in highly conforming agrarian societies than among highly permissive hunting and fishing peoples (Dawson 1977). Similarly, as industrialized United States has grown more permissive over the last three quarters of a century, so the percentage of left-handers has increased. And left-handedness has consequences for more clumsiness, greater creativity, and shorter life span (Coren 1992; Springer and Deutsch [1981, 1985] 1989, 142–71).

In spite of a remarkable similarity in the shape of cognitive development across cultures, there are remarkable differences in cognitive abilities and expressions (Super 1991; Gibson and Petersen 1991). Educational psychologist Manuel Ramirez III (1991) has developed what he calls "The Multicultural Person-Environment Fit Paradigm" (see figure 6.3). His paradigm helps orient the counselor to basic cultural variations in those who come for help. He draws on empirical research, which has distinguished a field-sensitive or field-dependent orientation and a field-independent or autonomous orientation. He connects these cognitive patterns with cultural expressions.

Ramirez suggests that a field-sensitive style is more traditional, more personal, and more communal. A field-independent style is more modern, more impersonal, and more autonomous. Without arguing respective values, Ramirez describes the importance of a therapist developing both a traditional and a modern style, utilizing both a communal and an autonomous style, and combining elements of both a personal and a formal style. Although these central tendencies of field-sensitive and field-independence are apparent, each person expresses these in a variety of ways. And the pastoral counselor is called upon to be aware of both the cultural patterns and the individual nuances.

BIOLOGICAL AND COGNITIVE DIFFERENCES

These cultural styles are strikingly similar to patterns of cerebral processing (Ashbrook 1984a; 1984b; 1988b; 1989a; 1989c; Springer and Deutsch [1981,

1985] 1989; see figure 6.4). Our conscious brain works in a pattern that alternates between all-at-once and item-by-item. The basic rest-activity cycle, which I describe in chapter 13, incorporates conscious symbolic meaning into nonconscious subsymbolic adaptation. But the rational mind, the new brain, is our distinctive human resource. With this we can sift and sort, anticipate and plan, assess and evaluate what matters to us.

The flow of experience engages these two contrasting and complementary styles. The dominant language hemisphere, usually the left, is vigilant. It works with a narrow attentional focus. The nondominant language hemisphere, usually the right, is responsive. It engages reality with a broad attentional focus. These reflect the older brain processes of arousal and relaxation, respectively (d'Aquili 1983, 264–65).

The left brain works a step at a time, analytically, sequentially, logically, conceptually. It is the interpreter (Gazzangia 1985; 1988a), the creator of consistency and coherence (Lancaster 1991). It derives primarily from the activity of the central nervous system and so is under direct conscious control.

The right brain works by leaps of imagination, synthetically, simultaneously, relationally, perceptually. It is the weaver of patterns (Perecman 1984), making connections and creating possibilities. It draws primarily on the activity of the peripheral and limbic systems.

Each process requires the other; neither works alone. The connecting fiber track of the corpus callosum lets each half know what the other half knows, thereby establishing collaboration between the halves (Levy 1985). That conscious connection is consolidated and integrated in the old brain in a subsymbolic and nonconscious way, as I suggest with basic rest-activity processing.

Neurosociologist Warren C. TenHouten (1985) has explored relationships between these neurophysiological processes and social structures. Like many, myself included, he has been intrigued by the two distinctive modes of thought of the two halves of the brain. He termed one mode "logical-analytical" and the other "Gestalt-synthetic."

Each person discloses a tendency to rely more on one mode than the other (TenHouten 1985, 342). This preference can reflect sociocultural experience. A preliterate society, for instance, will emphasize spatial or right-hemisphere reasoning, while an industrialized society emphasizes abstract or left-hemisphere reasoning.

Further, TenHouten hypothesizes that "in modern Western society the socially advantaged groups and classes will tend to appropriate the [analytical] mode of thought, with subdominant groups functioning in a relatively more [synthetic] mode" (1985, 351ff). Studies disclose that "socially subdominant and nonmodern groups and classes are relatively field-dependent" (TenHouten 1985, 353).

TenHouten distinguishes two additional aspects of hemisphere differences. One is the extent to which the two halves of the brain are specialized; and the other is the flexibility of response to specific cognitive demands—that is, an analytic task activates left-brain activity while a synthetic response activates right-brain activity. He speculates that in addition to the two modes of thought related to the two halves of the brain there is a third pattern. He calls this "dialectical." He believes the dialectical generates "a level of thought that goes beyond both the synthetic and the analytic" (TenHouten 1985, 344).

GENDER DIFFERENCES

My own investigations reject the dialectical complementarity as a third mode. Instead, I speculate, as I have described in chapter 3 on St. Ann's Home for the Elderly, a more integrated mode of processing, a bilateral pattern apparent in those in whom language develops early. That group consists primarily of females and left-handers, and there are more left-handed males than females. Females and left-handed males have been found to be more field-dependent or field-sensitive, to use Ramirez' relabeling, than right-handed males (Coren 1992, 32, 169–74).

Developmentally, by the sixth week of pregnancy basic human potential begins to differentiate (Benderly 1987, 14). This comes with the activation of male hormones, most likely testosterone (Konner [1982] 1983, 122). This activity prepares the emerging male for suppression of monthly cycling at puberty (Benderly 1987, 17–18). Further, it creates conditions that elicit different interaction patterns of socialization as soon as the sex of the fetus or newborn is known (Springer and Deutsch [1981, 1985] 1989, 213–25).

As a group, girls tend to mature physically and linguistically earlier than boys (Waber 1976; 1979). The result is a bilateral development of the neocortex. Each half of the brain uses both step-by-step and all-at-once processes. In addition, verbal and interpersonal skills are more readily accessible for girls and women. The social world is their sphere of confidence. Relatedness and connection thereby come to be primary values.

For boys and men, in contrast, the later maturation of language is accompanied by earlier physical exploration of the environment. The result is a more specialized development of the neocortex. Each half of the brain alternates between the interpretive and the impressionistic processes. Visual-spatial skills are more readily accessible for boys and men. The physical world is their sphere of confidence. Achievement and autonomy thereby come to be primary values (Levy 1980, 367–71).

These contrasts have another nuance that I consider to be significant (Kimura 1985). Girls and women tend to have thicker neural structures, especially in the general sensory areas. Both hemispheres are involved in defining words so that the source of their understanding is more diffuse, less conceptual, and more dependent on experiential processes. Boys and men tend to have simpler neural structures in the general sensory areas. Only the left hemisphere defines words so that their "naming" and "analyzing" makes the meaning of words more precise, more conceptual, and more specialized.

Because of these differences I contend that males and females construct different realities. Females construct reality in more nuanced and complex ways. This results in a view of reality as a web of connections and, incidentally, contributes to the idea of "women's intuition." Males construct reality in simpler and clearer ways, which results in a greater separation of spheres of activity (Springer and Deutsch [1981, 1985] 1989, 183–84), a more dichotomized and polarized view of the way things are.

In combining findings about gender differences, I arrive at two related yet distinguishable speculations. Males tend to be oriented more to an abstract and compartmentalized environment; females tend to be oriented more to an interpersonal and connected environment. Men tend to simplify and thereby stabilize reality; women tend to experience the real as more nuanced and thereby more alterable (Levy 1980, 367–71).

The pastoral counselor is respectful, attentive, and receptive to clients. These features are pulled together in a dominant image taken from the Christian tradition—namely, Pentecost. This image provides a paradigm, an archetypal prototype, of the assumptions with which the *pastoral* therapist works.

THE PENTECOST PARADIGM

People from every place and group gather in one place, expressing their experience in their own cultural ways yet understanding one another as belonging to the one family of God. "When the day of Pentecost had come, they were all together in one place. . . . Now there were devout Jews from every nation. . . . And at this sound [like the rush of a violent wind] the crowd . . . was bewildered, because each one heard them speaking in the native language of each. . . ." (Acts 2:1–13). Here we glimpse unity in diversity. No one way is the only way. The many cultures and many languages all are capable of bearing witness to God.

Paul gives a more precise definition of this Pentecost paradigm (Gal. 3:28): "There is no longer Jew or Greek, there is no longer slave or free, there is no longer male and female, for all of you are one in Christ Jesus." As Old Testament scholar Wolfgang Roth comments, this new reality overcomes ethnic distinctions, status distinctions, and sex-gender distinctions (personal conversation reported by John E. Hinkle). It is a metacultural vision, one that transcends the idea that any particular cultural pattern is universal.

In connecting with a client's world, the pastoral counselor must connect with what matters to the client. This initial task of empathic attunement (Basch 1988) is the basis of all that we do together. Without it we live in the old reality of the mythic Tower of Babel (Gen. 11:1–9). The word *Babel* itself derives from the root *bll*, meaning "to confuse." We do not think together, talk together, or share together. We do not stand under each other's experience.

Cultural and cognitive distinctives require varied ways the counselor connects with a client's world. Does one face the client directly or position oneself obliquely? Does one bracket out family and kin or include family and kin? Does one emphasize authority or foster partnership? Does a client ask for help or minimize need? Does a client express emotion or maintain a stoic stance? Does the counselor foster connection or allow the client psychic and physical space?

Similar implications apply to the relation between women and men. There is no nongendered and nonsex-related reality. How women and men are treated reflect different socialization patterns of reward and reinforcement. How women and men interact with their worlds reflect both socially and individually constructed patterns of meaning and managing. The pastoral counselor ignores these neurocognitive and socialization processes to the detriment of those seeking help.

As much as lies within the pastoral counselor, we are to become all things to all people, to use Paul's metaphor (1 Cor. 9:19–23). We are to empathize, to use our own experience to attune ourselves to the experience of others. We are to interpathize, to set our experience aside to enter more fully into the experience of others (Augsburger 1986; Hinkle 1989; Hinkle and Hinkle 1992).

In the next chapter we will turn to the process of engaging others as we move down into the reality of their pain. Once we connect, we can begin to explore more fully.

CHAPTER SEVEN

Hurting and Hoping

RESPONDING

■ ■ ■ ■ ■

The transition from first being let into another's soul and then being allowed to move around in that realm is always awesome. No particular intervention guarantees it, and almost any response may start it. Something within us wants to be known and lets us be known. We are made for relatedness (Buber 1937; Trevarthen 1990). This is the basis of reality and, most of all, the core of *human* reality. This religious conviction underlies and makes sense of the various psychodynamic views that inform the work of the pastoral counselor—drive gratification, adaptation to reality, internal representations of significant object relations, and self cohesion and worth (Pine 1985). Distinctive as each view is, each rests on the conviction that we are made for each other, and without the other we are not ourselves.

What characterizes the transition from initially connecting with a person seeking help and then responding to that person's inner resources? The person comes with ambivalence—wanting help yet wary of help. The counselor is respectful, attentive, receptive. Then, usually without fanfare, yet clearly experienced, the therapeutic process shifts from a connecting mode to a responding mode. What happens? The relationship shifts from a persisting ambivalence to an intentional approach.

Psalm 4 voices that transition from wariness to trust:

> Answer me when I call, O God of my right!
> > You gave me room when I was in distress.
> > Be gracious to me, and hear my prayer.
> > > (v. 1)

In this personal lament we find a note of confidence. Regardless of the circumstances of the pain—false accusation, the psalmist's doubt about himself and doubt about God—he seeks a real relationship. He expects truth in reality and reality in truth. The psalmist trusts what is really real and truly "right."

At moments in the past he has known the breath of life—"*room* when I was in distress," as he puts it. I interpret his "room" to mean "breath" or "oxygen." Breath or oxygen maximizes adaptation in an uncertain world. Because he has known living soul in the past, he trusts that he can know it again. This is the psalmist's prayer—and the unvoiced prayer of every person who comes seeking help: Give me room so I can breathe again!

HOLDING ENVIRONMENTS

As pastoral counselors, we answer that prayer when we respond to the seeker's invitation to come into her or his dwelling place. As we come into another's dwelling place, we are creating psychic space for the other to breathe again. By responding to the other's presence we are moving down into her or his painful experience.

The early exchanges between client and counselor, as I have noted, are at once preliminary and paradigmatic. They are preliminary in that we are getting acquainted. We are learning about the way(s) in which we present ourselves in a pastoral counseling situation. At the same time they are paradigmatic. These presentations of self reflect each person's defended self as well as each one's growing self. They are a work sample of the therapeutic process, a paradigm of what lies ahead. At the door of each other's psychic house of life we put our survival faces forward and keep our growth faces hidden.

In the case of the one seeking help that "survival" may be a picture of helplessness, a pattern of wariness, or a plea for companionship. In terms of ourselves as caregivers that "survival" may be a posture of goodwill, a glimpse of autonomy, or a desire for partnership. I described those survival responses more fully in Part 1 as basic emotional assumptions. Their growth aspects I described as basic theological assumptions.

Survival and growth are intertwined (Gilbert 1989) in these opening exchanges. The person in pain wants to be known yet is wary of being truly known. We counselors want to be present yet are limited in being truly present. However, once seekers experience our openness, we begin responding more explicitly to where they are and to what is happening to them. Their story takes on life. We respond to what pain is like for them.

CULTURES OF CARE

When we ask about the meaning of clients' pain, we are responding to the psalmist's prayer for hope. At a unconscious level we are calling forth the environments that have held them in the past. Sometimes that "holding" has been crippling; sometimes strengthening; usually both. Hope, then, relates to how we have been held and handled (Bollas 1987, 32–37). That "idiom of care," as psychoanalyst Christopher Bollas calls it, shapes our internal structure of what reality is like. It anchors us in the past even as it allows us to move into the future.

In asking people why they come and what they hope for, we are holding them and handling them in basically a "good-enough" way. We are reconnecting them with the natural sources of our development as human beings. Winnicott (1965) calls this life experience the "facilitating and holding environment." Developmental psychologist Robert Kegan refers to that environment as the cultures that hold us throughout our lives and that contribute to our growth (Kegan 1982, 256–61):

> the mothering culture which tends to us as a newborn,
> the parenting culture which nurtures our capacity for emergence,
> the role-recognizing culture which supports our exercises of self-sufficiency,
> the culture of mutuality which fine tunes our capacity for collaboration,
> the culture of self-authorship which creates our drama of self-expression, and
> a culture of intimacy which deepens our exploring interdependence.

These cultures are, in short, the transcultural culture of community and caring. They are the reality of our relatedness with one another and with God. They bring us into being and foster our becoming.

THE BIBLICAL GOD OF CARE

Because most people come to us for *pastoral* counseling, I make a basic assumption. They come because in them—however ambiguous and obscured it may be—is *that* culture that makes for growth, God at work in their lives. They long for us to respect and care for what matters to them. This is the point of the Gallup poll in which 66% of the respondents preferred a counselor who represented spiritual values and 81% preferred a counselor who integrated their values into the process (Gallup 1992; Woodruff 1992, 26).

Biblical images convey expectations of a caring context and parental-like holding and handling. Think of God as the Good Shepherd (Ps. 23; Luke 15:3–7) or the waiting father in relation to his two sons (Luke 15:11–32). Remember God as the diligent woman seeking a lost coin (Luke 15:8–10) or the discerning mother hen who would not force her little ones to gather under her protective wings (Matt. 23:37; Luke 13:34–35; see McFague 1987).

Whether or not those who come to the pastoral counselor are aware of these particular images, they expect the counselor to represent this kind of a caring reality. These images reflect both relatedness and individuation. In the shepherd and the woman we find an active seeking to hold and to handle the hurt and the lost. In the father and the mother we discern a holding back for the sake of liberating, an allowing of the children to experience their own reality. The *context* of pastoral counseling, as pastoral theologians Seward Hiltner and Lowell Colston (1961) demonstrated, awakens expectations of a caring and liberating reality. And the expectation of hope for healing adds to the possibility of that hope being realized (see Frank 1973).

SELF PSYCHOLOGY'S RELATEDNESS OF CARE

In the language of self psychology, those who come for counseling expect an idealized selfobject relationship. This expectation reflects both the core of their being and the conflicted level of their struggle. They hope the therapist will care for them, protect them, and make up for their deficiencies. They also hope that the therapist will encourage, liberate, and empower them. They long for a mirroring of their aspirations and a companion on their way. At the core of their idealization their identification with another is a growth-facilitating expectation of the counselor being dependable, competent, and a partner. Such holding reality manifests God as the Truly Other.

RESPONDING TO WARINESS

As pastoral counselors we assume that those who come to us expect to find in us a dependable, competent, and companionable selfobject. At the same time, we are aware of their anxiety and our anxiety. As I have indicated, people want help and fear help. People want to be known yet avoid being known. Ambivalence is ongoing. So counselors engage the conversation with the wisdom of a serpent as well as with the innocence of a dove (Matt. 10:16b).

We ascertain how conflicted are the unconscious forces at work inside the other and between us (see Ashbrook 1990a). While such an assessment may be more automatic than conscious, we can identify the process. Questions such as the following help focus the dynamics:

- Where are *we* hiding (Gen. 3:8–13)?
- What are *we* avoiding?
- What is going on *between* us?
- What is going on *within* each of us?
- What are *we* making known?

These unconscious forces, in part, are interpersonal maneuvers intended to maintain psychic balance and well-being (Sullivan 1953; Leary 1957; Anchin and Kiesler 1982; Ashbrook 1975, 86–103; Gilbert 1989, 37–77). When our exchanges become too intense and too limited, they reflect a survival dynamic and hinder our adaptation to reality. When the responses are appropriate to the exchanges, they reflect a growth dynamic, making for enlarged space and enhanced living. These interpersonal maneuvers apply to both those who seek help and us who facilitate help.

In terms of interactions, distancing or autonomous behavior is intended to provoke a distancing response; closeness or attached behavior is intended to elicit closeness. Simply put, like begets like—anger triggers anger, and warmth awakens warmth (see figure 7.1). Most people come wanting contact, an environment that hears their distress and cares to connect with them. A few come wanting control, an environment that respects their vulnerability and allows them their space.

In terms of power or status, deferring behavior is intended to pull out a directing response; a position of power is intended to produce a response of acknowledgment. Power and deference are reciprocal—when one person holds a higher status, the other positions him- or herself as lower status (see figure 7.1). At best, this positioning is more functional than hierarchical. (However, history has spawned a pervasive cultural pathology of power domination. Hierarchies invariably have been power oriented.) The person seeking help comes in hopes of finding someone capable of giving help. She or he looks to the pastoral counselor as a bearer of Being. Ultimately, both the client and the therapist are dependent on God.

These security maneuvers involve the autonomic nervous system (see Gilbert 1989). Too much arousal or too little stimulation (see Basch 1988, 72) results in an avoidance of reality. Then the person is fighting or fleeing or freezing. The autonomic nervous system's sympathetic arousal and parasympathetic relaxation are unbalanced and maladaptive. In contrast, appropriate excitement and relaxed openness enable people to move from a secure base out into an unknown world.

There are various ways the pastoral counselor might respond to the client's distress.

SIMPLE INTEREST

If the other is in the alert mode of nonanxious interest as P.S. seemed to be with Rogers, then we easily engage her self-disclosing, self-exploring, experiencing "self." We can attend to her in a direct, inviting, personal, and confident way.

I find the image of being invited into the psychic houses of people in pain helpful in guiding our responses as pastoral counselors. They show us around, taking us from room to room and talking about various objects and experiences associated with those rooms. These objects are symbols of what matters to them. The experiences are situations in which these objects have been taken into their meaning-making process. They are moments of intensified reality. They bear the being or weight of the person, providing clues to struggles and satisfactions. Instead of worrying about what to say and how to act, we respond to being shown around in the experienced worlds of those who come to us.

I invite those in pain to share with me what's happening to them: How do they feel about it? What do they think about it? What does it mean to them? I encourage them by asking for more detail. "Could you say more about that?" "What else is involved?" I expand their awareness by asking about what else was going on in them at the time. I connect an awareness of the present with an awareness of the past by wondering about emotional connections and continuities in their lives. In the midst of it all I listen for meaning and respond to feeling.

EMPATHIC UNDERSTANDING

If the other is more in the emergency mode of fight-flight as Mrs. White seemed to be with Collins (1982), I have to find a way to shift to what she or he might construe as a "safer" climate. I am respectful, attentive, somewhat formal, and receptive. My first task is to reflect—to mirror—what matters to her or him.

Self psychologists talk about "empathic understanding" (Basch 1988; Kohut 1971; Wolf 1988). By that they mean therapists' ability to find a way into others' experience via the affective signals they give off. We are to hear, understand, and use the emotional messages behind the spoken words (Basch 1988, 130). Empathic understanding requires that we convey a sense of acceptance and confirmation of others as they experience self (Wolf 1988, 125). That does not mean that we sympathetically support disorders of the self—empathy is not the same as approval (Wolf 1988, 131–32). Rather, we support others' sense of genuine self-esteem, as Kohut (1971) and Basch (1988, 183) put it, "until [others are] able to give [themselves] credit when credit is due."

Years ago Carl Rogers (1951; 1961) spoke of unconditional positive regard and client-centered therapy. That holding relationship and view from the inside were prerequisite for the therapist entering into the experienced world of the client as the client experienced it. Theologically, unconditional positive regard and empathic mirroring suggest *agape*, the Greek word for "love." *Agape* involves an intentional and intelligent cherishing of others' well-being apart from one's own, a neighbor love that includes love of enemies in an unconditional way (Arndt and Gingrich [1958, 1957] 1979; Kittel 1964). Pastoral theologian Christie Cozad Neuger goes further. She speaks of prevenient grace in the caring relationship, especially as it involves those who have been marginalized by the dominant and oppressive culture. In being marginalized, people have experienced "failure of the affective bond" and failure in affective attunement (Basch 1988, 131–34). Their world has neither supported them nor understood them. In truth, it has violated their basic being, their very existence (e.g., Grier and Cobbs 1968; Ruether 1983; Chopp 1986; Lerner 1986; Poling 1991).

Despite such marginalization, Neuger contends that God's love and assurance surround people before they know these exist. A culture of care is the basis of all culture because it is the culture of God. That conviction enables people to have "confidence in their own belonging and in their own truths prior to exploring their realities." Judgment is not suspended. Rather the pastoral counselor expresses a kind of care that takes the reality of others seriously, that values their experience, and that "belove[s]" their being (Neuger [1991] 1992, 36, 51).

Neuger ([1991] 1992) illustrates how she conveyed prevenient grace and empathic understanding to a client. Mary was a thirty-eight-year-old, white, middle-class, evangelical woman who had been hospitalized for depression. Because she had been affirmed and supported in the hospital, she found it hard to leave. Antidepressant medication seemed ineffective. She agreed to try pastoral counseling.

Mary's accountant husband and four children wanted her to fulfill the traditional gender roles of wife and mother. As her four-year-old daughter explained to her, "If you would only just keep the house clean and do the wash, Daddy wouldn't be angry with you anymore." Mary's case vividly expresses the "cultural pathology" of patriarchy. And part of her had bought into that mind-set.

At the beginning of counseling Mary tried to undermine Neuger's concern for mutuality and intimacy. She indicated that she was often late and often forgot things, and so might miss appointments. In effect, Mary was trying to talk Neuger out of caring for her. Closeness hurt more than distance.

Neuger chose to ignore Mary's resistance. She avoided insisting on Mary's adhering to the therapy limits of time and regularity. Instead, Neuger "saw it as one of the few ways she experiences any power and it is the power of the powerless because it damages her in the process." So she told Mary, "Sometimes I [have] a tendency toward lateness . . . so why [don't] we set an hour and a half for our session. That way either of us could be up to one half hour late and we still could get in a full therapeutic hour." Neuger went further and asked if Mary would like her to call her an hour before their appointment each week. While puzzled, Mary seemed relieved.

For the next four months Neuger called. They also kept the longer appointment schedule. Then Mary said she did not need to be called anymore. Further, she did not miss an appointment thereafter.

I discern strength in that flight-fight pattern. But the strength is more in the service of survival than growth. Empathic understanding transforms avoidance into excitement. In Mary's case, Neuger *behaved* empathically instead of interpreting empathically. She embodied an incarnational presence in contrast to an expert's attunement. Mary's "forgetting" was her way of caring for her self even as it was a way of getting back at her oppressive culture. Neuger joined her in her "forgetting," thereby freeing her to engage.

DIVERTING ATTENTION AND MAKING A POINT

In addition to simple interest and empathic understanding, stories are an effective way of shifting the emotional climate from threat to curiosity and then to growth. Besides slowing down the relentless observational drive of the left hemisphere, a story keeps the person intrigued with what is coming. Stories activate the imaginative pattern-making processes of the right hemisphere and the relaxation response of the parasympathetic nervous system. They connect directly with the limbic process of our taking in new experience and integrating that with ongoing meaning.

Some stories are paradigmatic, which means that they contain the predicament with which we struggle as human beings. They allow us to be in the story and to reflect on the story without becoming entangled in the life-story it reflects. In other words, in telling a story we are saying something about what is going on between us and the client. This emotional/meaning-making communication affects the climate of our collaboration.

Consider the following folk tale and my metacommunications (Ashbrook 1989d, 368–69). I used it in responding to a client who insisted I should work with him because his need was so great and yet his interpersonal maneuvers were skillfully avoidant of genuine contact.

Paradigmatic Story	Metamessage
Let me tell you about a colleague of mine. . . .	Reflect with me in a collaborative way about our working relationship. . . .
who arrived in a Persian village . . .	Your security operations with me can appear anywhere, with everyone. . . .
on a camel train loaded down with his luggage. . . .	You have arrived in my office with all the baggage of your past struggles and strength. . . .

Paradigmatic Story	**Metamessage**
He calls to a porter standing on the platform to come and assist him . . .	You are commandeering my services as a therapist to help you carry your past. . . .
"Here's my luggage. Now take it to my house." . . .	You have dumped your baggage in my lap and expect me to pick it up and carry it for you because you are frightened. . . .
The porter inquires as to where exactly the traveler lives, in order that he can take the baggage to its proper destination . . .	I intend to serve your genuine interests.
Upon hearing the porter's request, the traveler steps back and snarls, "I suspected you were a ruffian and a robber, and now I know that you are. I'll be damned if I'll tell you where I live. Now take my luggage there at once" (Shah 1972, 87).	You live according to the basic emotional assumption of suspicious vulnerability, which you handle by controlling the distance between us; to survive you fight and flee, depending on whether you can control the situation; the fearful part of you expects me to collude in ignoring your double bind request for help—you want it but won't tell me about your soul. We could play cat-and-mouse endlessly without finding "you"—my wanting very much to be of help and so overfunction and your wanting very much to ask-and-hide and so underfunction. At our best, neither of us wants to collude in such behavior.

Whenever I experienced us at an impasse or trapped in a power exchange, I would observe, "We seem to be caught in picking up your baggage but not knowing where your house is." Invariably, this intervention shifted the emotional climate from security to growth, from defense to exploration, from anxiety to curiosity.

Such a story engages a person's curiosity. Instead of being wary of what is coming, he or she is intrigued by what is coming. Instead of my pressing a point, I am relishing telling the tale. We are communicating in a meaning-making way that holds us together, that contains our anxiety, that allows us to breathe the breath of life.

Such sharing reflects the second great commandment. Love of neighbor and love of self are reciprocal features of one reality (Lev. 19:18; Mark 12:31; Rom. 13:9; Gal. 5:14; James 2:8). God is the creator and sustainer of both the helpee and the helper. In other words, when we change our survival mode into a collaborative mode, then God—as the future-generating possibility of meaning making—is openly discernible in realizing that loving others and loving self are each aspects of loving God. Together we are making a new reality (see Moltmann 1990).

This story suggests that what I as the counselor am experiencing between myself and the other person—at that moment—is very like the traveler and the porter. Something important has been placed on the platform, so important in fact that we find ourselves caught up in a survival struggle of approach-avoidance. God is present in a hidden way, known indirectly through our hiding-surviving. The story enables us to turn the impasse of "Reality is *against us*" into a signpost and symbol, a reminder of where we are and what we are about—namely, "Reality is *for us.*" We have been moving too fast. We need to slow down before we can go on.

Such a metaphor of meaning, specifically tied to our security maneuvers, provides a quick refocusing of impasses and power struggles. It names the "where are you hiding" for what it is. A gentle observation such as, "We seem to be tangling over the baggage again" conveys the metamessage that what is going on is very important. We are so close to significant material that we—like Moses—need to take off our shoes—tread gently—because we are approaching holy ground, the ground of our being, the Ground of Being Itself, Yahweh God in the wilderness (Exod. 3:2–5).

Such a reminder activates parasympathetic relaxation along with the all-at-once responsiveness of the nondominant hemisphere. In essence, with Kierkegaard, we take a deep breath in faith (LeFevre 1956, 36). Literally, we interrupt our rapid, shallow breathing. Shallow breathing makes for too much carbon dioxide in the bloodstream. In relaxing we return to normal breathing, which comes with a proper amount of oxygen. The result is two brains—the other person's and mine—working together on a shared task as part of the new reality God intends for all humanity.

ENLARGING PSYCHIC SPACE

In connecting with the client in such receptive ways as I have suggested, we are responding to his or her *kyrie*, the cry for help out of the misery of the soul, as Janet spoke of that initial spiritual/psychic crisis (cf. Boyce 1988). I describe this phase of pastoral conversation as a moving "downward," or deeper, into the psyche and soul. The metaphor of depth aptly reminds us of the Shamanistic roots (Laughlin et al. 1990, 269–76) of our similar, though less dramatic, experience as pastoral therapists.

GOING DEEPER BY ACTIVATING NONRATIONAL CONSCIOUSNESS

The initial Shamanistic move is a descent into what anthropologist Charles D. Laughlin Jr. and his colleagues call "experiential dismemberment." By that they refer to the process in which ordinary consciousness is torn apart by painful inner experience. In the symbolism of the mythic-dream world, shadowy figures—nonhuman and human—are set at odds, cut to pieces, and so disrupt routine and orderly existence.

Those images of "dismemberment," being "torn apart," and "cut to pieces" seem violent and destructive. This is especially so when we compare them to the basic trust and intent of respectful, attentive, receptive responding. The crucial point is that we as therapist, with the client, turn from the world around us to the world within us. We shift from dominant hemisphere consciousness to reconnect with nondominant hemisphere consciousness. We seek to recover this nonconscious resource for psychic growth. So we let go of rational consciousness and turn to elusive consciousness.

BIBLICAL IMAGES OF DEPTH

In biblical imagery, "the word of the LORD" coming to Jeremiah conveys just those elements of moving deeper into psychic experience:

> Before I formed you in the womb I knew you,
> > and before you were born I consecrated you …
> > [this is your gracious context]
>
> Do not be afraid [of your demanding context] . . .
>
> See, today I appoint you [to the meaning-making task] …
> to pluck up and to pull down,
> to destroy and to overthrow,
> to build and to plant.
>
> (Jer. 1:5–10)

Plucking up and pulling down, destroying and overthrowing, are more violent metaphors of the collapsing of one's cognitive structure, the experiential frame within which one has ordered one's world. In Western culture the collapse of our assumptive structure has been dramatized in Nietzsche's Zarathustra shouting in the streets "God is dead." The image declares that the implicit assumptions by which Western civilization has lived have died. There is a traumatizing quality to the loss of psychic certainty.

A similar dynamic is present in all mythic presentations of psychic disruption (see, e.g., Theissen 1987). Think of Jesus' being "driven by the Spirit" into the wilderness following his baptism, where he was "tempted by Satan" and "was with the wild beasts" (Matt. 4:1–11; Mark 1:12–13; Luke 4:1–13). In the face of tempting demonic illusions of grandeur, he stood fast, centered in God.

In Scripture the range of such disruptive images is vast:[1] being thrown out of the garden, wandering in the wilderness, being plunged into the watery depths, and being threatened by monsters and fiery serpents. Responding to the soul requires that the pastoral therapist move down into the anxious, threatening, frightening experience of unordered reality.

A REORDERING DREAM

The story of a woman in her mid-forties illustrates the dynamic involved in plucking up and pulling down in order to plant and to build (Ashbrook 1971, 188–89). She was facing the transition between her children leaving home and herself finding new ways of being a person. She reported the following dream:

> I was on top of a tall, thin tower. There was a woman at the bottom of the tower by the ladder that reached to the top. She wanted to climb up, and I told her not to. She did anyway.
>
> When she got to the top, the tower collapsed. Instead of crashing to the ground, somehow the bricks came together and formed a new structure that was more of a rectangle, lower and broader. We landed safely on the new building without any harm.

This woman's investment of herself as a mother had grown increasingly limiting over the years. She had neglected herself as a separate person with needs and desires of her own. Now the neglected side of her personality—the woman at the bottom of the ladder—was insisting on being taken into account. The conscious side of her personality—herself at the top of the tower—could no longer dominate. The old form failed to carry the new life force. It collapsed under the strain between the mother role from the past and the person-need in the present. But—and this is the basic core of hope in the midst of collapse—all the elements of her self were reassembled and recycled. The new building was lower and stronger than the old. In the midst of change she knew the continuity of her self.

In a demonstration interview I conducted as to how I work, my client, Karl, a man in his early twenties, spoke of "pieces of me."[2] The phrase "pieces

---

1. References to these images are: the garden—Genesis 3:4; the wilderness—e.g., Numbers 21:4-6; depths—e.g., Job 12:22; Psalms 69:15; 92:5; Isaiah 33:19; Daniel 2:22; Luke 8:31; Revelation 20:3 (see Anderson 1962b; Cirlot [1962, 1971] 1974, 364-67); monsters—e.g., Jonah 1:17—2:3 (Cirlot [1962, 1971] 1974, 213-14); serpents—e.g., Numbers 21:4-7; Deuteronomy 8:15 (Cirlot [1962, 1971] 1974, 285-90).

2. A Pioneer Workshop, The American Association of Pastoral Counselors, May 1987, New Orleans. Karl (not the client's real name) gave permission for use of the interview. A video-taped copy of the interview may be purchased from The American Association of Pastoral Counselors, 9508A Lee Highway, Fairfax, VA 22031. I appreciate Karl's willingness to put his experience in the service of pastoral therapists learning about the helping process. I also want to express appreciation to Dr. Walton H. Ehrhardt, who worked out the arrangements for the "live" demonstration.

of me" implied fragments of the self, unassimilated aspects of his psyche, behaviors and feelings that puzzled him, incongruencies, discrepancies, dynamics that made his life more painful than satisfying. Here we glimpse intimations of the cosmic dimensions I have just been describing.

The phrase "pieces of me" struck an associative cord in my own parallel processing. At the moment I was unaware of the link, though later the link became obvious. At the moment, "pieces of me" reminded me of the demon-possessed man who explained his pain by shouting at Jesus, "My name is Legion; for we are many" (Mark 5:9). I paraphrase that response to mean, "My name is Legion, for I am in many pieces."

There is a meaning-making link between the "pieces" of mythic metaphor and the psychic "fragmentation" of object-relations theory (Basch 1988; Kohut 1971; 1977; 1984). Each cognitive expression—the experiential voice of nondominant or right-hemisphere style and the conceptual voice of dominant or left-hemisphere style—adds something to our understanding of what is happening and our ability to be part of it in life-enhancing ways.

I noticed that Karl, in referring to these "pieces," used the past tense—namely, "pieces of me that I did not understand before." I inferred that he must be referring to "pieces" about which he had already gained insight. The fact that he was a client of another pastoral therapist reinforced this hunch.

Whenever such a reference to the past occurs, we are dealing with what I call "light from a distant star." The manifestation of the interaction, the reality being expressed at the moment, is not so much in the here and now as it shows something that has gone on back there and then. What is going on between us now reflects a return of anxiety whose source derives from elsewhere. More importantly, what is going on between us now contains a resource with which to engage the future.

CONNECTING EXPERIENCES WITH EACH OTHER

We can enlarge the psychic space of the other by making connections between the "now" of our interaction and the past the client brings. Inquiries on our part may seem relatively simple: "When have you experienced such 'pieces' before?" "Can you give me some examples of what you are referring to?" "Can you remember similar times when you have found yourself fluctuating between being scared and excited?" "What has the discomfort been like on other occasions?"

In terms of the brain, we begin to make conscious and explicit the nonconscious, parallel, distributed process of mental activity. The old brain subsumes and directs the new brain (Laughlin et al. 1990). Until our interaction shifts from connecting to responding, the one seeking help lives more at the level of defense than safety. His or her dominant cerebral hemisphere—usually the left—blocks the activity of the nondominant hemisphere, cutting him or her off from the rich experiential context of life.

But once there is a shift to moving deeper into the client's experience, responding fosters growth rather than safety. Both the client and the counselor experience breathing space. Such psychic space reflects the parasympathetic nervous system as mediated by the nondominant hemisphere. It blocks the defensive activity of the dominant hemisphere. Ego functions now incorporate "nonlinear, image- and affect-ridden thought processes" (Laughlin et al. 1990, 277) in a normal and restorative way. As Jeremiah described that shift from defense to growth, the Lord puts the right order of life within us, writing it on our hearts (31:33).

A vestibule opens into a multitude of rooms in the psychic house of clients. We move from "connecting with" their world to "responding" to what matters to them on the inside. Their soul begins to make itself known. The hardened mass of psychopathology loosens and starts dissolving into the softness of psyche-pathos-logos, the soul allowing its story to be known (Hillman 1975).

REMEMBERING ONE'S STRENGTH

A shift from survival to growth is the difference between a threatening cosmos— a wrathful God—and a liberating cosmos—a merciful God. The person coming to us moves more toward delight than dread, more toward being free than bound, more toward the liberation of an exodus than the slavery of an Egypt. In a Christian worldview, resurrection by divine action becomes more powerful than crucifixion by human calculation.

Like the psalmist, the people seeking help experience "room in . . . [their] distress." They experience us as an idealized selfobject. The pastoral counselor is indeed a symbol bearer of reality that can "hear [their] prayer" for what is "right," separating "truth from ego" as Janet so eloquently put it. Like the psalmist, they can recall the gracious context of God, who is the source and sustainer of their being (Ps. 4:1), the *gloria* as Janet described the transformation.

I assume that we and our clients get stuck because we have lost touch with what we have known in the past that has been helpful. An anxious present crowds out information we have acquired through previously disclosive moments. Our imagination runs wild. We "overread" and therefore "misinterpret" the meaning of a situation. We fill the psychic spaces of our lives with fear and dread.

In the language of general systems theory, the limbic system "oscillates" or "runs away." This is a pathological reaction in which our self-regulating processes break down. The psychic soul-making destabilizes and disintegrates (Hampden-Turner 1981, 84). In those moments the surge of adrenalin—the aroused sympathetic nervous system—takes over and we live in an apocalyptic state of pending catastrophe. Thus I try to tap back into that which the person has known in more adaptive moments. I seek to bring the hidden resources of life once again into the light of consciousness. I probe for what the other has forgotten in the face of a threatening situation.

"How have you been able to cope in the past?" I ask. It is a question of remembering—recovering—reconnecting with what is within. It is an invitation to the observing dominant hemisphere to look at more than the threat and to look back to other moments when it had observed different behavior, behavior of which it can be proud, behavior that it knew was "right" and "true."

Therapists Michael White and David Epston (1990) have expanded my understanding of such remembering. When listening to tales of woe, they listen particularly for "unique outcomes," for "what doesn't fit," for times when the person has failed to react in a survival mode. The alternative story—the story of competence and satisfaction, of loving oneself as one loves others—carries another meaning. This other meaning opens up space for the future. There can be a more adaptive response to stress now because there has been a more adaptive one in the past. In identifying these lesser-known "stories," the counselor assists the client in writing a new story, one told more like living truth than dead facts. The client breathes again the breath of life, the very breath of God.

Theological educators talk about "theological reflection." I suggest they are referring to that discovery of an alternative story, a new story, a new reality in which God liberates us from bondage (see Nelson 1987). Theological reflection includes attention to that which binds us—original sin, sin, tragedy, psychopathology, principalities and powers, limits and endings, cross, death, the old me in old reality. But more than that, or perhaps more accurately by means of that focus on constraints, theological reflection shifts our attention to God. Our relation to God quicken us—breath of life, exodus, Easter, transformation, new beginnings, potentiality, resurrection, a new me in new reality.

At the conscious level of culture our minds are simply unable to comprehend the greater resources that lie beyond (see Hinkle and Hinkle 1992). Only in an imaginative leap of faith—a trust in the reality that creates us, is within us, and works through us—only in that transcendence of observational analysis do we come upon that which we never expected. We think that which we could not imagine and discover that which we did not anticipate. We experience more than we have been able to handle under conditions of survival. We come upon the quickening, meaning-making possibilities of our soul. Transcendence replaces transference (Jones 1991).

We are not yet "established." We are to "become what we will be!" (Moltmann 1967, 162). We remember what life is about. *Gloria!*

SUMMARY

We move deeper into others' experience of hurt and hope by responding. This move reflects *agape*. We as pastoral therapists empty our "selves" for the sake of others' experiencing themselves, and we do so without giving our "selves" away.

This stance of peership and friendship reflects Jesus' saying to his disciples as his death loomed near, "I do not call you servants [or slaves] any longer, because the servant [slave] does not know what the master is doing; but I have called you friends, because I have made known to you everything that I have heard from my Father" (John 15:15). Here friendship means shared knowing. No one has a privileged status to which others have no access. The issue is not a personal and social intimacy. Rather, it is a divinely human understanding—"I have made known to you everything that I have heard from my Father." Everyone is "in on the know." And knowledge is power!

As client and therapist come to the rock of reality, there is little room for a *tabula rasa* relationship. In psychoanalytic orthodoxy, a blank tablet invites unlimited projection by the patient onto the therapist. In pastoral counseling, there is no role for a hidden therapist of superior knowledge and a vulnerable client of inferior knowledge. There is no place for one-way communication and individualistic interpretations. We are in this world—God's world—together. What makes for the meaning-making possibilities of one person contributes to the meaning-making possibilities of other people.

The holding environment of therapeutic relationships turns simple interest into empathic understanding. By responding to what matters to people in pain, we enlarge their psychic space. Experiences in the present are reconnected with experiences in the past and, in the process, people remember their strengths.

As we move more deeply into others' experiences of hurt and hope, we both summarize and support their own understanding. At this point we are encountering Yahweh God as rock and redeemer (Ps. 19:14). At this point object-seeking and meaning-making realities meet. We begin to plant and to build, to create new life, new reality, new possibility. We begin to find the rock of the really real—Yahweh God in the world. From such a base people in pain turn again to life, exploring and discovering the reality of growth.

CHAPTER EIGHT

Growing and Exploring

DISCOVERING

■ ■ ■ ■ ■

In therapy a psychic space and a meaning-making time exist between the counselor's initial connecting-with and responding-to the seeker and the seeker's subsequent discovering and acting. We cannot control that space and time, yet we can discern them. While we can't predict what will happen, we can cultivate the emergence of new reality. Here is the betwixt and between that anthropologist Victor Turner (1969) calls liminality.

One is on the threshold between an old structure of survival and an anti-structure prerequisite to growth. In this reality everything moves around, shifts, is seen and felt and thought in different ways. It is the place of transformation. With the Spirit of life itself it marks the elusive transition between breaking down and healing, between weeping and laughing, between keeping silent and speaking (Eccles. 3:1–8).

Once the person seeking help begins to do for him- or herself what he or she has been asking us to do, we are moving from a receptive relationship to a more active relationship. The seeker now knows—even though he or she may not realize it—what the therapist knows. Self psychologists term this "transmuting internalization" (Basch 1988,143–44). The client is gradually making his or her own the understanding that previously was that of the therapist. An inner voice replaces the authority's voice. The dynamics of the transference shift from idealization of the therapist and grandiosity in the client to more of a shared partnership in the therapeutic process.

While the transition from survival to growth has a universal quality, there are crucial distinctions between the experiences of men and women. For instance, let us look at what helped Janet move from *kyrie* to *gloria*. How did the cry of misery from the bottom of her soul change into a declaration of triumph?

That which made the difference reflects on the place and power of females and males in our culture.

A FEMININE HERMENEUTIC

I puzzled for years over that change in Janet (Ashbrook 1971, 65–81). As far as I could understand, I had been less than helpful, unable to discern a way for her to reengage her life. In spite of my inadequacy she blossomed. What made the difference? How did we get down into her inner cosmos, into that larger realm of soul-making? The thirty-year interval has brought clarity with the articulation of a feminine hermeneutic. Neither of us had the cultural and conceptual tools with which to understand. Now we are privy to such understanding.

Patriarchal and sexist cultures so constrain girls and women that they do not fully develop as persons in their own right. They abort their own selves, their own minds, their own voices, their own souls. Writers such as Jean Baker Miller (1976), Carol Gilligan ([1982]1983), Rosemary Radford Ruether (1983), Gerda Lerner (1986), and Carroll Saussy (1991), among many, have described the violation of the female soul. Boys and men—including brothers, friends, husbands, teachers, professors, pastors, and therapists—easily and often tell them what they (the females) think and feel. Since I was unclear as to what was going on, I was silent. Out of my silence came Janet's speech!

The nuances of our interaction deserve closer attention. They may illumine the transitional space between connecting and responding, initially, and discovering and acting, subsequently. Janet described the most silent of all my silences:

> One time I came here and I said, "I think I've told you all I have to say." And so I just sat here, and I couldn't think of anything to say. And, of course [laughing], you're not one to help in situations like that. And so, all I could remember you saying was, "Maybe you could feel the presence." And I said, "No, I can't feel the presence, and I don't ever expect to."

Janet left that session angry and frustrated.

By the next week Janet's mood had changed. Something had shifted in her psyche and so too in our relationship. That shift—metamorphosis—came with "sabbathing." Her soul needed breathing space. She had to sift out what was basic to her sense of self from what was culturally and socially encrusted. As she remembered, she told me a few things about myself that aggravated her. ". . . I didn't tell you I didn't like you, because that wouldn't have been true. Anyway, I think that after that, after I released my anger, which had to come out of me somehow. . . . Then I could go on deeper." The depth of anger and rage on the part of oppressed people cannot be calculated. Neither can it be bypassed. It is a major source of soul-making. It is a principal ingredient for healing.

ANGER AND RAGE

In the late 1960s I remember sitting in a meeting of women where women's issues were being discussed. Numerous women's meetings—both planned and spontaneous—were being held across the nation at the time. As the evening wore on, the intensity of feeling escalated. I began to experience a psychic dislocation. Those women seemed "possessed."

I was frightened, as I had been frightened in the face of black rage (see Ashbrook 1969; 1971, 157–83). I sensed something ground-shaking happening with the women even as it had happened with African-Americans. Only later did I realize how soul-shaking these events really were. My fright, I confess, reflected—and still reflects—evidence of my sexism and racism. While I work to get beyond the blindness of my privilege, I can never erase it from my psyche.

The shift from conventional niceness to unique power seldom occurs without emotional eruption. I was reminded of that by the experience of a married woman in her late twenties whom I was counseling. I will call her Matilda because she came to the place where, like "waltzing Matilda," she could dance to her own tune. In this psychic shift between moving deep and starting up—that realm in which everything is flip-flop—she shared the following.

Matilda had been shopping with her husband in an automotive store and suddenly became uneasy, to the point of growing panic. They returned home and she lay down on her bed. She told me, "I was scared. And John [her husband] knew I was scared, and he said, 'Why are you afraid?' And I said, 'Because I know I'm going to do it. I'm really going to do it.' And I'm not just going to. . . .'" Matilda began speaking very slowly and very deliberately. She was reliving the dramatic event of the previous evening.

> It's not just the books. It isn't books at all. And it isn't drapes. I was going to pull them down. It isn't your wastebasket. I was going to kick it over. And it isn't throwing glasses against the wall. It's people. And you're right. [She was referring to our previous session.] I do feel very, very pushed. And I let people push me, and there's a reason. . . . you said, "You really are afraid." And I said, "Yes, I really am." And I didn't really know I was being possessed. I didn't know there was so much hate in me.

At that point Matilda was breathing heavily. Her responses were slow. She was relating more to her own inner reality than to that which was between us. Her allusion to books and drapes and wastebasket implied rage against objects in my office and indirectly rage against me and all that I represented. Like an unfolding dream drama, she continued:

> And he [John] said, "I didn't either. I, I didn't think you could be so nice. And I used to get very mad at you for being so nice. Nice, nice all the time. But I didn't know it was bothering you so much."
>
> And I said, "Well, I guess I didn't know it was bothering me so much either." And then I told him a little bit about—about—the automotive store. How I looked at all the tools. . . . And I started to tell him about the tools. . . .

In the deep working of her psyche Matilda was reconnecting with her own energy. Her anger was the vehicle. She had been focusing on her anger at me. Suddenly she enlarged her awareness by connecting her experience in the present with her experiences in the past.

> And . . . I knew . . . it [the source of my pain] wasn't you. And I knew it wasn't John. And I thought maybe it was my father. And I thought maybe it was my brother. And I thought maybe it was Henry [a male colleague who had been harassing her] . . . .

Matilda had now moved into a trancelike consciousness in which inner experience was transforming external experience.

> And I began to go through the tools . . . . The first tool was . . . a sticklike tool. And my father used to keep it on the desk. It was for measuring things. And I thought about it. And I kept thinking about it. It was like a penis. But it wasn't. It was just a metal tool, too. It was *hard*. And I thought, I thought I could take that and I could . . . .

At this point the controlled quietness of her voice exploded.

> . . . I could *gouge* somebody's eyes out. I could GOUGE THEM OUT! . . .

Matilda was breathing very hard. I wanted to let her know two things: first, that I was there, and second, that I was with her in this eruption in her psyche.

Moments like this are decision points for therapists. Do we encourage the other to keep on or to draw back? Are we prepared to stay with the intensity of the pain/rage, or must we soften it to protect ourselves? Is the person's sense of self fragmenting and heading toward a psychotic episode, or is the unconscious at the service of the soul?

The clinical pastoral education movement had its cradle in the crucible of Anton Boisen's struggle with psychosis (Boisen 1960). Pastoral psychologist and pioneer Carroll A. Wise described being with Boisen during his second breakdown in the fall of 1930 (Ashbrook and Hinkle 1988, 7–13). He witnessed the disintegrating of Boisen's personality. He said, "[I had heard Boisen] talk about the experience of personal upheaval, the profound sense of isolation, alienation, and guilt. . . . I heard him talk about hell; now I experienced him in hell."

In the first twenty-five years of clinical pastoral education, we students found ourselves in mental hospitals with mental patients. We moved with them into the hell in their psyches. Since the mid-1950s, a biological revolution has come in psychiatry (Andreasen 1984). Jerold S. Maxmen (1985) describes it as "the new psychiatry." Its hallmarks consist of medication and a narrower focus on symptoms in contrast to symbolic expressions and meaning. This has been both blessing and bane. Much psychic pain has biological roots and is best treated with medication, supplemented with counseling. Because of this remedicalization of psychiatry, however, pastoral counselors are seldom exposed to decision points such as Wise had with Boisen and I had with Matilda. The deeper dynamics of the psyche can be compromised by too easy reliance on drugs.

Wise shared his memory of that moment with Boisen and in so doing voiced the dilemma the pastoral counselor confronts in the center of all therapeutic activity:

> I wondered when the constructive, creative forces, of which I had heard him speak, would appear. How would the living God manifest Himself in Anton? Frankly, I was frightened, very frightened. What could I do, what could I say? . . .
>
> In such a moment, understanding is not being able to formulate an idea or something in words. [It] is being able to communicate to the other person a sense of acceptance and being able to communicate by manner and bearing. (Hinkle and Ashbrook 1988, 8)

Because of my conviction of this creative force in the center of the psyche and because of my assessment that Matilda had the capacity to reflect on what she was experiencing, I chose to encourage her exploration of her rage.

> ME: Really *gouge* them.
> MATILDA: I (crying as she stammers for words) want . . .
> ME: Just jam it in there!
> MATILDA: (continuing to cry) . . . poke and poke and poke …

By then she was pounding the arm of her chair as hard as she could. She pounded and sobbed, sobbed and pounded.

ME: Just poke and poke . . . .

MATILDA: . . . and then there were wrenches.

She was speaking softly, hypnotically. But only for a moment. With each pass-
ing sentence her voice grew louder and louder. She seemed possessed by fury.
She smashed the arm of her chair. Her breathing became heavy, her sobbing
intense.

> I could hit and hit and hit. And I could make somebody bleed. I could
> hit . . . hit . . . hit . . . . And push . . . push . . . push like everybody—
> like I've let everybody push me. I'd push them back. Push and push
> and push.
> And then there were rubber hoses . . . . And I could take the rub-
> ber hose and I could tie people up and really kick them around . . . .
> *KICK* THEM . . . kick them around. And make them black and blue
> like I was black and blue. Like I *am* black and blue.

This was not the moment to turn back. This was not the moment to interrupt.

It is not helpful to encourage most rage (Patton 1990e). Rage is a first line
of defense against a wound to one's sense of self. Kohut called this vulnerability "narcissistic rage." The person is taken over by the need for revenge, for un-
doing the pain by any means possible.

In contrast to a narcissistic rage, Matilda was describing what I would call
a relational rage. She was including herself in the creation of her pain. After the
whirlwind, after the earthquake, after the fire, then and then only comes "a
sound of sheer silence," the voice of the living God, as Elijah experienced it (1
Kings 19:12). So I went with her fantasy. I encouraged her rage.

> ME: Just *kick and kick and make them black and blue.* (I pounded the
> arm of my chair.)

> Matilda: And I could take the rubber hose and I could choke them.
> Choke and choke and choke until they had no breath left in them. And
> just pull it tight. And they'd just die, just die. Just choke and choke.
> And hit them with the rubber hose. And hit them and hit them. Just
> hit them . . . . And then I could . . . I could dig their eyes out . . . .

She was now speaking very softly. We were in the eye of the whirlwind, the
quiet before the hurricane of hurt started moving on.

RECOVERY OF A PERSON'S OWN REALITY

Rage in itself is self-defeating. It exacerbates pain rather than resolving it. However, when understood as a signal indicating threat to the self (Patton 1990e), rage makes for healing and wholeness. This shock of recognition was working its transformation in Matilda. Without labeling her rage as a signal, she experienced it as a call to recover her own reality. Her voice began to take on renewed power.

> They were *brown* eyes. And I couldn't place the brown eyes. Were they my father's eyes or were they my brother's eyes or were they Henry's eyes? And I begin to think—whose eyes are they?
> And that's why I couldn't do it.

She broke down sobbing, crying with the recognition of whose eyes they were.

> Those are my eyes! And I have been doing all those things to me! I have been beating me and gouging my eyes out! And I would tear my hair out . . . .

Matilda's reference to her hair distracted me. I was feeling the intensity of her pain—and my own uncomfortableness. So I asked, "What do you mean?" Rather than side-tracking her, she used my detouring question to continue to voice the experience she had been denying. Her sobbing now sounded forth as insight.

> Well, it wasn't my *father*. It wasn't Henry. It wasn't my brother. Those are people I *let* do that to me. They didn't have to do that to me. I just *let* them . . . cause I thought I was so *bad* that I had to let them do that. And I couldn't be bad. I was so *damn* good . . . but I really thought I was a God-forsaken person. . . . That was really me, and I have let so many people push me around. And I let Henry push me around. I let him take my coffee cups when I didn't want him to take my coffee cups. And I got mad at him when he made—thought he could make—me take his coffee cups. . . . And when I would get so mad at him or so mad at me and . . . just hold it . . . just hold it all in . . . and . . . I really beat myself up. I really almost destroyed me.

"Nobody else but you," I affirmed.

> Yeah, it was just me . . . . I thought I would go crazy if I started this. I didn't . . . . But now it's almost done. The worst of it's done. I won't be able to let people push me. It's going to be hard to decide when . . . I won't have to decide. I'll just have to feel when they're pushing me. . . . And I thought about guilt and pieces of life. . . . What a surprise to find out it's me—the biggest surprise in the world. . . .

More, much more went on, but the whirlwind passed. Subsequently Matilda invested years changing killing herself into birthing herself. Like Jesus with Satan and the wild beasts in the wilderness (Mark 1:12–13), the turmoil passed until another "opportune time" (Luke 4:13).

The behavior of post-traumatic stress victims has some of this turbulence about it. They experience heavy breathing, hyperventilation, sobbing, aching, curling up in a fetal position. Associations can become loose. Strange and uncontrollable reactions appear—fugues, hysterical fits of weeping, spontaneous trances, catatonic-like states, and even alternate personalities.

A study of cerebral hemisphere functioning in a single multiple personality patient (Brende 1982; 1984) provides a framework for understanding the neurocognitive processes at work. There was overcontrol in the mechanisms of the left hemisphere and undercontrol of mechanisms in the right hemisphere. The protective personality came with left-brain activation; the victim personality with right-brain activation. Each personality was "associated with different ego functions and affective qualities." The lack of integration of cognitive and emotional processes contributed to frequent dissociative reactions.

Think of this lack of integration in victims of abuse and trauma as a person with a functionally split or not yet matured corpus callosum. Under stress one regresses to the terror and tantrums of a helpless child. The left brain tries to control the pain; the right brain carries the pain. Because one has been overwhelmed psychically, a barrier prevents the whole brain from working as a whole brain.

What Matilda experienced and expressed paralleled a Vietnam veteran's description of his induction into military service (Brende and McCann 1984, 60). He felt that he had to turn his back on "a civilian identity with moral standards for a combat identity without moral standards." He said: "They expected me to give up my old self in order to become a Marine. When I went into the service I cared about people, but when I came out I became a big bad Marine who killed people."

For many, the experience of killing one's self evokes basic survival modes of functioning. Regression to the reptilian (brain stem) and mammalian (limbic system) brains results in direct expressions of primitive aggression. Survival crowds out growth and adaptation.

Pastoral counselors cannot avoid working with victims of abusive and traumatic situations. In fact, evidence of violence and abuse in the 1960s and even in the early 1970s was more prevalent than most of us realized (Poling 1991). The Vietnam War surfaced the symptoms, named the syndrome, and opened our eyes to the presence of Post-Traumatic Stress Disorder (PTSD) in everyday society.

It is highly desirable that the therapist working with such victims have special skills (see, e.g., Brende and Parson 1985, 185–201; Courtois 1988). The wild oscillations of the autonomic system of arousal and relaxation defy conventional knowledge. The person can no longer experience what is happening. He or she becomes numb and denies the pain. Dreams, images, and emotions erupt into consciousness.

With a holding environment the victim develops a larger personal perspective on the trauma or abuse. In this reflective transition, one focuses more on the future and less on the past. With time the events are integrated into a fuller sense of self.

I have explored an illuminating movement in Matilda in order to underscore Janet's discovery of *gloria*. In helping people mind their soul, sophisticated therapeutic techniques are secondary to *respecting the reality of their reality*. Later in our reflective session Janet picked up the issue of my not speaking for her. The male not speaking for the female is the crux of the feminist critique of patriarchy. The way she put the issue is more elegant than anything I can say:

> JANET: . . . and I also think that it's just wonderful that you *don't* help more. How in the world that you can keep from it is more than I know.

> ME: What do you mean that I "don't help more"?

> JANET: Well, that you don't *say things* that would illumine the situation a little bit. Because ever since I have had this completely revolutionary experience, which gives me new eyes and new ears, I can see other people in the light—a little bit in the light in which you have seen me. And I see that I mustn't say what I see because you didn't, because help would hurt sometimes. [We laugh simultaneously.] So I think it's simply wonderful that you don't say anything.

Janet gave me credit I did not deserve. I did not say anything simply because I did not know what to say. Even so, the way she stated the issue intrigued me, so I inquired further.

> ME: But wouldn't it help if I did?

> JANET: Well, you'd think it'd help at the moment. . . . I'd really have thought at the moment that it would help if you'd just given me a little nudge or something when I was stuck. But in the long run it would not.

> ME: Why not?

JANET: Because I have to make my own decisions. I have to learn that
I am adult and that there isn't anybody else who's ever going to make
my decisions for me.

I could have said something if I had had anything to say and still have allowed
her to make her own decisions. Perhaps if I knew then what we know now, I could
have taken some of the edge off our pain in being stuck. Yet Janet's point stands.
In the final act she had to stand apart from everyone and on her own feet. So did
Matilda. So did the Marine. And so do each of us.

Janet's *gloria* of proclaiming, "I was I and was never going to be anybody else"
sounds like the thundering of the great "I AM" in the Book of Exodus (3:13–15).
By what authority was Moses to lead the Israelites out of Egypt? In whose name
was he acting? What power did he represent? The response of the Lord God has
been the liberating power of every oppressed person and people: "I am who I am.
I am what I am. I will be what I will be." And the word "LORD," the capital letters YHWH, are connected with the Hebrew verb *hayah*, which means "to be."
To be—to exist in one's own right and one's own power—is to become who one
will become, created in the image and likeness of God.

The feminist critique of conventional caregiving resources highlights the oppression of females by males. The critique also points to the oppression of males
by males, of those who have not by those who have, of laity by professional, of
everyone not in authority by those in authority, of minority cultures by a dominant culture. The issue is this: Who defines "experience" and its meaning—the
person? the expert? the culture? Who names what is and what matters? Feminist theology insists that the starting point of meaning-making is the validity of
one's own experience (Rhodes 1987, 31; Ruether 1983).

THE REALITY OF THE PERSON, NOT THE THERAPIST

The integrity of one's own reality can easily be misunderstood as an expression
of Western individualism. I am not describing an isolated, independent, autonomous, self-made male. Nor is the feminist hermeneutic falling into that
monocultural encapsulation.

Women's experience is connected experience, self-in-relation-with-others
and others-in-relation-to-self (e.g., Gilligan et al. 1988; Jordon et al. 1991). The
belief of self-versus-others or self-apart-from-others simply is a snare and delu-
sion. Identity and intimacy are simultaneous and sequential, from the beginning and throughout the life cycle.

The amygdala and the septum are inseparably intertwined in the limbic
system. Autonomy is never separated from attachment. This applies to men as
well as women. As psychologist Jean Baker Miller characterizes the autonomy
phase of development, this phase reflects more "an enlarged 'point of view' . . .

new configurations and new 'understandings' *in the relationship"* (Miller 1991, 26–27). The basic human truth is that there can be no alienating distance from others if we are to have life.

To connect with and respond to another's experience requires the caregiver to put one's own self—one's unique heart and soul and mind and strength (Mark 12:30)—at the service of the other's own self—her or his unique heart and soul and mind and strength. Instead of telling others what "is" reality for them or what they "should" do, we are to risk being open to their perception of what is and what might be. Those of us who are male must be exceedingly careful not to tell women what their experience is. We simply do not know firsthand. The same issue applies in all counseling and especially with those from cultures other than our own. Further, no conscious understanding—inclusive as it seeks to be—can contain the living God.

Pastoral psychotherapists John E. Hinkle and Gregory A. Hinkle (1992) make a claim and a case for pastoral counseling being *meta*cultural. By that they mean working with persons at a level of insight and faith beyond the egocentricism of the individual ego and the ethnocentricism of one's own culture. Cultures promise safety and certainty, which come as a result of fitting into the roles and expectations of the group. Faith promises risk and uncertainty, which come with the collapse of roles and the failure of expectations.

The pastoral counselor, thereby, is freed from needing the person in pain to behave in certain ways. The Hinkles defined the metacultural imperative:

> The metacultural holding environment allows both participants to cooperate in a process by which the self's cultural meaning (self as the culture defines and rewards it) is surrendered so that the soul (the I-Thou relationship) emerges as the dominant experienced reality. Hope shifts from the culture's promises about the future to the profound and terrifying intimacy and realized promise of the present moment. The faith that grows out of the soul's encounter with the Lord emerges as a deep bondedness, a trust beyond all reason and expectation: in the words of the translators of the King James Version, "Though [the Lord] slay me, yet will I trust [the Lord]" (Job 13:15).
>
> In this metacultural space grows the faithing/healing process. (Hinkle and Hinkle 1992, 115)

Once the pastoral conversation and therapeutic task reaches into clients' souls, we are free to put our experience alongside their experience in a more collaborative way. Exploring the inner world metamorphoses into engaging the wider world. We start up from the depths and reach out to the world, returning to that from which the seeker sought sanctuary.

Every session must involve "connecting" and "responding." These may include the panic arousal of confronting Yahweh God in the garden. Every session can activate survival mechanisms that help in the short-run yet do us in in the long-run. But once we have experienced the bedrock of reality—and have not only survived but have begun to find new life—we can move more quickly through the initial phases of every session. We can come more surely to the "outward" task of what it means to be created in the image and likeness of God. We can turn to how the seeker is to be and what the seeker is to do in his or her world.

STRATEGIES IN DISCOVERING

This turn around—*metanoia* in Greek—from living in the old brains to utilizing the whole brain comes as we get our heads and hearts together. The writer of Ephesians describes the experience as speaking truth to one another because we are "members of one another" (Eph. 4:22–27). The emotional mind will no longer panic in the face of pain, for we know that new reality lies in and through this experience. Relaxation replaces tension; a cognitive reconstructing transforms a threatening cosmos into a meaning-making cosmos.

We can engage this metamorphosis of soul-making in three ways: by adding on to the other's experience, by going beyond the other's experience, and by elaborating the emerging experience more fully (see Carkhuff 1969; Ivy 1971).

ADDING ON TO THE OTHER'S EXPERIENCE

As pastoral counselors we can now put our mind explicitly at the service of the other's search. The seeker will be able to take in what fits with his or her experience and sift out what is more the counselor's experience as we face the seeker's future collaboratively.

The counselor's responses are less mirroring and more a constructing or reconstructing of meaning. This active phase of "discovering" comes with an explanatory rationale or interpretation. Such a framing organizes the other's experience and permits the other to engage in new behavior based on that revised interpretation. Making sense of experience allows us to know and own who we are. An explanatory scheme is a crucial ingredient in healing (Frank 1973).

The importance of an interpretive frame—a cognitive shaping of affective-laden experience—is one of my major learnings in the last two decades. We are meaning-making creatures even as we are object-seeking creatures (e.g., Kegan 1982; Gilbert 1989; Mahoney 1991). Pastoral theologian Charles Gerkin (1984) helps us recover the central importance of "revisioning pastoral counseling in a hermeneutical mode." Explicit religious meaning has a key role in the therapeutic process.

In this exploring phase I tend to shift from short mirroring responses to longer responses consisting of my own parallel associations and wonderings. In the last chapter I referred to my demonstration interview with Karl. He had identified a growing ability to name his fear and so turn it into excitement. Later in our interview I picked up that theme of naming. I said:

> One of the things I think of in response to what you're saying about naming and getting through barriers is the creation story in Genesis. (I don't know how much you know about the Bible, and I won't run a Bible quiz on you.) God brought before Adam all the animals of the world and Adam gave them a name—hippopotamus or whatever. Naming is the capacity to turn randomness into a more focused reality. It sounds like you're able to do that.

I was adding my experience to his experience.

No mind is able to imagine the infinite possibilities in creation. We need to put our heads together. Although what I am about to say is more my own interpretation than an objective one, I believe Jesus is indicating a basic factor in new creation when he says, ""Where two or three are gathered together in my name [in the power of unconflicted presence for the sake of inclusive reality] I am there among them" (Matt. 18:20). This saying is preceded by his reflection about two people getting together—agreeing—and finding that what they ask is accomplished. I think of this synergistic phenomenon as tapping into the "group mind," the universal mind of how things can be. When that happens, we are on the way to fulfilling our being created in the image and likeness of God.

I reinforced and enlarged Karl's experience of naming his act of changing surviving into growing. When we can say what something is, then we are exercising responsible care over it. To give a name is to bestow reality. To be able to name our experience is to exercise power and to own our experience. In linking Karl's "understanding"—his consciously intended asking—with the Genesis story I made four distinct moves.

First, I began to educate him about my rationale or structure of understanding—namely, the Bible. In doing so I allowed the possibility that he might or might not know very much about it. More importantly, in referring to the Bible I did not intend to put him down—"I won't run a Bible quiz on you"—though I did let him experience something of my expertise. I wanted him to know that I was an authority as well as a believer. He had come for help to a *pastoral* counselor, and I was giving him my expert help.

Second, I shifted his awareness from an individualistic context to a communal context. His story was part of God's story. His search was humanity's search. He was unique yet not exceptional. His grandiosity had its origin in genetic human predisposition, the longing for meaning making that comes with object seeking.

Augustine voiced it for all of us: "Our hearts are restless until they find rest in Thee, O God" (Augustine, 1955).

Third, with my seemingly flippant reference to "hippopotamus or whatever," I was "normalizing" his "disturbance." I enlarged the context of our exploration from that of his being a sin-sick soul to that of our being created in the image and likeness of our Maker. We were not dealing primarily with psychopathology, present though it was in surface issues. Rather, we were dealing with knowledge of God's world, the depth of life itself, which includes knowing God and knowing ourselves. We were dealing with "psyche-pathos-logos"—the soul or psyche, suffering or pathos, its meaning or logos to be known (Hillman 1975).

For me to throw in "hippopotamus" as an example of the naming process suggested the fundamental reality of cognition itself. Consciousness in partnership with Yahweh God shows itself in our ability to name all that is, including God. Naming is not only telling and remembering who we are, it is the empowering that comes with saying who we are like: "I am who I am. I am what I am. I will be what I will be" (see Exod. 3:14).

Fourth, with Karl I moved to keep him alert but not aroused. He could not have anticipated my leap from his naming his fear to my naming a large, lumbering, chiefly aquatic African mammal. The immensity of the image could offset his mode of self-conscious survival. This technique has the same effect as the paradigmatic story. The mind-boggling demand to attend to the unexpected served to keep Karl from domesticating—*habituating* to use the technical psychological word—reality and thereby forgetting it.

I was introducing something novel. Every variation—or deviation—from what we expect triggers our signal system. Change gets the adrenaline flowing (see Pattison 1990). We wake up. If the novel is intriguing, we are alert, receptive, excited. If the novel is intimidating, we are vigilant, tense, fearful. I wanted to strengthen his excitement and minimize his fear. "Hippopotamus" was more likely to accomplish that renewing of his mind than my zeroing in on his obsessive self-consciousness. In effect, by sharing my association of the Genesis story I was consolidating his move toward psychic liberation. His excited response confirmed my understanding: "Yeah, yeah! I like that! I like that kind of connection. That's nice."

Karl's spontaneous "Yeah, yeah!" indicated that I had found an integrating anchor. His emotional mind and his rational mind cooperated. We were sharing in a liberating, transforming process of spiritual growth. We were combining the adjustment and coping focus of counseling, the renewal and growth focus of therapy, and the emancipation of metacultural concerns (cf. Strunk 1990). His eyes were opened with wonder, not fear.

Karl was experiencing within himself his partnership with God and our partnership with each other. In effect, I was incarnating Jesus with his disciples.

"I no longer call you servants but friends" (John 15:15). As Luther would put it, I was being a Christ to my neighbor.

Further, Karl's passionate conviction had come under the light of reflection. "I like that kind of connection. That's nice." Brief though the moment was, his reflecting ego—the observing left hemisphere and the evaluating frontal lobes—had surveyed, weighed, and found the "connection" worthy of his desire to understand. His inner experience of himself shifted from being fragmented to being whole.

GOING BEYOND THE OTHER'S EXPERIENCE

Having added to Karl's understanding, I moved into possible sources of his perplexity. I went beyond that of which he was aware to deeper dimensions of his life. I tried to map the complexities of what he was about—both their oppressive features and their liberating possibilities, their basic emotional assumptions of survival and their basic theological assumptions of growth.

I did this by an oblique association, oblique only by virtue of the fact that I was still associating with biblical material. I assumed that my association reflected the reality with which he was struggling. At the moment I made the association about naming I was unaware of its implications. Rather, I was picking up an earlier clue that Karl had given me. In the "connecting" phase, he had referred to "pieces of me that I did not understand." I said:

> The second association in the Bible that I have about this naming business is this. There was a story about Jesus crossing the sea, and upon reaching the other side, he encountered a demoniac (Mark 5:1–20)— we would say someone who had lost his marbles, today in more clinical terms—running around bruising himself. He was a very tragic person and, in fact, probably was the identified patient in the community. That is, they were all so scared they made *him* scared, and he was willing to sacrifice his sanity for the sake of *their* insanity. And so he was running around sick.

I caught an involuntary reaction on Karl's part to this crazy pattern of misplaced sickness. His head twitched, his eyes flashed, his body tightened. It seemed that I had touched a sensitive nerve in his psyche. I wanted to acknowledge his "recognition" without dwelling on it.

> Yeah, bad news. And he came up to Jesus and said, "What have you to do with me? Get away. Stop torturing me!" And Jesus said to him, "What is your name?" He said, "My name is 'Legion' because I am in many pieces."

What happened was that he had come apart. He had fractured. And [because of] the power of being with somebody who was nurturing—[he was] able to say "I'm out there," and "I'm out there," and "I'm out there"—he began to take them [the pieces] back into himself. And it sounds like you're discovering that for you.

I had just given Karl a highly condensed lecture on family systems theory (Friedman 1985), self psychology (Basch 1988), and interpersonal dynamics (Leary 1957)—all embedded in a biblical story. Of course this explanation is too much for anyone to take in quickly and calls for elaboration. But the promise of future fulfillment came close in the presence of this present reality.

"Scared"—panic, fear, fractured, psychopathology, sin, a runaway limbic system, unable to integrate concern for self and concern for others, however you want to name "fallen" reality—was the "gate" Karl used to frame his pain. Psychologist Perry London named the main object of treatment as "not so much surcease of pain as the establishment of a context of meaning in life, of which the pain is an intelligible part" (London 1964, 64–65). Again I "normalized" Karl's situation—or at least softened its psychopathological seriousness—by linking specialized clinical knowledge to the colloquial expression "lost his marbles." I intended this unexpected association between the biblical story and Karl's struggle to catch his attention and to keep him relaxed.

My reference to "a very tragic person" stressed the poignancy of the demoniac's—and by inference Karl's—situation. I took that association a step further by shifting from an individualistic framing of pain to a systemic framing—"the identified patient in the community." "Identified patient" is, of course, a technical term (Gurman and Kniskern 1981, 765–68; Friedman 1985). I was linking my biblical expertise with my clinical expertise. More importantly, I was integrating theological and psychological schema. I provided a rationale that combined aspirational commitment with causal explanation.

In this partnership mode of shifting attention toward the outer world of interpersonal relationships, I explained what an identified patient is. Others are "so scared of acknowledging the dysfunction in which they are caught that they make the patient scared, and he is willing to sacrifice *his* sanity for *their* insanity, and so the patient appears to be the sick one, when in fact it is the family or community system that is sick."

While time did not permit us to explore the interfacing of the demoniac's story with Karl's story, a later comment from his therapist confirmed the validity of the association. Karl was indeed sacrificing his individuality to keep the family system functioning. My parallel association had been attuned to his current struggle.

Such confirmation encourages me to risk these spontaneous parallel associations. If I am off, the person quickly reorients me. If my association fits, we have extended the realm of the understandable. I have come to trust peripheral associations, even when they seem far-fetched. In fact, far-fetched associations come close to home much of the time.

It is important, however, to allow psychic space for the other to assess the validity of our associations. I do that by prefacing my additive or multiplier comments with some statements like, "I may be completely off base with what I'm about to say, but let me try it," or "I found a funny—an unexpected—thought fleeting through my mind as you were talking . . . ." The qualifier keeps me from imposing my reality on the other. It also permits the other to be the evaluator of my comment's possible value.

Tradition-oriented believers may speak of such associations as "the work of the Holy Spirit." I agree. I identify such mysterious harmonizing as the working of God. Old Testament scholar J. A. Sanders describes this as everything unfolding within the purposes of a reality with integrity (Sanders 1987). I add to that conviction knowledge that parallel processes reflect shared experience.

ELABORATING MORE FULLY

In adding on and going beyond the experience of which the other is conscious, I intend to explore more fully what is emerging as the new and the old brains cooperate. I want to know more about the other's discovery of understanding. I want the person to give voice to his or her viscera. I want the other to make sense of his or her reality.

Self-psychologist Lallene Rector (personal communication) identifies parallels between my moves and Kohut's description of empathy. For Kohut, empathy is a process that involves, first, understanding, and, second, explanation. Understanding alone simply feels good; explanation enables a person to make use of feeling understood in ways that can be internalized. Explanation alone is simply a matter of conceptual understanding. It does not incorporate any of the affective dimensions of experience. Kohut said these may happen in repetitive micro-combinations. Often, a person may require a long period of understanding by the therapist before the narcissistic vulnerability can tolerate explanations.

The term *unconscious* has a mixed history of meaning—from Freud's view of the conflict between instinctual drives and repressive defenses to the blocking of information that has been evaluated "as threatening to arouse unmanageable affect" (Basch 1988, 122). Think of unconscious in terms of brain processing. Subcortical emotion generates the meaning of information. Such meaning mediates both the feeling and the cognitive framing of experience. Understanding and explanation combine.

To be assimilated, insight must be named. That leads me in this middle phase of counseling to shift from the relaxed processing of the right brain to the interpretive processing of the left brain. The therapist and the client shift from tension to excitement. It is as though the world suddenly takes on new reality—colors are brighter, feelings are surer, sensations are fresher, juices are flowing. They are "on a roll," so to speak.

The exhilaration of liberation from survival—from captivity in Egypt, if you will—finds its accountability in being responsible—that is, commandments at Mount Sinai, to continue the analogy. Grace can be cheap, as German theologian Dietrich Bonhoeffer reminded us. Ecstasy without ethics is destructive, while ethics without ecstasy can be empty. Eros and logos belong together (Walaskay 1977), even as do understanding and explanation. To love God, our neighbor, and ourselves with *all that we are*—heart, soul, mind, and strength—requires that we continue to work and rework the task of living out being made in the image and likeness of God.

All of us, counselors and seekers alike, have recurring moments or periods of fragmentation. Our psyche will be overwhelmed by what lies at hand or what we imagine ahead. All of us will skid back into a *kyrie* phenomenon. Yet most of us can experience that bedrock of soul—"I am I" which reflects Yahweh God. In the experience of the "burning bush" (Exod. 3), that loving reality that burns without being consumed, we learn the name of the really real. "I am who I am, I am what I am, I will be what I will be, I cause to be what comes into existence" (Anderson 1962a, 408–11). In knowing the name, we are empowered to be.

So in this middle phase the pastoral counselor encourages people to explore the "pieces" of their reality—probe them, connect them with one another, revisit and rework them. This expanded consciousness brings a sense of coherence, consistency, and, yes, power. The self is no longer overwhelmed. The self is capable of taking in and living with the scattered fragments of the self. As the soul grows stronger, the world grows clearer. One's "I am that I am" enlarges (cf. Laughlin et al. 1990, 272–73; see also Kelly 1955).

In such moments we and the person seeking help stand on the threshold of "acting." We glimpse a return to the everyday world of time and space. The next two chapters bring the counseling process to a close and then review the journey from *kyrie* through *gloria* to *credo*.

CHAPTER NINE

A New Engaging of Experience

ACTING

■ ■ ■ ■ ■

Minding the soul in pastoral counseling may involve only a single session or may stretch over months and years. Regardless of duration the process is cyclical, connecting and responding and then exploring and acting. Somewhere in that elusive realm between responding and exploring there is a working—and a re-working—of the same meaning-making process. The integrating activity enables the seeker to move out into the wider world. Whether integration comes in a flash of illumination—an "ah ha"—or gradually over time, the soul requires "sabbathing" in order to take in new experience and make it part of itself. Change requires breathing space, time, sleep, inattention, incubation, retrospective reflection in order to be bone of our bone and flesh of our flesh (see Gen. 2:23a). The result is an internal shift from a defensive organizing of experience to an adaptive organizing.

In this latter phase, therapy shifts from the exciting discoveries of the *gloria*—"I am I no matter what"—to the consolidating of the *credo*—the ability to affirm, as Janet put it, "what was real and true and determine truth from ego." People cope more adaptively. In fact, they experience exciting possibilities beyond sheer survival. The outward move into a genuinely meaning-filled cosmos prepares them to return to the ordinary world. They experience connection with others, coherence within the self, and competence in meeting whatever comes. They reengage their culture as a new world, a world known through direct experience (Laughlin et al. 1990, 276).

The psychic search for meaning is universal, based as it is on "neurognostic structures existent within the human nervous system" and dramatized in myths of magical flights and shamanistic practices (Laughlin et al. 1990, 273–81). The movement bears evidence of two phases: first, the receptive phase in which we allow primary experience—or primary process and subsymbolic processing—to be translated into feeling and intuition; and second, the more active phase in which we translate what is internal and implicit into active consciousness—or secondary process and symbolic processing. The translation then becomes the basis of new behavior.

This maturing sounds very like an "arrival," a "completion, a "perfecting." Actually, it is only a "sabbathing," a seventh "day"—or phase—in an emerging cycle of work and rest, reorganization and synthesis, celebration and renewal. Pain is being transformed into the power of possibility.

Those who seek help reconnect with their own ongoing experience. Their life space enlarges. They breathe again as living souls. They are empowered to be who they are in relation to what matters to what is genuinely human in themselves and others. As we have explored above, the relational context of special person and special place (Frank 1973) provides the ground of this new reality.

But love is not enough. We are meaning-making creatures as well as object-seeking creatures. We construct a frame of understanding and act on the basis of that understanding. Thus, the ascent phase of therapy involves an explanatory structure or rationale. The scheme makes sense of the seeker's pain. Based on that rationale she or he experiments with new behavior (Frank 1973).

RECONNECTING WITH ONGOING EXPERIENCE

Counseling in a multicultural mode shifts the focus from a more traditional psychodynamic long-term reorganization of the personality structure to a relational reality of social and cultural interaction (see Greenberg and Mitchell 1983; Strunk 1990). Couple and family dynamics deal with the system as "the client," not the individual in isolation from the system (Gurman and Kniskern 1981; Friedman 1985). In such an action-oriented approach to pain, the coping ego of consciousness becomes the locus of attention.

How do people live and act in concrete situations? The imperatives of religious and psychological understandings emerge in some form: "This do, and you shall live."

THE SOCIAL REALITY OF CLIENTS

Pastoral theologian and counselor Judith L. Orr (1991) emphasizes the social reality of clients in comparing working-class women and middle-class women. Middle-class women have the luxury of reflecting on life's purposes; working-class women struggle from crisis to crisis. Problem solving assumes more importance than purpose clarifying.

When middle-class women were asked how a minister could be most help-ful, they spoke of encouragement, reassurance, emotional support, kindness, trustworthiness. Working-class women spoke of honesty. More than *meaning* or *relationship* the word *honesty* places truth in the center of life.

> By honesty they meant the capacity to state clearly both how the min-ister saw the woman's problem and possible solutions to it, and what the minister would do in the same situation. Working class women do not want an authority figure to tell them what to do ("I want options, not absolutes"), or someone to give unconditional affirmation ("I want someone who can see through my bullshit"), or someone who is nondi-rective ("letting me flounder to solve it alone"). They do expect to get concrete, tangible results quickly with a counselor who is willing to en-gage actively in the mutuality of problem-solving. (Orr 1991, 351–52)

Class affects the expectations with which people come for help and the activity with which the pastoral counselor engages the person seeking help.

THE CULTURAL REALITY OF CLIENTS

David H. Bailey was trained as a pastoral psychotherapist at the Blanton-Peale Graduate Institute (BPGI) of The Institutes of Religion and Health in New York City. Along with a range of programs—marriage and family therapy, pas-toral studies, clergy consultation services—the institute's basic orientation con-tinues to be in-depth, individual, personal, psychoanalytically oriented pastoral psychotherapy. With that background Bailey became coordinator of counseling services of Bangkok, Thailand, in 1991. This agency has had to double its facil-ities in response to an all-time high of counseling sessions.

Bailey's experience may well be a paradigm of pastoral counseling in the 1990s and beyond. He writes to colleagues with whom he trained and worked:

> My work with clients is sometimes very different from what was the norm in NYC. Lots of cultural adjustments and ethnicity issues, more couple and family work than I've ever done before, less long-term "in-depth" work and more ego supportive treatment. But in all the change, I remain aware that the training I received at BPGI is stand-ing me in good stead at all times! (Bailey 1992)

Ego-supportive treatment—whether individual or systemic—in a particu-lar cultural context may be the greatest demand on our skill and contribution as pastoral counselors. Sheer survival for the person in pain takes on a priority greater than the exploration of intrapsychic and spiritual significance.

Contextual and crisis-oriented counseling focus on action or behavior change more than intrapsychic reorganizing of experience. The key lies in counselors' ability to mobilize clients' inner resources so they can take a hand in affecting their own destinies. As a resource, the counselor explores with the person the nature of the crisis, possible alternatives, and ways of engaging in new behaviors. The goal is not a dramatic transformation in the other's life. Rather, the goal becomes a slight change in the other's responses—not the maximum distance covered, but a minimum change in direction (Tyler 1961). After a while, a minimum shift in direction has a major effect on what happens.

In chapter 6 I referred to the experience in Acts 2 as the Pentecostal paradigm. Pastoral psychologist John Hinkle (Hinkle 1989, 145–55; Hinkle and Hinkle 1992) suggests that people from every nation translates into multicultural presence. This New Reality is *meta*cultural. Its aspirations go beyond the constrictions of every particular culture even as it focuses on the constructive presence of each person within a particular culture. Ethnic differences, racial, sex-gender, age and class differences are ever present and always impacting what pastoral counselors do.

The Rev. Christine Y. Wiley is director of the Center for Holistic Ministry of the Covenant Baptist Church in Washington, D.C. She has reexamined the traditional Eurocentric approach of pastoral counseling in her work with the African-American church and community (Wiley 1991). The center's services include a range of nine distinct programs: pastoral counseling and psychotherapy, substance abuse treatment and prevention, support and special interest groups, health and nutrition, spiritual disciplines, liberation theology in action, life skills, economic development, and children and adolescents. Wholeness requires and includes "different" people, different approaches, and different interactions.

Such variability goes beyond the scope of this orientation to pastoral counseling as minding the soul, a way of remembering who we are. Yet it is the widest context in which we do our therapeutic work. Therefore, we must be mindful of difference and diversity in our work with individuals and groups. Our task is to so empathize—or interpathize (Augsburger 1986)—with those who come to us that we accompany them on *their* pilgrimage. Genuine pilgrimage always takes us beyond our own constrictive culture into the emerging reality of God's kinship (see Hinkle and Hinkle 1992).

THE PSYCHIC REALITY OF CLIENTS

Within the social and cultural realities of those in pain is the psychic and spiritual reality of their being made in the image and likeness of God. Beyond survival lies the significance of human beings being human.

One woman's frustration with her psychodynamically oriented psychotherapy suggests a difference between cultural accommodation and spiritual searching:

> My own prayers have been real, hard pressed, not desperate, but aching, yes. All is turmoil and yet all has integrity. Ultimately I trust the larger resources will sustain; God knows I shall need it. Moreover I know in ever new ways I am made of stuff that can make good on what I turn myself to. And yet, that is also too big a claim. I am beginning to see I do have to let go—to quit twisting my own guts to make the non-workable, somehow workable.

Her analyst had been pressing her to adjust to a constricting culture.

> That [turmoil] is the reality of [being] 43, though not the one [my analyst] sees. She says reality is living with what you have and being satisfied with it—a moralist to the end. God, I am so tired of it! Oh, I *can* do it. . . . I am working hard to sort, to evaluate, to be, and to be faithful to what is happening inside. I have not taken *any action* other than to commit myself to look responsibly at what my experience means. That allows me not to blow apart.

She went on to describe some of her choices and more of her reservations about the direction of her culture-bound therapy:

> As you can see I have a quarrel with her which we will hammer out—perhaps with my going elsewhere to [get] help. I will not ultimately be boxed in by a mythological construct that says too much and explains too little.

In the words of Hinkle and Hinkle (1992), this woman refused to sacrifice her soul to her self. Inner integrity claimed priority over cultural values. And that wider and deeper contextualizing of the pain of those who come to us as pastoral counselors is an ever-present challenge.

AFFECTIVE ACTIVITY

Here, for instance, is one woman's experience of this process of reconnecting with the ongoing reality of her soul. Eloise, as I call her, was in her mid-30s. She found herself caught up in liberation issues, especially as they related to Latin America, for her, a sphere of psychic identification. She had discovered the work of Brazilian Paulo Freire in educating the oppressed (Freire 1970). In learning to read, the peasants were validating their own lives. (As one man reported in a group, "Yesterday I wrote my name. Therefore I am!") In response to this vision of humanizing, she found her own psychic boundaries relaxing and expanding. Ideas and images started bubbling up into her awareness.

Unexpectedly, Eloise realized that she was struggling for liberation from an inner oppression that colluded with social and political oppression. What she resonated with in Freire reflected what she was uncovering in herself. Toward the end of our working relationship Eloise reported a dream. She was walking on a street that looked similar to the one where she had grown up—a typical lower-middle-class New York City neighborhood in the 1930s. A little brown bear on the other side of the street caught her attention. She could not decide whether the bear was someone's pet and therefore harmless or an escaped animal and therefore dangerous.

Neurobiologically, her safety system and her defense system were at odds (Gilbert 1989). Relaxation and tension clashed around the emerging demands of her psychic reality. In her paralyzed state she caught sight of a huge, erect, black bear thrashing about, pawing at the door of a house at the end of the block. She wondered, "Shall I be afraid now?" She had moved far enough in her therapeutic exploration to reflect on the unknown and not simply react to it. She was reorganizing her emotional and cognitive processes.

Eloise decided to take her cue from the reaction of the little bear. She reasoned in her dream state that the bears were alike and the little bear would recognize the big bear's condition. As she glanced at the little bear, it fled. With that she raced fearfully to the nearest apartment, discovered she knew the woman, and asked for safety. The woman did not seem upset by the dreamer's barging in. With that the dreamer woke up.

On reflection Eloise regarded the little bear as her "child." It contained her early conditioning, which had helped her survive yet no longer seemed appropriate. For example, she was so afraid of death that she could not walk on the same side of the street on which a funeral parlor was located. She also feared that her father and God both had unlimited power to destroy her. Crowded places made her apprehensive. An empty house triggered panic. Similarly, she felt that the big bear represented objective reality. That would include crowds, authority figures (including me), suffering, and death.

Eloise's dream pointed out to her that as an "adult" she was still heavily influenced by her "child." She interpreted ambiguous and stressful situations as dangerous. When she felt anxious, the threat was intensified. She had learned early in life to organize her experience defensively. She discovered she could not get away from taking her cues from the little bear/child. She also realized that no one else could deal with the big bear for her. She had to engage both the oppressor(s) and the oppressed in herself.

About this time a week's separation from her husband stimulated Eloise's developing sense of self. During that time she experienced in her aloneness what she described as "a peculiar, unexpected joy." She became aware of a stretching out and exploring of her boundaries. She savored every decision. She felt the power of taking initiative. She experienced the warmth of responding to situations. She took more risks. Support came from inside more than from the environment. Suddenly she realized, "It seemed OK to look stupid, to make mistakes, to reveal 'herself.'"

In the midst of this week of waking up to who she was, Eloise had another "landmark dream." She was in a sunlit bedroom of her house early in the morning. The household was not yet stirring. The oldest of her children were with her—the boy looking about twelve and the girl about eleven. They were naked, though she was not. All three were in a playful mood. The children pranced around, laughing and teasing each other. She tried to get them to decide what to wear for the day. They kept on dancing, ignoring her pleas, fascinated with looking at each other's genitals to see how different they were. Her son playfully thrust his penis at her daughter's pelvis.

At that moment—in the dream—Eloise heard her husband's footsteps. "Hey, Dad's back," she nervously scolded them. "You've got to get dressed fast." With that she pulled opened the dresser and began tossing out clothes. At that moment one of her children woke her up so she did not finish the dream.

At first she was upset by the sexuality. Reflection suggested a symbolic integrating of her own masculine and feminine sides. She felt as though she were starting on a new beginning. The best was yet to come. Though her husband had returned, she no longer felt the need to "get dressed," to cover those parts of herself as she had tried to do in the dream.

Eloise realized she needed to find a room that was hers—a place to which she could go and in which she could commune with herself. That place had to be free of the shared side of her life. Yet she did not want to separate for the sake of separateness. Instead, she wanted to separate in order to return as a person capable of mutuality. Psychologically, that is called individuation.

As Eloise's sense of herself grew she experienced a reconciling of the active (masculine) and receptive (feminine) sides of herself. I use these Jungian concepts to frame her experience because she used them that way. The inner harmonizing reduced her fear of censure. She found a space of her own. And with that space of her own she experienced an expanding consciousness, ever widening and ever more engaging. As is often the case, a distant, judging God turned into an accessible, loving God (cf. Jones 1991).

COGNITIVE ACTIVITY

Eloise described her psychic struggle in terms of oppression and liberation. And her remembering who she was came via the old brain and rapid eye movement (REM) activity. In contrast, Ben, also in his mid-30s, described his psychic struggle in terms of "one-sidedness." He had come for therapy because his job as a high school social studies teacher, his religious commitment, and especially his wife were all calling into question his view of himself and his world. These challenges undermined his sense of self. He resented being forced to look at himself, because it hurt to admit his shortcomings. He was threatened to see that he was only half of what he could be, and his former confidence faded.

Trouble intensified at home and at work. No longer was Ben organized, disciplined, and productive. No longer did his wife agree with his directives. In terms of the Myers-Briggs type indicator, he became aware of the world through his five senses; his wife through what she brought to situations. He evaluated the world in terms of what he liked personally, she in terms of what was logical. He got things done by defining tasks and tackling them with a vengeance; she preferred to pursue possibilities. Their discussions mushroomed into arguments, each defending who he or she was. He was an ISFJ (Introvert, Sensing, Feeling, Judging) type, and she was an ENTP (Extrovert, Intuitive, Thinking, Perceiving) type.

In the midst of this turmoil Ben wrote a one-act play that gave voice to the inner dialogue he constantly carried on between the part of him he thought in control and the part that questioned his confidence. By giving voice to ignored experience he began to recover his truer voice. One-sidedness gave way to balance and buoyancy.

> *The Scene:* Ben, teacher, entering the faculty room at a suburban high school. Many colleagues are in the room.
>
> *The Plot:* One of the many dialogues that takes place in Ben's [my] head.
>
> *Characters:* Voice #2—The part of me that compels me to enjoy and know others; Voice #1—The part of me that withdraws from others.
>
> *The Act:* A dialogue.

Eloise had begun breathing into her soul through affective and subconscious processing. Ben began to breath into his soul through cognitive and conscious processing. This difference is supported by brain-mapping evidence that women respond to an active imagination activity from their central and visceral regions while men respond from their prefrontal and conscious regions (Smith 1989).

In both Eloise and Ben the basic rest-activity cycle was present. Both incorporated conscious symbolic meaning into nonconscious subsymbolic adaptation. With the new brain, the rational mind, they sifted and sorted, anticipated and planned, assessed and evaluated what mattered to them. They engaged the unbroken flow of experience in contrasting yet complementary ways. The left hemisphere focused their attention; the right hemisphere broadened their attention. Vigilance and responsiveness alternated. And these alternating orientations reflected the older brain processes of arousal and relaxation, respectively.

Recall that the left brain works a step at a time—analytically, sequentially, logically, conceptually. It is the interpreter, the creator of consistency and coherence. It drives primarily from the activity of the central nervous system. The right brain works by leaps of imagination—synthetically, simultaneously, relationally, perceptually. It is the weaver of patterns, the creator of connections and possibilities. It draws primarily on the activity of the peripheral nervous system and limbic emotionality.

Each process requires the other; neither process works alone. The connecting fiber track of the corpus callosum lets each half know what the other half knows, thereby establishing collaboration. That conscious connection is consolidated and integrated in the old brain in a subsymbolic and nonconscious way, as I explain more fully in Part Three.

What Eloise engaged during sleep, Ben engaged while awake.

> *Voice #1:* Well, here I am again. This is the second time this week that I've made it up here to the faculty room. Not bad. I hope that this time it is worthwhile; I've got a lot of work that I could be doing during this time.

> *Voice #2:* Time, time, time! That's all you think about! You know that there's more to being a teacher than just knowing social studies. You've got to be a person, too, *and not just with the kids!* Ninety percent of your time here you spend teaching them; when are you going to learn the value of personal relationships? You might enjoy your job more if you developed some friendships.

> *Voice #1:* Well, I didn't get hired to become Mr. Popularity with the teaching staff. I'm here to teach kids.

Ben is allowing the two sides of himself—the two sides of his brain—to express themselves. Since the right hemisphere tends to be the silent hemisphere, we could say that he is giving voice to the relational side of himself. The left hemisphere, in contrast, has no hesitation in saying what it thinks.

> *Voice #2:* OK! OK! You're right; you did get hired to teach. But let's cut the B.S. and get to the point! Week after week you come to school and put in endless hours. Your teaching and coaching experience have been pretty good—right?

> *Voice #1:* Right.

> *Voice #2:* But if you're honest with yourself, you'll admit that one big

problem area is your peer relationships. How many friends—good friends—have you discovered in your three years here?

Voice #1: Well, maybe one, and that's a hot and cold friendship.

Voice #2: And you haven't really gotten anywhere have you?

Voice #1: I guess not.

Voice #2: And don't you often feel kind of down and lonely because of this?

Voice #1: Maybe once in a while I get depressed about not having established any deep friendships. But I just don't seem to have the time to really get to know anyone. Everybody is so busy, and I've always got a ton of work to do; you know that!

We know that the left hemisphere not only interprets experience but also observes experience (Gazzaniga 1985; 1988a). In this dialogue, however, the right hemisphere is directing attention to what is present yet ignored.

Voice #2: Excuses, excuses!! If you really *desired* good personal relationships, you could make the time! Come on; be honest. It isn't a time problem at all; what is it?

Voice #1: Well, I guess I'm really hung up sometimes about reaching out to people in a personal way.

Voice #2: Oh, come on! Everybody here is saying hello; let's sit down and have a cup of coffee. There's Juan and Henrietta.

What matters is action, new behavior, different feedback, another reality. Talk is easy, action risky. So part of Ben—his right hemisphere linked with limbic connectedness—presses for new behavior in the old setting. But his organizing of experience has been too often on the side of self-preservation.

Voice #1: Naw, I spent the whole first period in a team meeting with them; besides I'm miffed at them. Juan was going to have the dittoes for the team done last night, and he had to race them off this morning. On top of that, I had to race down and get the filmstrip from Henrietta because she forget that I had asked her for it three days ago!

Voice #2: Yes, Judge! Boy, you're really upset with people when they don't meet their responsibilities, aren't you? That gets in the way of your getting to know people, don't you think?

Voice #1: Well, I know what you think, and maybe it is silly and a little too strict. But I'm hard on me, too. I expect a lot of myself and of others. But I guess my expectations can close me off and close others out sometimes, huh?

The right half of Ben is recognizing and appreciating strengths in the left half. At the same time, the right half is suggesting that what fits in one situation does not fit in all situations. Further, connecting present behavior with past experience fosters more growth-oriented self-organization. Ben's vulnerable left hemisphere is discovering breathing space. Pain is giving way to possibility.

Such conversations between these two voices began to alter Ben's interactions with others, including his wife. He came to understand that his "getting his head together" required that he face what he feared. His fearful and defended self—what I metaphorically refer to as his left hemisphere—desired order, duty, judgment, external success. His safe and adapting self—what I metaphorically refer to as his right hemisphere—acknowledged there is more to being alive than control. He began to experience the excitement of spontaneity, flexibility, and a vulnerable openness. As he shifted from needing to defend himself as right and good, he began taking in more of what was good. He added those qualities and relationships that he had been denying.

From a stress management point of view (Pattison 1990), Ben was engaging in positive "self-talk." He had accessed a cognitively mediated appraisal of his situation. He began to cope more effectively. He could be assertive about his wishes—wanting to get his head together—and effective in identifying his discomfort—"I'm afraid people will see. . . ." The alternating dialogue enabled him to regain a sense of control and to receive realistic feedback.

REINFORCING THE LIBERATION

A sense of the psyche's potential in reconciling opposites through new behavior is illustrated by another woman, Cynthia. Cynthia was almost ten years younger than Eloise. She had grown up in an upper-middle-class family. Both her mother and father exhibited genuinely strong images of themselves as individuals and as a couple. She had married a man whose quiet introversion loomed in stark contrast to her open extraversion. In fact, one professional urged them not to marry precisely because their differences were so great.

Early in our working together, Cynthia experienced the following:

I really feel panicked—like something is going to get out and start destroying everything in sight. Today I am having this conversation with myself: one self is pushing hard against my skin trying to get out, saying crazy things like "Just wait till I get out!" There is this blazing. It feels like destructive, pushing down, sheer energy. It feels like it's been simmering for a long time and is finally starting to boil.

Jesus, I don't know how I am going to face my in-laws for an anniversary party. I guess I'm really feeling me and mean. The inside me feels almost demonic, almost sheer destructiveness, yet, in fact, the only place in me with potentiality for creativity. I know that, but it feels like it's gnawing away at me, trying to rip through. I'm trying to realize it and let it come through, but all it does is scoff and threaten destruction and death and insanity.

An event such as an anniversary only exposed Cynthia's ongoing experience of "me and mean." Somehow, for Cynthia, destruction and creativity swirled together in her psyche. She continued:

I'm yelling, "Shut up! Shut up! Shut up! I can't be calm or aware or even understandingly disturbed. My stomach feels sick. All the nerves in my neck are tangled. I just want to crawl into bed alone. I'm yelling inside to everyone around: "Why don't you go away? Why don't you leave me alone? I don't even want to remember my dreams. I just want to forget."

This reference to remembering her dreams, obviously, is directed to me and our work together. In addition to looking at her interactions with others, I was suggesting that she needed to be receptive to her own psychic integration. That meant attending to her dreams as disclosers of her destiny. She continued:

What am I supposed to do? Feel schizoid twenty-four hours a day now? Jesus, I don't think I can take too much more.

Cynthia's use of "Jesus" reflected both resentment at religion and an unspoken cry for the resource of religion. As professor of religion and clinical psychologist James W. Jones (1991) suggests, the transferential issues in therapy parallel the transcendence issues of a judgmental or gracious cosmos.

Cynthia's reactive incorporation of compliance reasserted itself.

Be a good girl now [she says to herself]. Don't talk to me in that tone of voice. If you can't say anything nice, don't say it. Come on, act like my good little girl. Why are you always so uptight? You're always so out of it lately. That's the reason for seeing Ashbrook. There's noth-

ing the matter with you. Sometimes it's better to let bygones be bygones, to forget, be realistic. Life must go on. We can't just go around
"feeling" all the time. When would we get our work done?

So the battle surged inside of Cynthia. She struggled between being a mature
grown-up and an irrational child. She did not want her "old destructive self
coming out." That side carried too much power to be trusted. So she oscillated
between psychic opposites—the intellectual-rational and the mythical-intuitive.

During a fantasy trip Cynthia described the feeling of "being with it." As she
stood on a mountain ledge, the deep ravine below her slowly filled with water.
Then the lake began churning. A terrifying sea serpent—crusted and sickly yellow, with flaming eyes and a viperous tongue—burst through the surface. For
a moment her fright lapsed as she noticed the horrible monster bore a surprising resemblance to a Chinese dragon in my office. She had come to cherish that
dragon because of our work together. Even so, her fright grew as the sea serpent
swam toward her.

At my direction, Cynthia performed a magic movement. She stretched out
her right hand and made three large circles around the monster. Suddenly, a
golden-haired girl appeared in place of the serpent. The girl resembled her, although they were not identical. The two joined hands and walked from the
water to a quiet spot nearby. As they came near a tree, her companion turned
into a young man, a physically complete male counterpart of herself.

They had but a minute to become friends. She asked him, "Who are you?"
He replied that he was a person but that an evil spell had allowed his demon to
take over, transforming him into a sea serpent.

She knew exactly what that was like. Jumping up, she ran around the meadow
showing him the different faces, gestures, postures, and actions of her own different demons as they had been expressing themselves through her. Together,
she and he laughed, sensing but not saying that her demons were not really as
scary as a gigantic sea serpent. Then her companion said that because she had
accepted the sea serpent—his demons—she had allowed him to be himself—the
young man sitting next to her.

Again they joined hands. Her young man told her, "And now I shall always
be with you . . . inside." She brought her hand with his hand in it up to her
heart. That inner meeting and inner mating continued. Sometimes she sensed
the coincidence of opposites; other times she longed for it. Yet because her
inner life had been activated, her inner guide stayed with her.

As her journey gradually turned from flight into adventure, Cynthia looked
back. She wrote me about the process.

> Those months seemed longer than their actual span of time. They de-
> manded more than I was initially prepared to give. They raced faster

sometimes than I thought I could go. I delved deeper than I wanted at first to dig. I found myself asking questions, so many questions, there were so many places to go, so many miles to walk. Sometimes I had to swim through things, often with the feeling that it was hard to keep my head above water . . . choking, sputtering, angry, angry at you, angry at anyone, angry at no one . . . joyous, bubbling, happy, happy with me, happy with you, happy with significant others, happy with the whole wide world . . . mountains, deep oceans . . . sunlight and darkness . . . futility and aloneness, then meaning and closeness . . . here and there . . . hurt child—flat woman . . . unhappy child—full woman . . . the Intellectual-the Intuitive . . . the strong reflective man (my animus) and the beautiful I (quietly knowing woman).

It is as though all the poles needed to be played through, to be overemphasized, dominant, and recognized before any psychic center could emerge . . . before there would be a home inside me in which I, and others hopefully, may rest . . . a balance which comes only after the pendulum has swung from side to side, from right to left, and left to right.

Quite on her own Cynthia lifted up the experience of "coming to herself" and "coming home," which I described in the introduction. The exercise in active imagination confirmed and consolidated the more prosaic process of connecting and responding and starting to explore and act. We were attending to her changing conflicted opposites—a "mean" me and a "good" me—into delightful companions.

The process, understandably and typically, is exhausting. As she wrote:

No wonder I was so incredibly tired—emotionally and physically—a lot of the time. I was tired even after I had awakened from nine hours of sleep, but knowing full well how many questions I'd asked, how many tentative answers I'd supplied in my dreams those nights.

Running throughout the journey was an acceptance of a bit of reality that you, Jim, never stopped stressing: responsibility . . . a responsibility quite different from what is usually meant by the same word . . . to accept one's rightful responsibility for oneself in this world seemed the first step toward a healthier, wholer [sic] person. To acknowledge one's angels and one's devils as well. To acknowledge one's Ego and one's Shadow as well. To acknowledge the vastness of that which is largely unknown, the unconscious. To acknowledge these is to give them their own form, to make them your own in the truest sense.

Cynthia was experiencing and expressing the difference between controlling one's self and being responsible for one's self. She continued:

> And when [these angels and devils] cease to appropriate the shapes of self-destructive or unfeeling or grotesque or maimed monsters, they lose some of their terror and can be seen for who they really are and be heard for what they have to tell us. For too long people have projected their best and their worst outside of themselves.

But without the poles, she asked, how could the rest of the continuum of being have meaning? "What defines people's height and depth," she asked, "if the dynamics of their identity are external to them? Do we not, then, as my helpless child did, sell ourselves short by limiting the distance of our inner space?"

Having glimpsed her sea monster and having befriended her guide, Cynthia broke through the bondage of the defensive organizing of experience. She could activate the imagery potential of the growth organizing of experience. From vigilance to vitality. From having been a terrified traveler, she came to the point where nothing excited her more than the journey into the becoming of her own being.

I had mirrored her courage in facing her fear straight on. In what I intended as a theological framing, I shifted her attention from a catastrophic apocalypticism to a more fruitful sense of a realized eschatology (see Moltmann 1990). Fulfillment does impinge on our present in terms of decision making, but the decision making permits us more room for making the meaning of our lives meaningful. We take responsibility for remembering and attending to who we are in God.

Like Cynthia the person seeking help begins to learn how to transform being scared into being excited. Like Cynthia the person needing mirroring begins to experience the support of and affirmation by a significant other. Like Cynthia the person wanting direction begins to share in a partnership of engaging the world.

FINISHING TOUCHES

The work of coming to oneself and coming home never stops. Every ending marks a transition into a new beginning. How best to terminate?

Freud once characterized psychoanalysis as a chess game, in which there are a few standard opening moves and a standard closing move (check-mating the king). Pastoral counseling, hopefully, is less a game of competition and more a collaboration of helper and helpee exploring together what matters to the helpee. This is basically the kenotic model of God emptying God's self for the sake of humanity (Phil. 2:5–8) and the Christocentric model of Jesus establishing a pattern of friendship (John 15:14–15). Every ending is a new beginning.

Each stopping point is arbitrary, though hopefully not capricious. By that I mean whether we have a single session or the optimum of twenty-plus sessions or the unending program of analysis interminable (Freud [1937] 1964), there is always an ending. Each session has its cycle of beginning, working, and stopping. Each season has its cycle of coming, presence, and disappearance. As the Book of Ecclesiastes puts it, "For everything there is a season . . . a time to plant and a time to pluck up what is planted . . ." (Eccles. 3:1ff).

Always we could go on. Yet finitude—limits and endings—is basic to our being. In ending the counselor revisits with the counselee what their agenda has been. "What brought us together?" "What has taken place between us?" "What lies ahead?" "Is there anything unfinished between us?" In so doing the helper celebrates with the one who came in pain what they have done together. They have been minding the seeker's soul in order for that person to know who he or she is—with others, in oneself, in God.

CHAPTER TEN

What Awakens Hope?

INQUIRIES AND REFLECTIONS

■ ■ ■ ■ ■

In recent years continual give and take with professional colleagues has surfaced recurring issues on what awakens hope. Together we have inquired about and reflected on shaping ourselves into more adequate instruments of God's reconciling liberation.

In this chapter I step back from the actual process of getting from the here of pain to the there of possibility. I have described that in the preceding four chapters as connecting and responding and then exploring and acting. The professional practitioner carries this intuitive sense of movement within. It is the background of every interview even as it is the sweep of sessions stretching over months and years. Connecting and responding and exploring and acting crystallize the whole process of minding the soul. Yet these phases can be too simplistic in any specific relationship or at any particular moment. Life is richer than theory.

ORIENTING METAPHORS

I draw upon three biblical metaphors as ways of orienting myself to the task of pastoral therapy (Ashbrook 1989d). One metaphor comes from Genesis, one from Romans, and one from Acts.

Genesis provides a basic metaphor: "[Adam and Eve,] where are you hiding?" (Gen. 3:7–11). That is, what are the intrapsychic and intersystemic aspects of the pain of the person who comes seeking help? What are his or her security maneuvers, defense strategies, ways of avoiding the work of reality? The question of "where" the person is—as well as where I as the therapist am myself—is a task of discerning survival reactions.

The answer may involve a variety of interpretive schema. These include the psychodynamic views of drive theory, ego psychology, object relations, and self psychology (Pine 1985), or the Jungian analytic approach of persona and shadow and self (Jung 1960; Hillman 1975). The answer also requires a systems view that shifts the focus from what goes on within the individual to a homeostatic balance among the participants within a system (Gurman and Kniskern 1981; Friedman 1985), or a cognitive-behavioral approach that actively shapes clients' experience and expectation (Mahoney 1991).

Always, however, I take the relational reality between myself and the other as basic to reality as a whole. Philosopher Martin Buber (1937) has characterized this conviction in his famous phrase "I and Thou." British psychiatrist W. R. D. Fairbairn has posited object-seeking as the core of human personality (1953). Psychiatrist Harry Stack Sullivan (1953) has explored this assumption in his interpersonal theory of personality. Psychoanalysts Jay R. Greenberg and Stephen A. Mitchell have identified the relational matrix as the *"most useful way to view psychological reality"* (Mitchell 1988, 9; Greenberg and Mitchell 1983). And pastoral theologian Archie Smith Sr. (1982) emphasizes the reality of "the relational self" as the ground for ethics and theology. Anything less than an assumption of universal relationality, in my mind, reduces the potential of God to the particulars of the world.[1]

A second metaphor enables me to hold together religious language and a neurocognitive understanding. Romans 12:2 says, "Be transformed by the renewing of your minds." How can we reframe what's happening to the person in pain in order for that person to be transformed?

The brain is created to make meaning, to interpret what it experiences and make sense of what it knows. Unlike a blank tablet on which the environment writes its script, the brain actively engages what it experiences, taking in that which makes sense to the self and the soul and sifting out that which does not. How we frame experience determines the way we engage the world (see Capps 1990). When the survival process dominates, the limbic system no longer can adapt to reality. Only as survival and growth are integrated do we find our fullest maturation. Renewing the mind, or transformation, therefore, requires a cognitive shaping of affect in the service of community enhancement. We are meaning-making creatures as well as object-seeking creatures.

The other biblical metaphor that informs my work as a pastoral therapist comes from the experience of Pentecost, which I alluded to earlier. We read in Acts 2:1–13 that those first followers of Jesus *heard* something, *saw* something, and *felt* something, each in his and her own language.[2] An initial reading of this text suggests the synergistic utilization of the major sensory systems—auditory, visual, and kinesthetic. A fuller reading suggests a descriptive metaphor of mul-

1. My theological colleague James Will (1994) coined the phrase "the universal relationality of God." This theological conviction parallels the work of sociologist George Herbert Mead, among many, who conceived of *mind, self,* and *society* as inseparably linked (see Smith 1982, 55–78).

2. I am grateful to the Rev. Samuel Adams for first linking neurolinguistic programming and biblical experience in this way.

3. Charles V. Gerkin is the most articulate pastoral writer on the centrality of the hermeneutical mode.

ticultural reality and multidisciplinary discourse. That is, the many languages of Bible, theology and neuropsychology, and diverse cultural perspectives free us from every monolithic value. With such liberation we reengage the infinite possibilities of God.

These biblical metaphors of discernment, transformation, and liberation flow together. Each of them presupposes the other two. They are variations on a single theme, the theme of rebirth, of new creation. They keep me focused when I get distracted and oriented when I get lost.

With these orienting metaphors as background, I now address a few of the recurring issues that confront pastoral counselors: What provides direction in the midst of confusion? What about mutuality in the working relationship? What part does the biblical-theological play as an interpretive framing of experience? What about the delicate balance in intimacy and vulnerability? What fosters humility and inhibits cultural aggrandizement? Reflective practitioners have asked these questions of me and of themselves.

"Reflective practitioner" is the phrase of Donald A. Schon (1983), a leading social scientist. He examines five professions—engineering, architecture, management, psychotherapy, and town planning—to identify ways in which professionals handle problems in their area of expertise. In contrast to a dualistic split between theory and practice, a characteristic of virtually all academic and applied orientations, Schon demonstrates that the best professionals operate out of a style of improvisation. What they know, they learn in response to the concrete demands of their practice. These improvisations draw upon intuitive knowledge. They know more than they can ever put into theory.

Issues raised by colleagues (and myself) reflect this kind of pragmatic understanding. We seek insight into what is fitting given the givens in concrete counseling relationships. These questions make explicit basic issues in practice.

DIRECTION WHEN CONFUSED: NOT KNOWING THE "WHAT" YET KNOWING THE "WHERE"

An initial issue focuses on what is basic to every care-seeking and care-giving situation. We need to find out what the one seeking help is wanting and what he or she has done about that in the past.

I am not dealing here with those times when people experience chaos or violence. At those moments therapists become authoritarian and act with firmness. To restore stability we command what is to be done, no questions tolerated (Pavelsky 1990; Gerkin 1990a; Patton 1990b). We want to prevent the person from being overwhelmed by his or her runaway survival reaction. My point about the therapist being confused applies to more ordinary situations.

Early in initial contacts I ask, "What do you want?" Then I usually ask clients what they have done about their condition in the past. Often they describe a variety of ways they have coped. At periodic turning points in our work together I will ask again about what they want, what they have done, and how they have coped.

In responding to those coming for help counselors start with their conscious intentions. How do seekers view what they're wanting? At that moment what the counselor thinks is secondary. We are dealing with "soul." Soul means the making of meaning. Only each of us can know in the depths of our own being what is meaningful for us. So the focus of "what do you want" requires those in pain to connect their conscious awareness with their "guts," the visceral-emotional meaning of the world as they experience it.

Pastoral psychotherapist John Patton (1983, 90–93; 1990c, 852) summarizes the issue of what a person wants in three questions: "What are you looking for?" "Why now?" and "Why me or why here?" The question of "what" lets us know what is most urgent in the minds of others. The question of "why now" helps others focus on what has disrupted the balance in their lives. And the question of "why me or this place" names the way others "frame" or perceive the situation and the resources they have identified as being able to meet their need.

What people want may change in the course of connecting and responding. Regardless, what seekers want remains a constant. We are dealing with others' souls. We are continually calling forth the intent that constitutes the core of others. I must know what a person wants—really wants—in coming to me. The answer the other gives relates his or her perception of me as helper as well as points to clues to follow during our work together.

Having identified what the other wants as a point of access, I later ask how the person has coped with pain in the past. I assume the person is not facing a totally unfamiliar crisis. Because we have souls—core and characteristic ways of maintaining and enhancing what is meaningful in our lives—we construct a world reflective of our cocreating capacity. By cocreating, I mean cocreating with God as God works through that which matters to us. We do not create a world completely by ourselves alone. The world in which we live is one in which we always participate—whether crippled, well, lame, or blind. We have had a hand in making it what it is, at least in making it carry the meaning it bears for us.

The predicament with which people confront counselors is this: They ask for help because they do not know what to do and because they believe the helper knows what should be done. In my better moments as a helper—and also in my better moments when I am seeking help for myself—I know that the helper does not know what the one in pain should do. The caregiver is outside the psychic reality of the seeker. As an expert, however, I know that seekers know what they should do, but they do not know that they know. Therefore, the therapeutic task is to help them discover what they know even though they do not know that they know.

I find this an awesome truth. We usually have the directions, the clues, and the hunches about who we are and what we are about inside, in our souls. But most of the time we need a relationship with another person—a receptive presence—to help us put into words what lies implicit or dormant in our lives. Because we are anxious, the answer to the question of where we are hiding is unavailable. Only as we experience safety—sanctuary—are we able to breathe the breath of God again.

Further, we need an external demand to give voice to that primary knowledge. Only when asked to say what we know can we bring that truth into the light of consciousness. The reaffirmation of "I am that I am" is affected by another's presence. This is the cornerstone of community. Once we are conscious of what we want, once our anxious reactions and our inner resources are congruent with each other, then we "know" what to do because we have been able to do it before. Our soul has caught up with our body. We are "one" again, with ourselves and with the world around. We can disengage from what entangles us. We can reengage in more fully functioning behavior (Anchin and Kiesler 1982; Watzlawick, Beavin, and Jackson 1967).

I recall leading a workshop for a group of U.S. Air Force chaplains in England in 1969. I thought the group was doing wonderfully well in getting out ideas about what ought to happen in certain pastoral care situations. When I gave them an opportunity to ask questions, someone complained, "You haven't told us what we're supposed to do."

I was dumfounded. They had come up with so many excellent ideas—many more than I could possibly have generated alone. I had nothing to add. However, until I underscored—verified, legitimized, authenticated with my authority—the "right" ideas, what they were looking for went unrecognized and unappreciated. Fritz Perls called this "random communication." In random communication a person has no way to understand and evaluate what he or she is saying. Only when I "named" the strategies the chaplains had suggested did their suggestions become valued ideas. In our working together they discovered what they already knew and also gave me input to recognize what was important to them and for them.

We only know together. We combine our knowing that "we do not know" with others' "not knowing that they know." I think of this as an exercise in basic humility and active curiosity. No matter how much I would like to "know, really know" what is what for others, I never can "really know." Ignorance, then, is not so much a strategy as a fundamental epistemological reality. And humility is a fundamental theological stance. We cannot know for others what their relation to God involves.

In the incarnate presence, God gave up omniscience and omnipotence, entering fully into *our* human struggle (Phil. 2:1–11). In that process we find the concrete truths that make for life for each of us in our life together.

So I continually ask those who come to me: What do you want? Help me understand where you are. What is this pain like for you? How have you managed to cope in the past? What really matters to you now?

MUTUALITY IN THE RELATIONSHIP: WE'RE BOTH HUMAN

Just as the initial response identifies "not knowing yet knowing" as a basic truth of therapeutic work, so a second response points to the relational context of every working task. Ultimately, the relationship is based on mutuality. To draw on Martin Luther's insistence, we are to be Christ to one another and to serve as priests for one another. No one can be Christ to oneself; we can only be Christ for others. So in a counseling relationship both seeker and counselor are human in our need for others.

Not every working relationship develops easily. A client with a sense of anxious autonomy distances and controls our interactions. This person defends against his or her "perceived" vulnerability, as I illustrated in chapter 7 with the paradigmatic story I used with the person whose perceived need was so great. The same can be said for those exhibiting an anxious inclusiveness or an anxious attachment. An exaggerated sense of one's own responsibility or an idealizing of the therapist's ability to be responsible reflects an anxious defense against interdependence. When these survival mechanisms are on overdrive, connecting is not easy.

Before connecting and as part of getting started, I assume a basic mutuality between myself and those with whom I work. Each of us is a human being in our own right, with our own hurts and hopes; and we each need other human beings, in their own right, with their own hurts and hopes. We all need help in being the persons we are meant to be. The difference between my being the therapist and others being clients lies in this: hopefully, I as the therapist am not quite as anxious as they are as clients.

Therapy, like life itself, is a collaborative task; we are in this process together. The issue, from my point of view, is that I not get stuck in socializing, to put it as positively as possible, nor in using the other to help me with my pain, to put it negatively. Such contamination of role responsibility is termed *countertransference*. The survival needs of the therapist can get in the way of serving the well-being of the other.

In a straightforward way, social work professor Alan Keith-Lucas (1972, 48) put his finger on the cul-de-sac of sociability in therapy: "The attempt to keep the relationship on a pleasant level is one of the greatest sources of ineffectual helping."

In an effective helping relationship we do not swap stories of struggle. Instead, the helper focuses her or his attention on the soul-making requirements of the one seeking help. Mutuality is not sociability. Rather, mutuality is the reality of shared humanity—in all our vulnerability and all our grandeur. I have been helped by parishioners and students and clients in my own struggle of soul—sometimes directly, often indirectly through my own parallel processing of that with which they are dealing. At times I am not able to cope in my life as well as they are coping in their life. But at the moment the task is my helping them, not their helping me.

Sometimes I link clients' experience of fear with my experience of fear. I have shared with some clients my dream of being a prisoner on a Russian train the night before returning to therapy. I have used that particularly when a client is overwhelmed with shame at being in my presence. My message is clear: Each of us is a human being. And to make the point explicit, I occasionally declare, "We all have two eyes, a nose, a mouth, two ears, and insecurity." I put that commonality on the table rather than letting it just be "the other's" problem. A division of task responsibility between helping and being helped is only a temporary separation of our deeper relatedness.

We all are vulnerable; we all are capable of nurturing. In truth, we are most fully human when we are faithful to the necessity of nurturing, which is basic to our being the creatures that we are. From an evolutionary point of view, the nervous systems of all mammals, ourselves included, are tuned to nurturing the young and the vulnerable, and to caring for one another in the service of the continuity and community of the species (MacLean 1985).

BIBLICAL IMAGERY AND SPIRITUAL LANGUAGE: CREATING AN INTERPRETIVE FRAME

Which language do we use to voice the truth of a situation—street parlance, neuroscience, psychological, sociological, biblical, theological, religious, spiritual, philosophical? How do we say what is to be said? How do we interpret the making of meaning? How do we explain what is going on within the psyche in relation to the environment?

I have made much of the context in which pastoral counseling occurs (see Hiltner and Colston 1961). The religious dimension is explicitly present, either by the therapist being ordained or being part of a staff that is known as a "pastoral" counseling center. Some professional therapists, however, are also invested in the "spiritual" dimension of therapy. Although their context does not convey that conviction, they want to include the spiritual in their approach. How, they wonder, can they make the implicit spiritual dimension explicit in their therapy? Is the religious more than the relational?

The religious or spiritual dimension—whether institutionally or individually oriented—calls for discussion. It deals with Frank's (1973) third component of "persuasion and healing"—namely, an explanatory structure. What language do we use with clients to help them make sense of their experience?

Naming. In my Pioneer Workshop interview I referred to my associations with Karl's reference to "naming." Later I was asked whether I was "conscious of criteria in using biblical stories" and how frequently I would "typically use the story early in the [therapeutic] encounter."

I have no preplan for engaging people in pain. I have no specifics in mind, whether the use of biblical language, psychological language, or the language of the neurosciences. I simply intend to be present, receptive, and responsive to whatever emerges. This, I assume, is true of every counselor of whatever persuasion.

As I indicated previously, pastoral psychotherapist John Karl and I have developed a model of professional development that combines religious resources and clinical functioning (Karl and Ashbrook 1983; Karl 1989; Roth 1989). In it we explicitly ask the professionals, "What biblical images, events, people, or experiences come to mind in response to what you have just heard in the case presentation?" We further ask about theological themes—for instance, such as pastoral theologian and clinician William B. Oglesby Jr. identifies (1980), initiative and freedom, fear and faith, conformity and rebellion, death and rebirth, risk and redemption—as well as particular psychosocial theories—such as developmental, ego and self psychologies or systems.

The method models a multilanguaging process in specific steps: (1) our projective identifications with the client(s), (2) theoretical organizing of impressions from the data, (3) biblical and theological associations and amplifications, and, finally, (4) concrete strategies in working with the client(s). As a result, practitioners find themselves thinking in multi-perspectival ways, including a more confident use of their own spiritual resources.

I do not consciously think to myself, *Now, what biblical story might relate to this? What psychological theory might make sense of what I'm hearing?* Rather, I find myself drawing upon biblical experiences at any and every point in the "connecting-and-responding, exploring-and-acting" process. Quite simply, these are images and meanings that emerge and orient me to reality. They help me engage the experiential truth of situations. In contrast to psychosocial theory with its narrower focus, biblical images open up nuances of more universal meaning. They widen the horizon of understanding (cf. Gerkin 1986).

In making such linkages I am saying to the person, "We're not here by ourselves. We're dealing with reality with which generation after generation has dealt. Your story and my story and our story are part of the human story." I draw upon my own associations to provide the client and myself with metaphorical anchors.

These open us to multiple levels of experience and integrate the various dimensions of our lives.

Patton (1990d) writes that our personal stories are ways of sharing who we are, with whom we are identified, and how we function. Stories provide a way to see "the dignity and humanity of a person in situations where dignity and humanity seem almost lost." I believe that as we link our personal stories with biblical stories we discern the divine dignity in situations in which people feel bereft of that presence.

At the same time, these metaphors give us a language that allows us to elaborate issues. All therapists teach an interpretive language to those with whom they work. In teaching an interpretive language pastoral counselors are no different than other therapists, for therapists of all persuasions teach their own language to their clients. Our language represents the interpretive schema with which we order experience (Gerkin 1984). Along with the importance of a special relationship with the therapist, an interpretive scheme explains—makes sense of— the confusion in one's life (Frank 1973). Making sense restores order or what we can speak of in religious terms as a meaningful cosmos.

Most of us know the importance in counseling of a caring relationship (Bergin and Lambert 1978, 180, quoted by Gilbert 1980, 252), one characterized by warmth, acceptance, respect, genuineness, empathy, and concern for the client (Truax and Carkhuff 1967, 23–143). In fact, many therapists—including pastoral therapists—believe that a way of interpreting one's experience is less crucial than the supportive relationship.

Morton Lieberman (1972; Lieberman, Yalom, and Miles 1973, 226–67) is only one research therapist among many who has identified the importance of people being able to put into words what they experience. Being able to say what is going on transforms a confusing and/or conflicted world into an orderly and meaningful one. The interpretation or rationale provides concepts that frame, name, clarify, and give meaning to what is happening.

Our brains are wired to "name" and interpret what we experience. It is misleading to separate thinking or cognition from feeling or affect. The whole brain combines emotional impact with interpretive language.

Interpreting. Meaning-attribution or interpretive language—*hermeneutics,* to use the current term (Gerkin 1984; 1986)[3]—does not simply order experience. An interpretation creates a structure of the way the world is put together. It

---

3. Charles V. Gerkin is the most articulate pastoral writer on the centrality of the hermeneutical mode. In *The Living Human Document* (1984) he examines its relation to pastoral counseling, while in *Widening the Horizons* (1986) he directs attention to the task of pastoral care. For a succinct overview of the issue see *DPCC*, Capps, "Bible, Pastoral Use and Interpretation of," 82-85; Gerkin, "Interpretation and Hermeneutics, Pastoral," 591-93; and Southard, "Religious Language in Pastoral Care," 1068.

tells of our mysterious origins and our meaningful emergence. Rationales of healing explain the cause(s) of a sufferer's pain, spell out desirable goals for the person, and specify steps to take for attaining these goals. Built into the rationales—or *myths*, as Frank (1973) terms them—is an implicit optimism about life. We do not need to be as pained as we are; we can be relieved of our demoralization; even more, we can be restored to the land of the living and be a part of loving relationships.

For those of us who believe, "God" is the power of our organizing myth. God overcomes absurdity, randomness, chaos, alienation, demoralization. As pastoral counselors, we ultimately affirm with Paul that nothing—not death nor life, not the powerful good nor the powerful bad, not what is nor what might be, not ecstasy nor despair, no "thing"—can separate us from the love of God in Christ Jesus our Lord (Rom. 8:31–39).

When a client speaks of "naming" his or her fear, that word *naming* triggers in me the two biblical associations I have noted above: first, Adam's naming reality as Yahweh presented it to him, and second, the panic people project on others as dramatized in the account of the demon-possessed man—"What is your name?" "My name is Legion for I am in many pieces."

I intend that clients re-cognize and re-connect with the importance of naming their experience. To name bestows the power of being able to give voice to what is. Liberationist and feminist thinkers stress the power of those who have been marginalized to name their experience (e.g., Freire 1970; Ruether 1983; Belenky et al. 1986; Jordon et al. 1991). In the beginning of creation is the Word, the power of naming, and we bear the *imago* of that Power.

From brain studies (Laughlin et al. 1990) we are learning to identify various patterns and structures of consciousness. The active processes of the whole brain create the illusion of a stable, unified world outside of us and of a single, centered self inside of us. In point of fact, most brain processing occurs outside of our conscious awareness and in widely distributed ways (Rumelhart [1986] 1987). If we attend to them, many of those processes are capable of becoming conscious, and we gain some capacity to monitor them. Further, we integrate them into a growing and an adaptive model of our self-world relationship.

Psychic and spiritual integration is an adaptive process of taking in information and selecting out stimuli. We make such selection in accordance with what we perceive to be necessary for the survival of what matters most. We are constantly matching new and novel experience with familiar and organized experience. We are always processing sensory and emotional information in two ways: simultaneously and in parallel fashion on the one hand and sequentially and in step-by-step fashion on the other. What we experience consciously combines both a mental discontinuity or fragmentation of experience and a bodily totality or unity of experience (Laughlin et al. 1990, 130–40).

However, we can never focus *all* of our bodily processing on any selected object of consciousness. As Paul described Reality, "we see in a mirror dimly, . . . [so that we] know only in part" (1 Cor. 13:12). As we bring separate streams of information into the light of consciousness—that is, as we name, identify, make distinguishable, and organize what is going on by matching the new with the old— we experience a deep visceral sense of expansive relaxation. This is known as a knowing altogether.

Phenomenological psychologist Eugene T. Gendlin (1978, 8) says this change process of feeling good is "like inhaling fresh air after having been in a stuffy room for a long time." We experience an internal bodily awareness—"a felt sense" (Gendlin 1962)—that feels right because "whatever is," which means that which is going on both inside and outside of awareness, becomes full of recognized meaning. To name something is to bring it into consciousness—to bring it into being—and thereby connect it to that which makes sense. We are more for having named it and are empowered by having been able to name it.

Correlates of Brain and Belief. In its maturest form, naming develops into interpretive schema. These schema become systematic, connecting the diverse pieces into a coherent whole. They also possess analytic power. With analyses we are able to discern subtle dynamics. Such discernment enables us to move more confidently from the known into the unknown.

The basic rest-activity cycle involves incorporating conscious symbolic meaning into nonconscious subsymbolic adaptation. But the rational mind, the new brain, is our distinctively *human* resource. With this we can sift and sort, anticipate and plan, assess and evaluate what matters to us. The flow of experience engages two contrasting yet complementary patterns (Springer and Deutsch [1981, 1985] 1989). One is the vigilance of a narrow attentional focus—the left brain—and the other the responsiveness of a broad attentional focus—the right brain. These reflect the older brain processes of arousal and relaxation, respectively.

The left brain works a step at a time, analytically, sequentially, logically, conceptually. It is the interpreter, the creator of consistency and coherence. It derives primarily from the activity of the central nervous system.

The right brain works by leaps of imagination, synthetically, simultaneously, relationally, perceptually. It is the weaver of patterns, the creator of connections and possibilities. It draws primarily on the activity of the peripheral nervous system.

Each process requires the other; neither works alone. The connecting fiber track of the corpus callosum lets each half know what the other half knows, thereby establishing collaboration. That conscious connection is consolidated and integrated in the old brain.

I suggest an affinity between these cognitive processes and patterns of belief or theological assumptions (Ashbrook 1984a, 1984b, 1985, 1988b, 1989a,

1989b, 1989c). The right brain style parallels a sense of wonder, a belief in the locus of the holy being present in every nook and cranny of the universe, in every cell and synapse of the body. Philosopher Paul Ricoeur and theologian David Tracy have called this a phenomenology of manifestation (Tracy 1981). I associate it with savoring the goodness of creation. In the dynamics of the evolving self, it emphasizes identification with others and an idealization of the authority.

Similarly, the left brain style parallels a sense of urgency, a belief in the locus of the holy being known in definite commandments and imperatives. Again, Ricoeur and Tracy have called this a hermeneutic of proclamation (Tracy 1981). I associate it with saving a broken and fallen world, reconciling that which has been torn apart within us and around us. Again, in terms of the evolving self, it points to one's competency and the mirroring of that autonomy.

When savoring and saving, receptive affirming and active shaping, are combined, we discern the whole-making process of the old emotional mind. Tracy (1981) has called this a belief pattern of prophetic action. I suggest that it has its origin in prophetic mysticism. From an evolutionary perspective we are in touch with the context of making real that which matters most. We center by integrating strategies to nurture one another in ways that are environmentally adaptive. I associate this with caring for the world in which we are cocreators with God. Finally, in terms of the dynamics of the evolving self, we discover our connectedness and the experience of being like each other.

Biblical associations and theological assertions link our experience with that of others through the ages. We are human by virtue of being "generational human beings." We have responsibility to care not only for our own generation but for those that come before us and after us (Patton and Childs 1988, 24). Similarly, theological identifications—themes about our life within the context of a gracious God—discern ways in which God is actively liberating us from our limited and limiting lives (see Hiltner 1967; Nelson 1987).

Brain studies provide information about the neuronal substrates—structures and functions—which create and carry out the meaning-making process of our lives. Psychocultural theories of personality and systems enable us to think more analytically about what locks us in and what opens us up. All of these are ingredients we use in creating a context of meaning.

Two other issues call for comment in reflecting on what awakens hope. One deals with the vulnerability that comes with the intimacy of therapy, the other with the humility required in knowing the limitation of every cultural value.

INTIMACY AND VULNERABILITY:
HANDLING SEXUAL FEELINGS

I have already alluded to the issue of potential abuse in the therapeutic relationship. This is more true for male therapists than female therapists (Foy 1983). Socialization patterns have persistently reinforced male dominance and female subordination. The difference in power easily gets sexualized. Consequences include the exploitation of the woman client by the male therapist (Marecek and Johnson 1980, 84–85) and harm to the well-being of both.

Every helping profession struggles with this issue—medicine, psychiatry, law, psychology, social work, ministry, pastoral counseling, teaching. It becomes most acute in the care-eliciting relationship of vulnerability. Because of the climate of violence in family life, many women—and some men—have experienced only an abusive relationship with a father. Thus, to find themselves in the presence of an attentive male is to know for the first time an authority figure who cares about them. The male therapist feels tender and strong; the female client feels cared for and important. That combination makes for emotional confusion, which may lead to personal and professional tragedy.

Pastoral psychotherapist Thomas McFarland has helped clarify the source of such confusion (personal conversation). He suggests that when a male therapist feels sexually stirred by a female client, the issue is not so much a matter of physical sexuality as a matter of personal intimacy. At a deep emotional level the woman client has let down an inner protective barrier and allowed the male authority access to her inmost being. She has allowed herself to be vulnerable to him in an emotional rather than physical way. She feels personally intimate rather than sexually desirable.

The very structure of the counseling relationship fosters the letting down of barriers and the development of intimacy. Because so many women have been pressured by dominating or abusive males, beginning with fathers, they are taken off guard by an attentive and nurturing male. The male therapist, in turn, has been so marginalized by a macho culture that he is energized by the client's idealization. He confuses psychic tenderness with physical excitement.

Boundary violations in the early years of life create a readiness for a reenactment of those violations. Mutuality is a goal more than a reality for such people. Newly crafted professional codes of ethics, therefore, question the possibility of a postcounseling romantic or sexual relationship between a client and a therapist. The mix of a client who has been abused and a therapist who is attentive makes for a potentially explosive and exploitative relationship.

Supervision and vigilance are called for when vulnerability and intimacy emerge. The female client cannot *not* experience the warmth of being held psychically; the male therapist cannot *not* experience the stirring of closeness. These responses come at the level of the old emotional mind (MacLean 1985; 1990a), the locus of nurturing, the loosening of boundaries, the excitement of sharing with another.

The physical stirring is a signal of emotional responding. Something of primal importance is going on, but it is psychic and spiritual, not physical and sexual. The male therapist needs to be alert to its presence. At the very least one can observe, "We seem to be standing on holy ground. I am experiencing a special openness and intimacy. I wonder what you are experiencing at the moment?" To name the intimacy is to respect the boundary.

Counseling psychologist Janet Foy (1983) raises a caution about male therapists working with young, single women. Research on the impact of the sex of the therapist on patient outcome lends some support to her concern (Orlinsky and Howard 1980; Marecek and Johnson 1980, 87). Single women and young, single women, especially, appeared consistently to benefit most from working with a woman therapist (Orlinsky and Howard, 1980, 27). Single mothers tended to do better with male therapists. The crucial difference, however, came with the experience of the male therapist. Those who were highly experienced (seven or more years) were as effective as their female colleagues, whether moderately or highly experienced. However, sexual ethics violations are highest among middle-aged male therapists. By contrast, the moderately experienced men (two to six years) had "at least twice the others' rate of worse and unchanged patients and half the others' rate of considerably improved patients" (Orlinsky and Howard 1980, 29).

An early study (Howard, Orlinsky, and Hill [1969], cited by Marecek and Johnson 1980, 81–82) examined the feelings of nineteen therapists in response to female clients. Both therapists and clients were experienced in the therapy process. In general, the male professional reported "more frequent unpleasant and 'personal' (vs. 'professional') feelings than female therapists." Further, the men "tended to feel 'disturbing sexual arousal,'" while female therapists reported mainly feelings of 'uneasy intimacy' and, secondarily, positive affect, feelings of resignation, and nurturant warmth."

In light of such potentially harmful consequences, is any physical contact appropriate in the therapeutic relationship? This question applies most especially to a male pastoral counselor with a female client. Certainly no sexual contact is justifiable. Such contact is unethical, exploitative, harmful (Marecek and Johnson 1980, 84–85). But what of "appropriately timed hugs, hand holding, and other physical expressions of assurance and affection," which cognitive psychotherapist Michael J. Mahoney believes "can be valuable and [have] beneficial experiences for many psychotherapeutic clients" (1991, 311)?

Experience and research suggest caution where there has been abuse or deprivation in the early years. The undertow of ambivalent feelings may catch both client and therapist in dangerous waters. If the two have no contact with each other beyond the counseling sessions, which is true of most counseling, then physical distance ought to be guarded. Because of socialization a woman client can experience a male therapist's embrace as sexually motivated rather than his wanting to reassure her in the face of her psychic pain. It is better to name the inner experience than to express it—"I feel so moved by your pain that part of me wants to hug you to let you know how deeply I'm feeling for what you're going through."

The early church had a tradition of greeting "one another with a holy kiss" (Rom. 16:16; 1 Cor. 16:20; 2 Cor. 13:12; 1 Thess. 5:26) as an expression of love (*agape*) for one another (John 13:35; 1 John 3:14) and of the "laying on of hands" as a ministry of healing and reconciliation (Mark 16:18; Acts 28:8). In ritual, the physical and the psychic dimensions are held together (Couture 1990; Ramshaw 1987). Intimacy and distance are integrated in a way that makes for shared empowerment. In therapy, the physical can express the recovery of human contact (Ashbrook 1971, 43–63). To reach out to touch a client, thereby, can be a form of support or it can be an expression of exploitation. Which it is depends on both people being aware of what is being expressed, its naturalness, its mutuality, and its expression of the community's values (Graham 1990). In comforting a client the male counselor especially must be careful not to undermine her confidence and competence (see Brodsky and Hare-Mustin 1980, 396–97).

CULTURAL LIMITS AND HUMILITY

Difficulties in cross-cultural pastoral counseling match those of gender differences. Status and power powerfully affect all interpersonal activity. Our ability to be present in healing and liberating ways is compromised by cultural blinders (Augsburger 1986; Ramirez 1991; Hinkle and Hinkle 1992). There is no easy way to avoid imposing our values on others.

To counsel with those who live in contrasting cultural worlds only accentuates the humility that is at the heart of Christian theology. We are to enter into the life experience of clients by respecting their worldview, their values, their way of knowing, their balancing of closeness and distance, their openness to prophetic liberation (see Augsburger 1986, 311–12). The issue is not getting people to mend their ways, since that may be disruptive to themselves and to others. The issue is enabling people to mind their souls. Openness need not preclude authority (see Augsburger 1986, 338). What matters in the therapeutic process is what matters in the life of the client, in her or his integrity as a person in relation to other persons in the community and in the community of humanity, the family of God. Pastoral counseling embraces intracultural, cross-cultural, multicultural, and metacultural concerns and convictions (cf. Hinkle and Hinkle 1992).

Pastoral counselors can err on the side of helping too much. "One of the conditions under which help can be given," insists Keith-Lucas, "must be that the helper does not too passionately wish to give it. This does not mean that [one] is indifferent or does not care. It means that [one] cares so much that the help given is real help that [one] will not insist on it being given when it is inappropriate" (Keith-Lucas 1972, 53).

The Christian tradition carries images of God caring so much that God refrains from imposing on humanity. Christ Jesus gave up godly power, humbling himself and suffering "even death on a cross" (Phil. 2:5–8). The early church father Irenaeus insisted that Jesus Christ became flesh and blood like we are in order to make us genuinely human like he himself is (Bettenson 1958, 106). Jesus said to his disciples, "I tell you the truth: it is to your advantage that I go away, for if I do not go away, the Advocate [Helper] will not come to you" (John 16:7).

As therapists, we are to give up our need to be needed. We are to let go of our desire that others be like us. We are to put ourselves at the disposal of those who come to us even though we do not allow ourselves to be mastered by them (Keith-Lucas 1972, 117). We are to give up our power that they might live *their* lives.

A TESTIMONY TO PASTORAL THERAPY

Here, then, are basic components that I find useful as I put myself at the service of those who come to me in pain:

1. The locus of meaning lies with the person seeking help.
2. We work together in a context of mutuality in which our relationship solidifies a shared humanity even as it provides data for untangling dysfunctional behavior.
3. We draw on a variety of languages in organizing and framing the client's experienced world but especially the biblical/theological language of making the meaning of our lives part of the ultimate meaning of life itself.

In addition to these concerns that awaken hope, I attend also to the dynamics of intimacy and vulnerability, especially in relation to female clients. I want to put myself at the service of that which best serves the reality of the other. People come to counselors to live *their* lives, not to be clones of our lives.

Pastoral psychotherapist John Patton suggests a useful guideline for assessing effective therapeutic work. He says that although the generalization cannot be universally applied, *"pastoral care involves assisting persons to move from talking generally about themselves and specifically about their problems to talking specifically about themselves and generally about their problems"* (Patton 1990c, 894). An example of this shift to talking about oneself was manifested in a young man I saw in pastoral therapy over a period of three years. On the anniversary of our terminating he wrote a letter telling me what the process had meant to him.

Being in therapy in so many ways helped me to make that oh so very hard transition from a boy to a young man. I am thankful for your support, for your guidance, for your thoughts, for your love.

But now that I have made that transition and am in mind and body a young man, I still am sad sometimes and scared and confused and frustrated. And I still have dreams at night, and I still make mistakes, and I still forget sometimes to love humans (my enemies, my friends, and myself included). Basically I am like anyone else who is fortunate enough to be alive.

What I have realized is that in the hour or two we would spend together each week, more than talking about my weight or money or my becoming more disciplined (all the reasons I thought I was going into therapy) *we really were talking about hope, dreams, love, and in some way faith.* [italics added]

I am gratified to hear echoes of our times together, most of all, that in and through the concrete problems this young man discerned that we were dealing with ultimate issues—faith, hope, dreams, love. In fact, the last time we met I had asked him to reflect on what had gone on between us and within him. After some thought, he quietly said, "Hope. I have experienced hope."

In his letter he filled me in on what had transpired in the intervening twelve months. Part of that was his trying to identify "what our relationship should change to." He regarded the letter as a continuation of our therapeutic work. As he put it:

On the surface [the letter] is all about me: my problems, my thoughts, my life. But in another way it is about us; our shared vision of the way I am choosing to begin my adult life. And that vision in many ways incorporates you and your thoughts and dreams in addition to all of mine. *It is as if we have used my life as a common vocabulary to discuss bigger issues.* [italics added]

Self-psychologists would point to my serving as an idealized selfobject for him—"our shared vision of the way I am choosing . . . incorporates you . . . in addition to [me]. . . ." He could become more truly who he is because he had been able to relate and incorporate my mirroring of his needs and aspirations.

Finally, however, no one lives unto oneself and no one dies unto oneself. As we live and as we die, we live and die together. Our lives constitute what this young man calls "a common vocabulary," a vocabulary in which we "discuss bigger issues." The issues always embrace more than our own limited and individual lives.

In therapy as in life, we explore what it is to be the human beings we are. We do that within the human community that we have created. Most of all, we share an obedience to the gracious context in which we become aware of ourselves. In the next section I turn to the pastoral counselor beginning with her or his self. For our stories help us make sense of our soul and thereby enable us to help others make sense of their soul.

PART THREE

Making Sense
of the Soul
Beginning with Oneself

For it was you [O LORD] who formed my inward parts;
you knit me together in my mother's womb.

Psalm 139:13

I will put my law within them, and I will write it on their hearts; and I will
be their God, and they shall be my people. No longer shall they teach one an-
other, or say to each other, "Know the LORD," for they shall all know me, from
the least of them to the greatest, says the LORD.

Jeremiah 31:33-34

CHAPTER ELEVEN

Stories

LEARNING WHO WE ARE

■ ■ ■ ■ ■

Counseling is a personalized way of helping people in pain. It assumes the participation of the person coming for help and the presence of the person giving help, for without these little of significance can occur. In fact, evidence suggests that the relationship between the one seeking help and the one giving help sets the context and influences the process more than any other factor (Frank 1973; Hiltner and Colston 1961).

In Part Two we explored the actual interaction of the counseling relationship. After sitting with others in pain, the process begins to be familiar to "the reflective practitioner" (Schon 1983). One has more psychic energy to think about what is happening as it happens. "What is the meaning behind this person's misery?" "How can I facilitate the reorganizing of this person's mind-set in more appropriate ways?" "What may enable me to be a channel of grace to empower this person for God's purposes?"

With experience the pastoral counselor begins to realize the importance of herself or himself as a resource. "Who do I represent for the other? Who do I represent for myself?" The symbolic dynamic takes on increasing importance. Who the professional is as a person constitutes a basic resource in help giving. This, of course, is equally true of the more general task of pastoral care. Both the specialist and the generalist must depend on the resource of their own personhood. An intimate and explicit knowledge of that resource is prerequisite for effective counseling.

So in this final section I turn specifically to the person of the counselor—who we are, what we are about, how we come to be invested in the specialized ministry of pastoral counseling. In minding the souls of those who come to us, we are called upon to mind our own soul.

Minding our souls involves remembering and attending to who we are. That means where we have come from—our personal history, our family of origin, our cultural origin, our origin in God. We know and draw on who we are when we talk about ourselves—sharing our stories, discerning the person we are through our own particular history. These stories are a way of making meaning for ourselves, our life, our soul.

We bring to the pastoral counseling task a life lived communally. We are in this world together, whether we like it or not. Philosopher Jean Sartre ([1946] 1956) identified that inescapable togetherness as "No Exit." "Hell is other people." But the faith that undergirds our work refuses to settle for such pessimism.

In 200 C.E., the woman martyr St. Felicitas reminded the faithful of the nature of God's world: "Another for me and I for [another]." Less than a century later St. Anthony, first of the Christian hermits, spent ten years in the wilderness between the Nile River and the Red Sea. There—alone, ascetic, emaciated—he gave the faithful the same formula: "Your life and your death are with your neighbor" (Williams 1939,48). African theologian John S. Mbiti voiced the kinship variation of that truth: "I am because we are; and since we are, therefore I am" (Mbiti [1969] 1970, 141). Only in relatedness are we who we are.

Jesus summarizes the two great commandments in a similar way: first, we are to love the Lord our God with all we are, and second, we are to love our neighbor as we love ourself (Matt. 22:34–40; Mark 12:28–34; Luke 10:25–28; 20:39–40; cf. Deut. 6:4–5). In the imagery of Paul, "the body is one and has many members, and all the members of the body, though many, are one body" (1 Cor. 12:12). Despite our differences we are part and parcel of one reality.

Recent work in evolution and human development supports this view of our connectedness. Basic to all mammals is the phenomenon of the separation call (MacLean 1990a). Inevitably the infant and the caregiver get too far apart. One or the other experiences the loss of support in the face of the unknown. That one lets the other know by a cry, a signal, a gesture, a movement the necessity of reconnecting.

I call this the cry for connection (Ashbrook 1993). Despite the enormous range of behavior shaped by learning and experience, there is built into our very being, our neural system, care-eliciting and caregiving activity (Gilbert 1989). We need each other, and we respond to each other—both in our vulnerability and in our strength (see Mitchell 1988).

The question for the pastoral counselor, as for all who care about life together, is how do we tap into that resource of our being for each other? How do we find God in the midst of our struggle for survival and in our search for meaning? How can we care for those who come to us by minding our own soul?

The key to a care-giving life lies in our being able to share ourselves with others: share our experience, explain why we act as we do, tell how we keep going, allow others to know our hopes and discern our dreams. As we tell our stories and share our histories, others are able to share their stories and tell their histories. We discover we are affirmed in the process. So too others are affirmed in their life because of shared storytelling (see Gerkin 1986; Groom 1980; Patton 1990d).

Without a story a person has no soul. James Baldwin wrote powerfully of "Nobody Knows My Name" (1961). And Ralph Ellison relates that experience of namelessness to the experience of being "The Invisible Man" (1952). Without a name one is invisible, a nobody. To be invisible is to not exist, to be a nonentity. Whether seeking help or giving help, if we have a story we are a person who is known (Keen and Fox 1973, 2). To have a name is to be a person who has a story that makes sense (see Howard 1991).

My point is so obvious that it is a truism. The power of its truth, however, struck me anew when I was seeing a couple in marriage therapy. While each had a professional career, asymmetry remained in their lives, as it does in the lives of most of us. He was the more visible and admired professional, she the more sustaining and taken-for-granted homemaker.

During our second or third session, in the midst of a painful exchange about the "good" father who took the children out to play to give his wife a rest and the "taken-for-granted" mother who hounded the children to get their schoolwork done, she suddenly said to me, "When you called me Claire that first time we met—and said it on three different occasions—I felt so good. It was as though you knew I existed, that I was important as myself." I had not used her name deliberately. Rather, I automatically use a person's name as a way to connect. Yet the power of one's name struck me with fresh importance.

To have a name is to have a story. To have a story is to be an individual. To be an individual is to be unlike anyone who ever lived. Yet we are also like some others as well as like all others. Anthropologists view us through these three lenses—the individual, the cultural, and the universal, respectively (Augsburger 1986, 48–78). In some ways we are unique; in certain ways we are like some others; in basic ways we are like all others.

On a national level we share a common language, an idea of how we are governed, a common legacy of events that made us a nation. This sharing makes us citizens united by a common background and purposes. At best it keeps us from being strangers. If we meet abroad, we immediately recognize each other. This sharing of who we are through common language and history gives us meaning as citizens, as people belonging to a certain homeland. To have this story to tell about our beginnings and to call it our own gives us our name as citizens of a particular country.

This sharing also applies to the families and faith communities of which we are a part. Each group has its stories to tell, how it got started, what has happened to it, where it is now. When we get together in family gatherings or church meetings, we tell about who we are by recalling what has happened to us. To have been "nobody" and find oneself "somebody" is to be transported from a life without resources into a life with abundant resources. We have a story to tell to the nations, as the old gospel hymn puts it:

> You are a chosen race, a royal priesthood, a holy nation, God's own people, in order that you may proclaim the mighty acts of him who called you out of darkness into his marvelous light.
>> Once you were not a people,
>> but now you are God's people;
>> once you had not received mercy
>> but now you have received mercy.
>>
>> (1 Peter 2:9–10)

In technical language the stories of faith are now referred to as "narrative theology" by writers such as Gabriel Frackre (1978), Robert Alter (1981), and Michael Goldberg (1981 and 1982), to name a few. Simple as that key of having a story is—to finding our life with God, with each other, and with ourselves—we keep losing it. Our stories go awry (Howard 1991, 194). A folktale makes my point (Shah [1966] 1972, 26; [1964] 1971, 62).

One evening a neighbor saw Nasrudin searching for something and asked, "What have you lost?"

"The key to my house." With that they both got down on the ground on their hands and knees and began hunting for it.

After a while the neighbor asked, "Where exactly did you lose it?"

"In the house."

"Why, then," asked the neighbor with some annoyance, "are you looking for it out here?"

"Because there is more light out here."

We have been conditioned to look outside, in the environment, for the key to life—to God, to ourselves, to our relationships. Yet all the while the key lies inside the reality that is ours. At one point in his *Confessions*, Augustine voiced that classic misconception of the locus of reality, "Belatedly I loved thee [O Lord]: For see thou wast within and I without, and I sought thee out there" (Augustine 1955, 3.6:68).

How can we help those who come to us get inside themselves? How can we together discover their story? How can random bits of pain come together into a journey of the soul? How can we provide conditions enabling people to come to themselves and find their way home?

These are the issues in *pastoral* counseling. Beyond specific problem solving, the *pastoral* therapist attends to the deepest issue of minding the soul. Of course that is the issue of life itself. It is not enough to talk abstractly about people in process or pilgrims on the way. It is not enough to read what I or others write.

It is not enough to look to others to let us know what's inside of us. We get inside our soul by telling about our own life in particular. We enter the souls of others by listening to them tell about their own lives in particular. It is in the telling and listening, the reflecting and feedback, that we come to know we who are.

In the powerful phrase of theologian Nelle Morton (1987), the inside story comes with "hearing into speech," being so present with each other that we are freed to say who we are by sharing what we are about.

The locus of the really real—the holy of holies, the inner sanctuary of the soul—is found in the midst of our stories. To be a bearer of God requires that we be ourselves with one another. To be in specialized ministry requires that we have a story to tell—even if most of it remains unvoiced in the counseling process itself.

Two questions may help identify that key to each of our unique stories. The first is "What brings us to the specialized ministry of pastoral counseling?" The second is "What do we bring to this specialized ministry?" The first question asks about our motivation, the second about our resources. Each in turn will be explored, and then I suggest how to tell our stories and how to listen to the stories of others.

WHAT BRINGS US TO MINISTRY?

We can respond to the question of "what brings us to ministry" specifically through stories. We also deal with that question through psychological and theological assessment. Stories and assessment are important for different reasons.

Through psychological and theological assessment we examine our own desire to counsel in the framework of the representative role of bearer of God. It is not enough that I want to express specialized ministry; a community of faith must want me in that role. We can too easily confuse egocentric and narcissistic needs with supposedly altruistic purposes. The perspectives of others help sift out dysfunctional motivations from those that are appropriate.

In recent years there has been a surge of interest on behalf of nonordained and lay pastoral counselors. The American Association of Pastoral Counselors has a special committee on recruitment especially charged with sorting out the issue of "justice, empowerment, and inclusivity" of minorities in pastoral counseling. A call to a generic ministry is minimized and a call to specialized ministry is emphasized. Even so, the desirability of a supportive religious context out of which a counselor comes and which a counselor represents requires clarification.

For the still normative view of a call to ministry in general, a board of ministry or an association or a judicatory conducts an outside or objective search to corroborate and confirm the authenticity of one's call (see Malony, Hinkle, and Hunt 1990). Some kind of community consensus is right and proper, even when such a group may disagree with an individual's sense of calling. Amos was physically isolated from the community. Jeremiah stood in the center of the community. Yet the ministry of each of these prophets was unacceptable to their respective communities. History, however, has affirmed that they both bore the presence of Yahweh God with exceeding power. The legitimacy of Paul's call to apostleship was also questioned, as have been the calls of countless saints through the ages.

In this book I bracket the larger issue of call to ministry in general by assuming it. That is no small assumption. I can think of many I have known who have been convinced they were "called" and yet church officials did not agree. I can also think of some whom church officials blessed whom I thought ought to be rejected. Even so, I believe pastoral counselors cannot create a new community of faith nor establish a new meaning to ministry. We in specialized ministry are dependent on the wider communities of faith to give shape to the meanings of ministry in their basic connotations. Such is the unavoidable tension between an inside key to reality and an outside key.

As individuals, we can use standard assessment tools in an inside way. We can examine the gifts and graces that brought us to this specialized ministry. This personal understanding of our motivation can enable us to deal more intelligibly with what we have in relation to what is needed.

Again, the key to understanding the reality of "being called" into pastoral counseling can be related through and in story form. Each of us can tell about experiences that crystallized our desire for the specialized ministry of counseling. Many have known care, having been sustained or supported in times of crisis and moments of growth, but not everyone is so fortunate. Some bring stories of abuse—physical, emotional, or sexual. The devastating experiences of being adult children of abusive parents can become transformed in the alchemy of grace into the determination to make life different for others. Some tell of a grandmother or an uncle or a neighbor or a pastor who provided breathing space and sanctuary from a desolate environment and who also pointed the abused to the promised land of making a difference in the world.

In sharing stories it is important that we identify our strengths, those resources of experience that bring us to where we are and from which we can draw in our counseling. These resources of experience carry intimations of our own soul making. We may ask those who "hear us into speech" to listen for the treasure and grace in what we tell. How is God using what has happened to open up our future and to make us a bearer of being? Their feedback gives us clues about how we have minded our soul.

As I have told my story and others have listened to it, we have identified clues to what I bring to pastoral care and counseling: intimate acquaintance with chance and accident, the benefits of convergent resources and providential possibilities; gratitude not only for different people with different gifts, but also for people of different faiths and different resources; the synergy that comes when caring and competence combine; faith that gives courage and courage that gives faith.

Our motivation for pastoral counseling, however, is always more complex than we tend to recognize. Sigmund Freud and dynamic psychology remind us of conflicted and questionable motivation. We have been hurt; we want to help. We have sinned; we want to save. We struggle against unruly impulses—aggressive, sexual, ambitious—by "doing good" or by "being good." Karl Marx and critics of society remind us of systemic privilege and vested interests. We are advantaged—and disadvantaged—by forces in society and culture that we do not create yet we continue to perpetuate.

For instance, I have been made aware that no African-American has not suffered and no white has not benefited from racism in our society (Grier and Cobbs 1968; Pannell 1990), and I am white. No female has not suffered and no male has not benefited from sexism in all cultures (Ruether 1983; Ellen 1990), and I am male. Being an advantaged white male in the richest country on earth, I am aware that no disadvantaged person has not suffered and no advantaged person has not benefited from unequal distribution of the world's resources (Chopp 1986; Barnette 1990), and I am an advantaged person. These are certain truths in our society and culture, yet I am the person I am in spite of them—perhaps at times, because of them. And I too have to learn how to walk justly with my God.

Thus it is, given the intense psychological and sociological analyses of our society and culture, we are made aware, especially as pastoral counselors, of the darker sides of our personalities where motives are suspect and belief in God an aberration. Such realities call for a hermeneutic of suspicion (Ricoeur 1974a, xv–xvii), a questioning of the self-serving assumptions on which every person and every group rest and in terms of which they live. Jesus calls us to "be wise as serpents" (Matt. 10:16), while Paul declares that we have all sinned; "there is no one who has understanding, there is no one who seeks God" (Rom. 3:11–12).

In such a framework we examine our motives for counseling. What makes us tick? What hidden need drives us in this "call" to counseling?

At times I have understood my behavior as a manifestation of my own survival needs. I *will be* needed no matter what the situation warrants; I *will be* helpful regardless of whether others want it or not; I *will respond* to all requests for help as people ask for it. It is that willful drive to respond that becomes such a terrible burden for those with whom we counsel and for whom we care. It also turns into the source of counselor burnout.

Our stories, however, carry the blessing of strength as much as the residue of curse. In telling them we are sharing our best, idealized though it may be. The new being in Christ always incorporates the old me of the past. And as in any new birth, the beginning is fresh and new, the scales fall from the eyes as mind and memory transform conflicted motives into a bonding in Christ and a resultant resolve to follow in his path as a disciple.

The father of psychoanalysis reminds us that not only are we all far more immoral than we suspect, but we are also far more moral than we know (Freud [1923] 1962, 42). In the language of interpretation theory such reality calls for a hermeneutic of espousal (Ricoeur 1974a, xviii), an affirmation of all that is good and true and just and loving. In terms of the beloved community of Yahweh God, Jesus calls us to be "innocent as doves" (Matt. 10:16), while Paul insists that "from now on . . . we regard no one from a human point of view. . . . if anyone is in Christ, there is a new creation: everything has passed away; see, everything has become new! All this is from God, who reconciled us to himself through Christ, and has given us the ministry of reconciliation" (2 Cor. 5:16–18).

Psychopathology, as Jungian James Hillman points out (1975), consists of three Greek words: *psyche, pathos,* and *logos. Psyche* refers to soul or self, that core of identity that is uniquely one's own. *Pathos* refers to suffering, more accurately "allowing" or "permitting" as in the King James rendition of Jesus saying, "Suffer the little children to come unto me" (Matt. 19:14; Mark 10:14; Luke 18:16). And *logos* refers to order or meaning or story, the Word that creates and sustains life together. When the one word *psychopathology* is reexperienced as three words, *psyche—pathos—logos,* then the soul allows its meaning to be known. As that happens, survival behavior is transformed into behavior that makes for growth.

As we examine the how and why of ourselves through stories, memory clothes them in this new meaning making of ourselves. Ultimately, this process of meaning making transforms our soul. We recognize what matters most to who we are and let go of that which matters least. Deadening pasts become vibrant futures, graced with possibilities. Thus in our stories about being called to a counseling ministry, we mind ourselves in a context that renews ourselves and our relation to God.

WHAT WE BRING TO THE MINISTRY OF COUNSELING

Because what brings us to the specialized ministry of counseling is so mixed with questionable motives, it is important to set that call in the fuller context of our lives. As a bearer of God we are still ourselves. And it is that "self" that is the instrument through which grace flows, providing the resources with which we carry out our responsibility. Again I seek to identify what we each bring to counseling through story, the story of each life.

To tell and listen is to find soul. Further, stories reflect the implicit yet guiding metaphors by which we organize and live our lives. While we develop our stories by ourselves, we need others to whom we can tell them. Others call forth our soul as well as reflect back what they hear and see and feel about us through our story. The give and take of telling-listening-learning how we are received adds to our story by connecting us with others in community. We experience being more than we are individually. Without that connectedness we live isolated and alienated lives, lost in the web of our own imagining.

The one resource we bring to pastoral counseling that is truly our own is personal experience. Even the grace of God is mediated through our experience and does not operate apart from that. In storytelling we affirm—hopefully celebrate—that resource. In storytelling we connect with others, and the sharing deepens trust and creates bonding. The openness makes meaning sacred. In truth, we authenticate who we are with one another.

The ways we can tell our story are many. We can start with basic facts: name, age, where we were born, what schools we attended, which church we belong to. We can chronicle developments year-by-year. We can string together associations of experiences. We can tease out threads of thematic importance. Various guides are available, each of which is detailed and extensive (see Fowler 1987; Progoff 1975, 1980; Keen and Fox 1973). For the most benefit with the least effort, I suggest a highly structured process. I learned it from Marya Barr of William Glasser's Educator Training Center in 1971 and have used it regularly since. The exercise set the context for teachers learning how to teach in "Schools Without Failure," settings in which nobody—students, teachers, nor administrators—was forced into a corner with no option but to fail.

You begin the process by dividing your life into thirds. This is a phenomenological task. The division depends entirely on your own way of organizing your life. You may simply decide to divide your life into equal time segments. You may frame that in terms of phases of a life cycle—beginning, developing, maintaining. You may struggle with a more experiential division that takes into account what you regard as meaningful "chunks" of your life. Thirds is an arbitrary division, though it does suggest a trinitarian bias. Its value lies in suggesting changes through the years while requiring continuity of experience.

Take ten minutes or so to identify two stories, events, experiences, incidents—however you want to label them—in each of the three periods. These are to be stories of things you found difficult or satisfying, successful or frustrating. Do not wonder whether they are similar or different. Simply select six in all. This is an arbitrary number, restrictive since you will have many memories from which to choose. A restricted number forces the mind to focus and select.

I find it helpful to draw a life line, specify the years, and in a word or two identify the events. For example, below is my current time line:

Years:	0–18	19–55	56–present
	1. Old Oak Farm	1. Ronald	1. Move to Evanston
	2. Call to ministry and W.W.II	2. Call to teach and leaving the parish	2. Cancer (Ashbrook 1988c)

Once the stories are identified, get together with three or four others in a group and have each person share one story from each period. The telling ought to take about two minutes per story, or six minutes per person. In sharing events across the life span we set the stage with small details and circumstances, describe the people in the event, and identify, if possible, the importance or significance of the story for us. The structure is strict, the intimacy surprising.

I'll use my story as an illustration:

> From the period 0–18, I tell about Old Oak Farm, a fresh air camp for underprivileged children from metropolitan New York. In the summer of 1943 I served as head boy counselor there, a position a bit over my head yet necessitated by so many males being in the service. One noon as I ate at the head table a counselor came over and asked if I would cut my bread into four pieces. It turned out that the boys at his table refused to cut their bread in fours, which he was insisting on, because I cut mine only in twos! I had been unaware of the "visibility" and "modeling" of the authority role. While I try to keep from pretending to be what I'm not, that experience keeps me mindful that I am seldom only myself. I have responsibility because of the role I have in relation to others.
>
> From the period 19–55, I tell about Ronald (Ashbrook 1971, 29–42), a neglected child, damaged by family chaos. Because of special circumstances, we took him into our family. He was four, while our children were three, five, nine, and eleven. He behaved at a two-year-old level, spoke only a few words, wolfed down each meal as though it were his last, soaked his sheets with the perspiration of terror each night, and when thwarted resorted to self-destructive acts such as jamming his hand in small spaces and once even trying to gouge his eye out. My wife and I had thought of ourselves as loving people, yet our inability to cope with his dysfunction eroded all sense of competence. After Ronald had been with us about six weeks, our five year old asked my wife, "How come everyone in the family accepts Ronald except you and Daddy?" Our children were the ones who saved him, transforming him from a traumatized animal into a delightful youngster, with their presence and their resiliency. After a year and a half, the couple who had adopted his older brother adopted him. In the years since, our children often refer to "the wonderful times we had when Ronald was with us." In such blessed naivete does grace abound.
>
> From the period 56-to-the-present, I tell about our move to Evanston, Illinois. At the beginning of this period we had remortgaged our house with the intention of retiring where we were. We de-

signed a new porch to replace the one falling off; we remodeled the bathroom after eighteen years; and since the backyard had gone to grubs, we transformed it into an oriental garden for rest and renewal. Then came the events of this story. The preceding year had been one of those harvest times, an expanse of brilliant colors radiating the vigor of life. Home and work and church and community all were sources of satisfaction. Unexpectedly the direction of the school where I taught collided with where I thought we ought to be heading. In retrospect I suppose the collision was inevitable, given a history of differences and disagreements, though support and affirmation as well. I was enraged at what I regarded as an act of betrayal. Instead of blowing up—and I confess I did some blowing up on more occasions than I care to recount—I channeled my rage into developing an alternate proposal to that of the long-range planning committee. My proposal was rejected, but I felt the satisfaction of being constructive instead of simply destructive. I had engaged the process rather than being victimized by it. When people wonder what made me move, since I had been so identified with that setting, I reply: "Two things—a kick in the stomach and a call from God; neither one by itself would have been enough for us to pull up roots and move rocks. But that's what did it—a collision and a call."

As each person shares her or his stories, the listeners find themselves expectant and attentive. They ask for more detail or understanding. At the same time their role is discerning the teller's strengths and/or spiritual resources as shown through the stories.

After each finishes his or her three stories, the listeners jot down on a card strengths and spiritual resources they perceived as they listened. The recording ought to take about a minute. Then each of the remaining people tells stories in turn, while the listeners record on separate cards what they perceive in the stories of each teller.

When all have told their six minutes of the making-of-the-meaning of their lives, the same rotation is followed, only this time the listeners tell the teller what they have discerned. The supposedly separate stories turn out to be a single story—*the story*. The soul is allowing its meaning to be known. The stories are a mosaic of the meanings of the person's psychological and spiritual resources, "an unfolding tapestry," as faith developmental theologian James Fowler (1987) images it. The reflections add meaning, making implicit processes of character explicit, even meaning hidden to the teller.

Again I use myself as an illustration. When I have told these stories in the context of shared discernment, people have indicated to me that I have some of the following resources:

- awareness of others' needs
- initiative
- keeping on under pressure
- family support
- reconciliation through sensitivity and perseverance
- optimism and confidence
- a sense of responsibility
- determination
- courage

I wish these were truly true of me. In the midst of stress I wonder. But I cannot dismiss the accrued evidence of my story across the years. Nor can I dismiss what listeners identify as resources in the reality of my life (limited as their knowledge of my reality might be).

A final learning about community comes as we step back from telling and listening, from giving and receiving, and reflect on the process itself—what has gone on inside of us as we have framed our life, identified our stories, told them to others, received their feedback, and in turn heard their stories, identified their resources, and given them feedback?

People report surprise at the clarity that comes from sharing supposedly so little information about themselves. They are awed at the intimacy that is generated in such a brief period of time. They are energized—empowered—by the very process of experiencing and expressing their "life and death" with one another.

In telling about ourselves we may make the meaning clearer by speaking of the feelings and thoughts and imaginings we had during the experiences. Identifying these in the here and now makes the meaning more explicit. We tell "why" we tell the stories and "what they mean" to us today. However, it may not be clear immediately why we tell them and what they mean. Others can help by focusing on: "How come this story comes up now?" and "Why is this the story you want to share?"

Memory is not the impersonal recording of isolated facts. Memory is ever and always an organizing and a reorganizing of experience in terms of its significance for us. Even when we are mistaken about what happened, we are conveying what it means to us. In storytelling, our narrative "stories" the meaning of our life.

"What" we remember may not be precise details so much as perceived meaning. It will be what psychoanalyst Donald Spence (1982) calls "narrative truth," that which accurately reflects "some overall characteristic of the situation" (Neisser 1988, 365–66). Post-Enlightenment theology avoids "proving" that certain events happened as the Bible records them, for instance, Moses dividing the Red Sea, Jesus turning water into wine, or Adam and Eve in the Garden. Instead, contemporary theology gives voice—"testifies"—to the experienced truth of the biblical "myth" by use of the hermeneutical or interpretive approach (Ricoeur 1980).

What we know of ourselves appears to be a "by-product" of everyday memories. These recollections provide our life themes and sense of self (Barclay and DeCooke 1984, 91–92; see Barsalou 1984). Our sense of coherence (Antonovsky 1981; 1987; Squire 1987, 223), of having a sure identity (Erikson 1968), is the result of our knowing our own life stories. Other people have access to these memories only to the degree they share our experience of the world. Events that may seem isolated to the listener make sense for us "only because [these events] fit into a broader framework of self-knowledge" (Barclay and DeCooke 1988, 120).

Others may discern in what we tell more than we ourselves are aware of. That is why our listening to the listeners can be so important. They hear with other ears, see with other eyes, feel with other hearts. When they tell us what they discern, they are condensing stories into statements, making implicit meanings explicit. Psychological processes now carry theological themes. Those who listen to us can take the pieces of our lives and discover a pattern, a tapestry, a thread of providence (see Pruyser 1976). They may discern more than we discern. However, their discernment may not illumine our perception. Therefore, their discernment must always be confirmed by us if it is to be genuine.

We give structure to our world through the stories we tell. The stories we remember to tell also tell about the situation in which we find ourselves in the present. The past is always present when we remember it. The stories we tell are metaphors that implicitly convey the meaning of how we view what is happening to us now (Savage 1987). Like dreams, stories combine psychic meaning from the past with the psychic significance of what we are dealing with in the present. The stories are less important for their historical accuracy and more significant for their making known the meaning of our life in the present.

Again I use myself to illustrate the point of our stories "back then" being metaphorical resources of our "here and now." I told three stories, one from each of the three phases into which I had divided my life. The first was my discovery of the responsibility that goes with leadership; the second was our taking a disturbed youngster into our family; and the third was our pulling up roots and moving to an unknown territory. What might I be disclosing about my life now by telling about my life then?

The visibility of being in a leadership role is self-evident. Writing this book is an exercise in responsibility, as is teaching pastoral counseling. I am putting together what I know about a public role. At the same time, I am aware that my personal life impinges on that public task. I cannot keep who I am as an individual out of this process. I cannot keep who I am separate from what it means for me to be a minister, an authority, a professor, a pastoral counselor, a selfobject representation, a bearer of the Holy. In fact, the very way I "butter my bread" influences the way others "eat." The years since my days at camp have only made that story truer and truer.

My family's taking in a disturbed youngster is a less obvious metaphor of the meaning of what is happening with me as I write this section. Although our family is fairly intact, like most (if not all) families, we are struggling with "taking in change," as my wife puts it, especially taking in the changes that come with grown children. When I did this exercise in 1989, our youngest child (age thirty) had just gotten married. For the first time in several years the whole family gathered—our three other children (all in their thirties) with their spouses, plus three grandchildren (ages three, six, and eight). Then (and now) we are mindful of differences in our backgrounds—ethnic and class. These differences are sources both of tension and enrichment. My wife and I had to learn that to care meant to set limits with Ronald. Now we struggle with knowing that to care means to set limits on trying to direct our grown children's lives.

We are disturbed by the pain in family life—our own, our children's, friends', acquaintances'—caused by the stress of unexpected and overwhelming demands. Yet we are also reminded of and reassured by the unexpected resources of our family. We are resilient in the face of disruption. What seemed devastating has become part of the celebration of who we are. I suspect in sharing this story I was—and am—reminding myself of the resources in our family. An uncertain present calls forth who we are and have been.

Our packing up all our worldly goods and setting out like Abraham and Sarah, not knowing where we were going (Heb. 11:8–16), was traumatic. We spent almost two full years grieving. We knew the move was right, yet it meant separation and loss. The satisfactions have been beyond imagining—for me, for my wife, and for our children. In the face of my cancer (the second story of this later period) and the approach of retirement, life continues to require us to pull up stakes. In leaving life behind I discover that life goes before me.

Pastoral theologian Charles Gerkin (1986, 72–75) schematizes narrative hermeneutics, human praxis, and the praxis of God. He calls that "widening the horizons" of pastoral care in "a fragmented society." The process of storytelling and story listening that I have described above fits into that formal structure— a structure that takes *our* stories into *the story*.

Pastoral counseling—and all pastoral care—begins with our present situation, the story of what is happening to us now. In telling where we have been, we are also disclosing how we are going. Retrieval from the past allows us to understand ourselves in relation to our future. This is the "gate" into the here and now. By my allowing the story of my soul to be known, whatever psychopathology has distorted my being a genuine bearer of God is modified and transformed— reframed from random events into a meaningful pattern.

Our brains are made to make sense of experience (Ashbrook 1989a). We organize what happens to us in ways that make emotional sense. Then we construct a story of the world and our part in that world. By moving around—literally as an infant and then increasingly in our imagination as adults—we shape what matters, and we are shaped by what happens. In short, we live in the world as we understand it—as we story it—and not with the "world as it is" apart from our part in it (Lakoff 1987, 212). We live out our own narrative truth.

Biblical faith—and every faith for that matter—provides metaphors and images. These illumine the imperatives and obligations of "normative" life, guiding standards of what matters. These also set before us a vision of the future, a vision of what God is doing in the world. In theological language that is called the eschatological "not yet."

As I drew on the image of Abraham and Sarah when my wife and I pulled up stakes and moved into unknown country, I draw on them continually as "parents of our faith." I make a discovery at the limits of my consciousness—the known world of my everyday competence. I find that as I can let go of my life, my soul, my reality, my control, unsuspected and awesome new realities emerge. This is the "new reality"—the cosmic context—of my situation as seen and known through the Judeo-Christian stories. While my life is uniquely mine, my life reflects and shares the life of people in all places and all periods. As psychologist Carl Rogers once put it, the deeper we go into the personal, the more we find ourselves in the midst of the universal (1961, 26).

The final step in allowing the story of our lives to be known is that every metaphor, like every dream, carries an imperative. Praxis or lived reality is the result of storytelling. Individual and group life are transformed by a new or renewed understanding of the way ahead. In reappropriating the narrative of our tradition, we are transforming our present for the sake of the future. There is no life without life together; our life is only lived in life with one another.

The format and value of narrative hermeneutics are not restricted to those who represent God. Nor does the process unfold necessarily in a formal way. But the story scheme does identify how what we say about ourselves is ultimately important. We are not simply talking about ourselves. We are really telling about God and how God is at work in us. This applies in a limited way to our work with clients and in a broader way to our part in the whole creation.

In the next two chapters I explore the concept of soul, its meaning and its making, as relevant to the task of pastoral counseling. How are we, as representatives of the community of faith, to mind the souls of those who come to us? I have set forth the experience of storying our lives. Now let us turn to the neuropsychological basis of the making of that personal meaning that depends on memory and helps us make sense of soul.

CHAPTER TWELVE

Soul

MEANINGFUL MEMORY

■ ■ ■ ■ ■

Our stories—the outward expressions of our inner reality—convey the heart of who we are. As we know our own stories, we are able to listen to others' stories, especially the painful stories of those who come to us for help and want their life stories to be known. With them we want to transform psychopathology into psyche-pathos-logos (Hillman 1975), their soul making its logic known. If we can discern their story, then they can discern it. To have a story is to have a soul.

Soul is the basic image and concept of this book. It has provided the lens through which we have explored pastoral counseling. Yet the word evokes strong feelings, both positive and negative.

AMBIVALENCE ABOUT THE CONCEPT SOUL

As a religious conviction, many have believed the soul and its immortality to be crucial. Others have dismissed it as unimportant. As a socio-theological concept, soul had its origin in a Hebraic belief in the resurrection as communal. As a political idea, in recent times soul has come to mean the free spirit of a people.

In our day, the experience of African-Americans has brought *soul* back into widespread usage (DuBois [1953] 1968; Pasteur and Toldson 1982). They have celebrated its expressiveness and rhythmicity, its spontaneity and emotionality, yes, and its stress-reducing contribution to survival in a hostile world. Soul has inspired people by expressing spiritual longing. Soul has been the vehicle of cultural and political rhetoric. Soul has affirmed the integrity of a group and awakened the hopes of those who have been oppressed.

Yet most modern scientists have dismissed the idea of an immaterial and immortal soul in order to deal with actual conditions of living (Kolb and Whishaw [1980] 1985, 304; Bergland [1985] 1988, 139).

As pastoral counselors, what are we to make of this simultaneous resurgence and rejection of soul? Does it make the difference I have insisted upon in our work with those who come to counselors in pain? Is soul primarily a mystical quality of spirit—an elusive essence of a person or group? Or is soul primarily a material feature of life—a specific bit of tissue or a literal continuation of oxygen intake? Perhaps soul is merely folk psychology carried over from a prescientific past?

Is soul as central for pastoral counseling as I have maintained? What difference might it make to those who come to us for help? How might minding the soul be the core of what we are about in pastoral counseling?

Soul refers to our making the experiences of our lives meaningful, a task that is not simple. So pastoral counseling as a specialized ministry of helping people make the experiences of their lives meaningful requires two aspects at least: a sense of the sacredness of each person and the knowledge of the process by which life is made meaningful.

THE SACREDNESS OF PERSONS

Although a sense of the sacredness of each person cannot be taught like geography or spelling, we can try to create conditions that encourage a sense of sacredness. Such a sense comes as a response to our experiencing a gracious context, a respectful environment, an empowering God.

First John states the truth: "We love because [God] first loved us" (4:19). We reflect back that which has mirrored us. Developmental psychology underscores the point: the foundation of life is trust (Erikson 1968; Ainsworth 1979; 1982; 1989; Bowlby 1969; 1973; 1980; Stern 1985). Without trust, life is precarious at best and terrifying at worst. A sense of respect for the well-being of others is caught, not taught. That is why the quality of a counselor's inner life is so central to the task of counseling itself.

KNOWLEDGE OF HOW LIFE IS MADE MEANINGFUL

If a sense of sacredness cannot be taught, a knowledge of how life is made meaningful can be. Such knowledge comes as we combine the wisdom of the ages with the evidence of the sciences, especially the neurosciences and the human sciences.

In the preceding chapter I described how the stories we tell reflect the continuity of our lives. They reinforce and support who we have been over time, and they also provide glimpses of our inner core—our heart—our soul. Stories depend on reminiscing, and reminiscing depends on our ability to remember what matters to us. In addition to storytelling and story listening, then, I add another aspect in making sense of soul: meaningful memory.

The care of souls has a long and varied history (Mills 1990). In its broadest use it has referred to the work of the priest or pastor. In a narrower sense it has described pastoral care. In this century the emphasis in the care of souls has shifted from salvation as a theological and religious concern to self-realization, a shift shaped by popular psychology and culture (Holifield 1983; Stokes 1985). Running through the soul's several expressions is a special caring for the soul on the part of the community.

This book brings a unique addition to that vision. Along with the historical understanding of soul, it adds current understanding of how the brain works. Empirical research gives backbone to experiential reality. It helps make the soul more sensible, more plausible, more crucial to human well-being. Further, it makes soul central in counseling and psychotherapy (Ashbrook 1991; 1992a). In understanding the neurocognitive basis of soul, pastoral counselors may enable those who come to them to tend their souls more mindfully. Simply stated, experientially the state of the soul is reflected in the conscious experience of the states of the mind, and from an empirical view soul has its physiological correlates in the states of the brain. This chapter explores this intersecting of the experiential and the empirical.

An anecdote and an experience focus my conviction. The anecdote, which I believe was recounted by Quaker philosopher Douglas Steere, comes out of Africa. During the last century a caravan of traders had been pushing their porters hard. Eventually, the porters stopped, efforts to keep going failed, and the traders demanded to know what was wrong. The Africans explained, "We have been traveling so long and so fast that we need to wait for our souls to catch up with our bodies."

The experience I use to illustrate my view of the soul is jet lag. Everyone who travels by air has suffered from it. After crossing two or three time zones one is groggy, out of sorts, not oneself. Too far and too fast upset one's entire biopsychological system.

Jet lag is an empirical equivalent of the cultural expression "wait for our souls to catch up with our bodies." It is that phenomenon of getting and keeping ourselves together—body and soul. Getting and keeping body and soul together constitutes the core of pastoral counseling. This, I submit, is "minding the soul."

The meaning and making of soul are at the heart of our being the human beings that we are (cf. Gerkin 1984, 97–117). We sense the loss of soul, or self, in a loved one's inability to care for her- or himself because of Alzheimer's disease. We sense that loss in those who are confused about themselves and what they are about. Their eyes are dull, faces listless, bodies wilted. We know the resurgence of soul in those who, having been denied full participation in society, fight to be visible and viable members of the human community. Their eyes and faces shine and their bodies are charged. The recovery of soul was symbolized in the dramatic tearing down of the Berlin Wall.

TO WHAT MIGHT SOUL REFER?

If soul is not an entity, what is it? How can we know it? What difference does it make? How does minding the soul relate to pastoral counseling?

Anne Harrington opens her *Medicine, Mind, and the Double Brain* (1987) by stating, "The Double Brain [left and right hemispheres] began its history, not so much as a scientific or medical problem but as a theological one." The earliest physiologists, and later Descartes, sought to find a unitary organ in the body that would correspond to "the indivisible unity of the ruling conscious self." All organs—heart, lungs, kidneys, hemispheres—were composed of pairs. Thus the pineal gland, as a unitary organ, became "the site of the soul's interaction with the body." The body was assumed to be passive, while the soul was active and thereby outside of nature (Harrington 1987, 6–7).

What began in theology as a search for active, integrating, unitary coherence passed into the neurosciences—from the philosophical to the empirical. The theological concern for the core of human beings became irrelevant. No wonder clinically oriented pastoral counselors had little patience with concern for the soul. Today, however, we are recovering the centrality of subjective experience—of active, integrating, unitary, coherent consciousness (Sperry 1990; Barrett 1986). What has been separated for centuries—namely, body and soul, soma and psyche—is emerging as a new reality because of the explosion of activity in the neurosciences.

Soul refers to core and characteristic ways people experience and express reality. It is not a "thing," separable from all that people are. Molecular biologists, according to brain researcher Richard Bergland, are discovering that the molecules that "give life to the *soul* and guidance to the mind" are in every cell of our body (Bergland [1985]1988, 139, emphasis added). As philosopher Holmes Rolston III puts it, "The whole organic program is inlaid into nearly every cell" (1987, 85). These scientific descriptions are matched by Paul Tillich's theological conviction that "we are totally present in every cell of our body. You cannot have a 'soul'—or whatever you call it—without a body" (Ashbrook 1988a, 144–45).

If soul is not a "thing"—a specific entity with definite features and fixed boundaries—then we can only think of soul as a process or an experience. But what might it mean for soul to be the core and characteristic ways people experience and express reality? To ask to what process soul might refer shifts the focus away from an assumed realm of Platonic essences—a dualistic split between an immortal soul and a mortal body. To inquire about the reality of experience—a stabilizing image of self-world interaction—is to explore that which is most immediate and meaningful—namely, our experience of ourselves and our life in this universe. Soul expresses "meaning," and the making of meaning depends on memory.

In a reflective personalizing of the link between soul, memory and meaning, my editorial consultant Barbara Stinchcombe shared the following:

> Is soul the repository of memory? Memory can extend to all systems of the body, [to every cell of the body]; can be the nerve endings that pain in the stump of the arm that has been amputated; can be ancestral memory such as the fear of falling; can be the dread of darkness.
>
> Is it just my stomach that remembers the fullness of fasting; just my taste buds that carry the succulence of watermelon in the heat of summer? As I understand it, it is the mind and senses together that ritually make the first bite into the first apple of the season real and ritual to me, so that the season, the taste, the recognition of change all celebrate the occasion as ritual event calling on memory as it reaffirms me living in this event of the apple season from the past, and moves me along in the reality of life in this new apple season.
>
> Memory draws from my gut, from my physical senses, from my brain, from my knowledge of time's passage in the instance of the apple season, forming an experience of life that is my life, that bears my history. (I draw on memories of apples stored for winter in the straw above the horses' barn; the wind-fallen apples in the orchard; the memory of baking apples for supper the night I received news of my sister's death, so I don't bake apples anymore because of this memory. I remember going with my father with a wagon load of apples to the cider mill, sensing his excitement of this event, which now I call his richness in the world.)
>
> All of these are part of apple memory. But it's brain, senses, gut— all the systems [and cells] of my body together—that form an image of the person I know in the name I bear. Thus might soul be summed up as all the parts of the body creating in unison a particular view of the reality of being with memory as the linchpin that holds all in place.

Quite simply, *soul* expresses *meaning*, and the making of meaning depends on memory. To mind the soul is to attend to meaning making.

MEMORY AND LEARNING

In 1953 a twenty-nine-year-old man with the initials H. M. was operated on in a final attempt to relieve the effects of severe epileptic seizures (Scoville and Milner 1957). The procedure involved cutting some of the connecting neural pathways between the frontal lobes and the old mammalian brain, more particularly the amygdala and the hippocampus (see figure 6.1).[1]

---

1. The amygdala contributes to arousal, especially to survival and the sense of self. Although the amygdala "plays as large a part in memory as the hippocampus" (Mishkin and Appenzeller 1987, 4), without the hippocampus, newly processed information is not "stored in an enduring and useful form" (Squire 1987, 194; Lynch and Baudry 1988).

H. M.'s seizures stopped, but so did his memory. He continues to remember remote events, those up to three years before the operation. But his memory of events during the three years prior to the operation appears vague and unreliable. Even though he can learn new tasks—procedural memory—"he cannot remember new events" (Winson [1985] 1986, 12). Cognitive functions, however, such as attention and perception, and general intellectual ability are not affected.

Patients suffering from amnesia show the same pattern. Memory for distant events remains normal. In addition, the ability to reproduce information immediately after it is presented can remain normal, provided the amount of information is not greater than immediate memory capacity (Squire 1987, 176–77).

Immediate memory capacity embraces only seven separate pieces of information, plus or minus two, at any one moment (Miller 1956). This is probably the reason telephone numbers consist of no more than seven numbers, three for an exchange access and four for a particular location. Patients such as H. M. can recall six digits at a time, a number within the normal digit span. For him to remember more than six, however, becomes not only difficult but impossible (Squire 1987, 141).

In sum, we have different kinds of memories. Immediate short-term memory forms within milliseconds and lasts from a few seconds to minutes at the most. Intermediate storage memory forms within minutes and can last for hours. Long-term permanently stored memory forms within hours and lasts from days to years (Popov and Matthies 1983).

The meaning or significance of information depends on learning and memory. Learning has been defined as "the *process* of acquiring new information, while memory refers to a *persistence* of learning in a state that can be revealed at a later time" (Squire 1987, 3). In short, think of memory as the result of learning. We selectively combine stimuli from the outer world with expectations from the inner world. Together they result in a coherent sense of continuity over time and across space.

To achieve such a coherence we need proper rest. When we lose sleep, especially rapid eye movement (REM) sleep (see chapter 12), we exhibit disturbed behavior (Hauri 1979; Dement 1979; Arkin et al. 1978). We become irritable, disoriented, anxious—uncertain about where we are, what we are doing, and what we intend to do. In extreme cases we forget everything, including who we are.

MEANINGFUL MEMORY

We all know the frustration of faulty short-term memory: "Where did I put my keys?" or "I forgot to pick up milk on the way home." We also get flustered at the loss of long-term memory: "Who was it who said . . . ?" "I recognize the face but the name escapes me." "I can't remember anything of my early life." Meaning and the making of meaning are linked to memory. Meaning depends on memory, and memory is neither a single phenomenon nor a single process. As one researcher puts it, "Memories are . . . like chocolates. They have many different forms and characteristics, and contain many different types of information" (Olton 1983, 335).

In part, memory is associated with the hippocampus, so named because of the Greek word and the structure's resemblance to the small, marine sea horse (Seifert 1983; see figure 6.1). The process involves incorporating highly organized and emotionally significant information into a sense of the continuity of reality (Winson [1985] 1986, 30–34, 201–2). What is novel and uncertain gets our attention. With the amygdala serving the "gate-keeping function" of "selective attention" between our senses and our emotions (Mishkin and Appenzeller 1987, 10), we select information, sort it, filter it, and perhaps take it in, depending on whether it is interesting and pleasurable or dangerous and painful. Is it to be approached or avoided? Then, unless the hippocampus computes that information, we lose it (Squire 1987, 194).

Memory has been divided into two major types (Squire 1987, 162–63, 170): *declarative memory*, or what we can declare and bring to mind as an idea or an image, and *procedural memory*, which involves skills and things that improve with experience. These two types differ in the kind of information stored, how that information is used, and which neural systems are involved. Procedural memory is more automatic and adapted to learning in small increases over time; declarative memory is more cognitive and capable of immediate learning.

Declarative memory embraces both a short-term and a long-term stage (Squire 1987, 242). In addition, researchers distinguish between episodic or working memory and semantic or reference memory (Olton 1983). Reference memory ignores the context by processing information that applies to many similar instances. Significant for my speculation about the link between soul and meaning, working memory involves the specific personal context.

I am dealing here with working, or episodic memory, the memory of meaning making as the core of experienced reality. This memory refers exclusively to "autobiographical" remembering and ordinarily permits a sense of personal relation to that of which we are a part (Squire 1987, 169, 173). Our view of what goes on is more constructed than photographic, an inside process that organizes and interprets outside information (Loftus and Yuille 1984, 168). This is memory for past events, events that are "specific and personally experienced" (Neisser 1988, 357).

By storing and retrieving the cumulated events of our lives we develop individual histories, our own unique, self-repeating styles and stories that contribute to the emergence of models of self-world interactions. We are particular individuals; we are particular communities. These stable internal images inherently resist conditioning and accommodation. Here are the continuities, the essences, the core characteristics of ourselves.

As discussed in the preceding chapter, knowing who we are and sharing who we are is basic to pastoral counseling as well as to pastoral care. People tell us their stories, and as we listen we discern their souls making the meaning of their lives known.

People have access to each other's stories and the personal meaning of their lives only to the degree they share their experience of the world. Events that may seem isolated to others make sense for them because these events "fit into a broader framework of self-knowledge" (Barclay and DeCooke 1988, 120). People remember what matters to them in terms of their sense of who they are.

The context of one's life is another way of identifying working memory. From an experiential viewpoint, context comes into focus when we ask such questions as: "Where are you (in terms of physical space and psychic space)?" and "What time is it (in terms of chronological time and the meaning of the time of your life)?" The answers orient us to what is happening inside the other and enable us to act in adaptive ways (Kubie and Ranch 1983). Evidence suggests that the hippocampus—that mediating structure between short-term and long-term memory—defines "the continuing presence of a particular context" (Lynch and Baudry 1988, 80). Without a sense of context we are lost in space and time.

In some sense H. M., the twenty-nine-year-old man who underwent an operation to relieve his epileptic seizures, lost the picture his memory had made of him in time—the picture that let him know who he was and where he was. He became a person without a known context, at least no context of which he himself was aware.

Without working memory, nothing is personally meaningful. A person has no unique identity and no sense of continuity, since the person cannot connect his or her present with a past. Such a person lacks a sense of self (Winograd 1988, 17). In truth, the person loses his or her soul—that basic structuring of one's unique self-world interaction (Nelson 1988, 266–67)—and becomes soul-less. When this happens the person seeks help, longing to recover his or her soul, the sense of self.

Working memory, and its consolidation (Weingartner and Parker 1984), make up the core or essence (in an experiential sense) of a functioning person. The mother of an amnesiac patient expressed this point when she observed her son: "Everything surrounding [him] is a memory thing . . . . You've got to have a memory to remember" (Squire 1987, 177–79). People have to have a working memory in order to remember who they are.

Without long-term memory, like H. M. and other such patients, we live in the hell of an eternal present, a present without a future because it is a present without a recoverable past (Kolb and Whishaw [1980] 1985, 481–94).

REMEMBERING

Perhaps the integrating of a novel present with a stable past neurobiologically reinforces, and helps account for, the centrality of the biblical imperatives to remember. I think immediately of Moses' instructions to the Israelites, "*Remember* this day, on which you came out from Egypt, out of the house of slavery" (Exod. 13:3, italics added), and Jesus' request in the face of betrayal and love, "Do this in *remembrance* of me" (1 Cor. 11:23–26, italics added), and the importance of one's name being "*found written [remembered]* in the book of life" (Rev. 20:15, italics added) (Ashbrook 1989a, 72).

The making of meaning involves purposeful behavior, and purposeful behavior comes because of a working memory. Consolidation takes time, specifically from about one to three years (Squire, Cohen, and Nadel 1984, 188; Eccles 1983, xv). To be retained, memories must be dreamed, and dreaming involves intense emotional appraisal over time (Fox 1986, 38). (I say more about the process of dreaming in the next chapter.) Perhaps that consolidation process is the neurobiological basis for the typical experience that it takes about three years to assimilate major changes in life—be they death, divorce, moves, failure, or success. Think of the process as similar to transplanting a mature bush in the yard. It takes about three years to reestablish a fully functioning root system. In consolidating meaning making we are reorganizing earlier memories.

This synthesizing process is affected by the ability to store in memory what goes on in daily life. Memory is dynamic in that it changes over time (Squire, Cohen, and Nadel 1984, 206). We keep interpreting our lives in terms of what happens to us. That is, we re-member, re-connect, and re-cognize what has happened to us in light of what is presently happening to us. That is why in counseling we return again and again to the *same* events, experiences, frustrations, and yearnings. We reshape them according to the meaning we make of them. In consolidating our stories we reorganize our relationship with the world. And it is this synthesizing process that is affected by the ability to store in memory what goes on in daily life (Squire, Cohen, and Nadel 1984, 206).

Life crises upset, distort, even cancel our personal picture of ourselves. H. M.'s operation is the physical equivalent of every form of psychological damage. From Vietnam we have come to understand the post-traumatic stress syndrome (Brende 1982; 1987). Massive trauma blots out memory. People suffering from this disorder have little or no memory of the past. Then suddenly they are overwhelmed with flashbacks, waves of pain and terror sweeping over them so that they literally gasp for breath.

Cognitive psychologist Michael J. Mahoney vividly describes the experience of a woman client reconnecting with the memories of brutal sexual abuse by her father, several of his friends, and finally her mother (Mahoney 1991, 259–65, 296–301). Over time her discoveries of abuse moved her from chronic and intense depression to chronic grief over the death of her cat, to stomach cramps, to fetal regression, to medical confirmation of repairing vaginal tears, to allowing her mother's "touching game" of genital fondling as a way to avoid her father's abuse. She had had to forget in order to survive. Eventually, in order to accept herself as a "strong-spirited" person she had to remember.

From individuals suffering from multiple personality disorder (MPD) we have come to understand the way in which the inner self creates subpersonalities— guardian angels in my way of thinking—to intervene between the assaultive world and the vulnerable self. In less extreme—though acutely painful—ways, crises such as death, failure, and divorce also erode our memory.

One woman reflected on the impact of her divorce on her image of herself and her memory of who she was:

> My definition of myself was as a married person having a certain re-
> lation to another married person who was my husband. I was a mother,
> not alone, but with the presence of a father. Though the divorce it-
> self was the result of a rupture and incompleteness in these images of
> myself and my husband, divorce in and of itself totally negated and can-
> celed out those images in the context of who I was when I was mar-
> ried and a mother in that married state. *Who am I* then became *the* ques-
> tion in my life. And that person whose name I am and bear had to be
> rediscovered.

What this woman described—and it is the experience of almost everyone un-dergoing the trauma of separation and divorce—is the loss of a personal context. What the operation on H. M. accomplished in a permanent way, trauma ac-complishes in a functional way.

Imagining a future requires remembering a past. As one researcher says, "Memory development is about the future, not the past" (Winograd 1988, 17). Without a past there is no future, no sense of purpose, no awareness of anything as personally significant. It is only in retrospect, only in remembrance, that we discover and create a universe full of meaning. The pattern of events comes as we sift and sort what happens, taking in what matters to our well-being and let-ting go of what does not matter.

SOUL AND UNIQUENESS

Forty years ago, psychologist Rollo May expressed dissatisfaction with the body-mind split that arose with Cartesian thought. May believed that an affinity ex-isted between the "capacity for self-conscious affirmation of [our] own being" and the classical meaning of the term *soul* (May 1951, 315, 312). With his urg-ing I undertook a study of "the functional meaning of the soul in the Christian tradition" (Ashbrook 1958)—that is, in the way people used the term through history. I found that the idea of soul identifies our uniqueness—our capacity for centered decisions, our capacity for taking initiative, in short, the primacy of the whole over the parts. It conveys a sense of the "inside" or uniquely personal meaning of events.

Those who question the validity and value of soul tend to do so on an assumption that reflects Greek dualism rather than biblical holism. Generally, people who have been reflective about their faith have used the term *soul* in ways that do justice to higher cognition, personal meaning, and brain processes (Browning 1987; Hillman 1975; Jones 1985; Niebuhr 1951, 2:294–98; Walker 1971; Sherrill 1951). They have kept open the issue of the separation of soul and body at death. Rather than believing in an immortal soul as a substance or entity distinct from a mortal body[2] they have affirmed the *experience* that personal reality is more than physical reality. I too hold a functional view, not a substantive one.

As I have indicated above, African-Americans have resurrected the power of soul. Soul is the heartbeat of identity (DuBois [1953, 1961] 1968; Cleaver 1968; Tutu 1979; Pasteur and Toldson 1982; Gooden 1990). In describing "The Black Mood," for instance, Lerone Bennett (1965) points out that *soul* defines our living, "the spirit—a certain way of feeling, a complex acceptance of the contradictions of life, a buoyant sadness, a passionate spontaneity, and a gay sorrow" (Bennett 1965, 89, quoted by Pasteur and Toldson 1982, 103–4). St. Clair Drake puts these abstract yet poetic ideas in more concrete language:

> The beat of "gut music" spilling into the street from ubiquitous tavern juke boxes and sound of tambourines' rich harmony behind the crude folk art on the windows of storefront churches give auditory confirmation to the universal belief that "We Negroes have 'soul.'" (quoted by Bennett 1965, 89, cited by Pasteur and Toldson 1982, 104)

Augustine provides a historical-theological view of soul. He described that intuitive awareness of the union of body and soul by saying "the soul . . . is the life of the body" (Augustine 1873, 93). In other words, soul has the power to affect and change bodily substance. It is at once present in the whole body as well as in each of its parts (Oates 1948, 766). While Augustine thought of soul as lacking measurable dimensions, he believed it was located within the body (Morgan

2. *The Encyclopedia of Religion* (Eliade 1987) provides an excellent survey (with bibliographies) of the concept of *soul* from the viewpoint of comparative religion, including ancient Near Eastern concepts (431-34), Greek and Hellenistic concepts (434-47), Chinese concepts (447-50), Jewish concepts (450-55), Christian concepts (455-60), and Islamic concepts (460-62). These concepts vary in their ability to hold together an essential unity of body and soul with belief in an afterlife.

1932, 127). Recall the earlier statements of neuroscientist Richard Bergland and theologian Paul Tillich about the soul being "scattered everywhere" throughout the body and in "every cell." Where there is living body, there is soul; where there is soul, there is living body.

What remains is the making of meaning. As it makes meaning of our experiences, soul makes us who we are. As it is forming we are formed. It is this process that can make us in the image and likeness of God.

Augustine's understanding of soul is very like what we are learning about memory. Memory, understanding, and willing come to mind apart from the information the brain receives from the outside. By the very act of understanding the experience of knowing, the mind knows itself. It is impossible to doubt that one lives, remembers, understands, wills, thinks, knows, judges. The mind beholding itself is inherent in its very nature (Oates 1948, 794; Augustine 1873, 254, 256, 354).

For Augustine, the soul has been endowed with the ability "to feel and to measure . . . time" (Augustine 1955, 255). Therefore it must be both within time, in a chronological sense, and beyond time, in a gathering together of future and past into a present full of meaning. To have such a sense of time is to stand above it and to shape it simultaneously.

People seek a center of meaning and power inside themselves—that is, within, yet beyond, consciousness (Augustine 1952, 225, 1). I link the idea of "beyond consciousness," as I explain more fully below, to subsymbolic processing and the rhythmicity of older brain activity. From the standpoint of faith, here is the power of God, the ultimate creating activity of the universe (see Ashbrook 1989b). This transcendence frees us from bondage to the isolated external stimuli of space and time.

Sometimes a sense of transcendence comes as we stop working on a project because nothing productive is happening. We put it aside and turn our attention elsewhere. Later, when we return to it, we are amazed that it has mysteriously come together. Sometimes a sense of transcendence comes when we are baffled by a problem and then wake in the morning to discover our sleep has taken care of it. Sometimes that sense comes as we give up struggling with a crisis only to experience an unexpected source of breakthrough.

Apart from that transcendent center of meaning and power we are "torn piecemeal," to use Augustine's words. We lose ourselves in the multiplicity of things (Augustine 1952, 59, 20). Self psychologists identify this phenomenon as a "fragmented self" (Basch 1988). People are limited in their ability to distinguish and to decide between various aspects of experience. They are subject to conflicting or chaotic forces inside and around. They experience the "jet lag" of soul.

In the court of memory, to continue Augustine's imagery, we confront ourselves with ourselves: what we have done—when something has happened and where something has happened, and under what feeling and with what meaning that something took place (Augustine 1955, 209). Augustine believed the image of God did not reside in the capacity for abstract thought (Browning 1987, 23), but rather in the capacity for self-knowledge and introspection. When people lack memory—as in amnesia or in not taking time to remember—they have lost their soul and are living "soul-less" lives.

The Augustinian tradition is more mystical than rational. It unites "the experience of the identity of subject and object," as Tillich put it, with "Being itself" (Tillich 1959, 14; see Dourley 1975). The German philosopher and mystic Meister Eckhart (c. 1260?–1327?) expressed that experience of continuity as an ontological claim. In other words, what we know in experience reflects what is true in the universe: "There is between God and the soul neither strangeness nor remoteness, therefore the soul is not only equal with God, but it is . . . the same that [God] is" (quoted by Tillich 1959, 14–15).

In the language of brain processes, here is an awareness of the unconditional, parallel, distributed, subsymbolic, and symbolic processes (Ashbrook 1989a, 77; see Rumelhart et al. [1986] 1987). As working memory, soul is a certain awareness—a knowledge *of* the really real manifest in right-brain activity rather than knowledge *about* the really real as we observe it with left-brain activity. Working memory is an unconditional knowing, a knowing without qualification. It is immediate.

The limbic system may be the most identifiable, though not exclusive, locus of the core of self-world interaction. To use the philosophical language of Tillich (Dourley 1975, 55), it is there, in the older brain, that "the infinite and finite interpenetrate." Evolution and history combine, and we become "at one with our own essence." The transcultural soul and the cultural self combine (see Hinkle and Hinkle 1992). In the older brain we take outer and inner stimuli and organize and modify them for optimal adaptation with the integrity of our own unique model of self-world interaction. I describe how this process occurs in the next chapter.

This integrating is an active process that includes the peripheral nervous system and the subsymbolic processes. It initiates and integrates cortical and symbolic activity. It is bodily knowing, that which is deeper than consciousness itself. It is here that God is present in a way that is certain, and in that certainty we are made whole.

In sum, people have used *soul* when talking about that which is central to our being the humans that we are. Quite simply, *soul is that which each of us can call our own*. It is our own unique essence, that which distinguishes us from everything else in the universe. For me, this faithful knowing is our experiencing what matters most in life. That certainty appears below the conscious level, coming as a result of what goes on in the older brain. We sense that certainty in vague feelings of conviction or discomfort. We glimpse it in fleeting images of possibility or apprehension. In whatever ways the older brain communicates with our consciousness—bodily feelings, visual images, verbal flashes—we know that something that matters to life is working in and through us.

We voice that sense of bodily reality in terms of what we believe. As the Letter to the Hebrews puts it, "faith is the assurance of things hoped for, the conviction of things not seen" (11:1). "Assurance" and "conviction" about what matters most are right-brain responses to limbic activity. They integrate concern for the self in the service of the species. When we say what matters to us we transform older brain processes into the left brain's language of explanation (Ashbrook 1988b,150–155; see Rumelhart et al. [1986] 1987).

If the experience of soul depends on memory—the making of personally meaningful history—how does this come about? What is the means? What are the biochemical processes? Of what might soul making consist? How can this link between soul making and brain processes help the pastoral counselor? The next chapter explores these issues as the experience of "sabbathing" or "God's way of making meaning." We will see that the making of meaning is the equivalent of integrating our experience.

CHAPTER THIRTEEN

Sabbathing

INTEGRATING THE EXPERIENCE

■ ■ ■ ■ ■

We have explored stories and soul. Yet the question remains: How are stories and soul united? What biological processes bear the weight of psychic integration? On what spiritual reality can counselors depend in their work of minding the soul?

I suggest *sabbathing*. In advancing this idea I am aware that modernity has eroded sabbathing as a way of life. Pastoral counselors may even feel that the use of "sabbath" is too explicitly religious and would only add to the oppressive religion with which many clients struggle. When the meaning of sabbath has been retained or recovered, interpreters have moved beyond its being a historical institution to articulate its cultural and psychic significance (Edwards 1982, 26). I join that task of reinterpretation, except I link its validity with biological rhythms and neurocognitive processes. This linkage gives the idea specific therapeutic importance.

Pastoral counselors can use the meaning and means of sabbathing in helping people discover who they are. In fact, I believe the meaning and means of sabbathing to be the key to our therapeutic activity. *I define sabbathing in its broadest sense as the integrating and transforming activity of stories and soul, of meaningful memory and each person's own unique identity in the service of community.* As pastoral counselors, we are to attend to this basic process of minding the soul.

The neurocognitive process expresses the biblical commandment: "Remember the sabbath day, and keep it holy. Six days you shall labor and do all your work. But the seventh day is a sabbath to the LORD your God" (Exod. 20:8–10). I take this commandment as a metaphor of how we keep body and soul together. In terms of biological processes, sabbathing can be understood in the context of the resting state of mind in nonrapid eye movement sleep (non-REM) and the reorganizing state of mind in rapid eye movement (REM) dreaming.

In pastoral counseling, as in life itself, we are to mind the meaning of our lives—our very nature, that which we are in the fullest and truest sense of our being made in the image and likeness of God (Gen. 1:27). In short, we are to be mindful of—to attend to—our souls. This minding is never simply an individual task, personal though it is; it is also a communal task, that which inheres in the nature of the whole species, male and female. To mind the soul is to attend to that which matters to people in their separateness and their togetherness. For the pastoral counselor to mind the soul, she or he brings to bear on this task knowledge of the working brain and the intuition of faith.

The minding of soul is as mysterious as the phrase sounds yet as intelligible as the way we are made. A neurotheological approach to pastoral counseling holds together soul and memory, on the one hand, and sabbath and biorhythms, on the other. First, I will say more about the role of the religious phenomenon of sabbath, and then I will describe the mediating brain processes of the basic rest-activity cycle.

SABBATH AND SOUL MAKING

From a biblical and theological viewpoint, the phenomenon of sabbath is the means of making meaning (Morgenstern 1962; Andreasen 1978). Think of sabbathing as the imaging of soul, God's way of creating us in God's image.

BIBLICAL-THEOLOGICAL BACKGROUND

The symbolic meaning of sabbath (Gen. 2:1–3) links the natural order affirmed in Genesis 1 with the historical order detailed in Genesis 2. These two myths of creation provide a picture of the God-world interaction and the generating of emergent meaning.

Genesis 1 sketches the glory of the natural world in all its goodness; Genesis 2 portrays the ambiguity of the socio-historical order in all its anxiousness. To use philosophical language, essence (in Genesis 1) precedes existence (in Genesis 2). And what connects our origin in God with our activity on earth? The seventh day (Gen. 2:1–3), its presence and its purpose!

> God saw everything that he had made, and indeed, it was very good. And there was evening and there was morning, the sixth day.
>
> Thus the heavens and the earth were finished, and all their multitude. And on the seventh day God finished the work which he had done, and he rested on the seventh day from all the work that he had done. So God blessed the seventh day and hallowed it, because on it God rested from all the work that he had done in creation. (Gen. 1:31—2:3)

The order may be taken as an implicit theological statement. That is, the sequence of essence-sabbath-existence reflects the order of importance from the standpoint of our relation to God. The chronology of Genesis 1 and 2 is secondary to the interpretation carried by their structuring. Even though the narratives were composed in reverse order, from a theological perspective the supporting cosmic context of Genesis 1 precedes the disrupting human presence of Genesis 2. Although we start with our selves and our experience, our origin lies in God and God's creating.

Sabbath holds together the natural order (depicted in Genesis 1) and the socio-historical order (described in Genesis 2). Simply put, the Sabbath bridges culture and nature. Only a stopping of what we are doing creates the meaning of what matters.

The fourth commandment makes the centrality of the seventh day explicit. It comes between the first three commandments, which focus on our relationship to God, and the last six, which deal with our relationship to each other. In Exodus the commandment is linked with creation (Exod. 20:11), while in Deuteronomy it demonstrates Israel's being free to rest because it has been redeemed from bondage (Deut. 5:12–15) (Jacobs 1987). In short, the Sabbath is the means God uses to connect heaven and earth.

Transforming the word *sabbath* from a noun, a known entity—*the Sabbath*—into a verb or process—*sabbathing*—reflects a periodic recognizing of a transcendent context of human origin and responsibility. The term *responsibility* joins the inner capacity to respond with the external context of accountability, specifically, symbolic consciousness. This reflects "a transcendent context." I locate access to that transcendent context in the neurocognitive processes that cannot be contained by conscious intention—namely, in subsymbolic, nonconscious, transcerebral activity.

The distinctions between "inner" and "external" and between "symbolic" and "subsymbolic" serve an analytical purpose. They are not separate and distinct spheres, ontological entities reflecting a dualistic structure. Rather, reality is an integrating realm of activity. It incorporates everything, depending on various perspectives—inner/outer, symbolic/subsymbolic.

The Sabbath is an institution found only in the biblical record (Andreasen 1978, 23). That includes Canaanite and Babylonian analogues as well. To understand soul as meaningful memory, I summarize interpretations of Sabbath history and its institutionalization. Then I identify ways in which that tradition has been understood in terms of psychic and cultural dynamics. Finally, I link these phenomena with brain processes.

HISTORICAL AND INSTITUTIONAL BACKGROUND

Despite changes (see Barack 1965), here is the basic structure and meaning of the Sabbath in Hebrew Scripture.

First, the Sabbath is both given and commanded—"remember."

> Remember the sabbath day, and keep it holy. Six days you shall labor, and do all your work. But the seventh day is a sabbath to the LORD your God; you shall not do any work—you, your son or your daughter, your male or female slave, your livestock, or the alien resident in your towns. (Exod. 20:8–10)

Sabbath is fixed in nature, in the created cosmos, and found in history, in the commandment at Mount Sinai. We are directed to attend to this given. Although it is ever present, we can forget it, and in forgetting it we lose the power of its presence.

Because Moses broke the first tablets containing the commandments in frustration over Israel's unfaithfulness, God gave them a second set. As the rationale of each differs, so does the imperative. In the first, the Hebrew word is *zakhor*, or "remember"; in the second, it is *shamor*, "keep" or "be watchful" (Barack 1965, 6). The difference reflects the gap between how we are made and how we act.

Therefore, we are instructed to "remember," which means to "*re*-member," to *re*-connect, to join together again conscious intention and continuing existence. Such attending to reconciling symbolic essence and subsymbolic existence requires vigilance. Sabbath is "the only institution linked with creation and even with the Creator . . . [and] the only holy day commanded in the Decalogue" (Barack 1965, xii). We are commanded to keep watch that we truly are the image God has created us to be. In sabbathing we are reconciled with God.

Second, the Sabbath is special, different, separated from everyday living. In religious language it is to be kept "holy," set off from the ordinary and profane. As God hallowed it, made it whole and intrinsically valuable in and of itself, so we are to remember to punctuate time with a regular break. We are to set aside a timeless time, to create a space for catching our breath and savoring life.

That whole-making intent includes the quality of fulfillment. God sees all that God has made and judges it to be "very good." "Satisfaction" reflects the completing, the consolidating and fulfilling, of what has taken place prior to that point in time. Now the cosmos is "all together," of a piece, which makes for peace (*shalom*). The holy and hallowed time of sabbath embraces what is intended in the beginning, what emerges along the way, and what is brought to completion as an "eternal now."

When the Midrash asks, "What was the world lacking at the end of the sixth day?" it answers, "Rest, Sabbath . . . and this was the completion on the seventh day" (Barack 1965, 1).

Third, the Sabbath is clearly a day of rest. We literally stop the work of the world, assuming, of course, that we have actually been engaged in the work of the world. The Sabbath is no excuse for "goofing off." Good, hard, responsible work is what is assumed—doing what one can do regularly, routinely, continuously, week after week, month after month, year after year.

In counseling that assumes regular sessions of intense engagement with the pain of people's lives. But work is always to be interrupted by a period of rest. "Six days you shall work, but the seventh day is a sabbath to the LORD your God." *Day* may be a metaphor for a period of time and not a literal entity.

In resting we recognize that we are not the whole show. In relaxing we acknowledge our dependence on that which is more than our conscious selves. In stopping we give sway to that which is other than our conscious intent—namely, the Lord God working through subcortical biogenetic processes. We cannot make meaning simply by willing it. We must allow for the working of nonconscious activity.

Fourth, the Sabbath equalizes both people and animals. Parents and children (wives are conspicuous in not being mentioned), masters and servants, friends and strangers, those who have and those who have not, and even work animals—all are liberated from unrelenting toil. There is no double standard, no privileged man and no superwoman. Here is a radical recognition that we are all dependent on that which we did not originate and that which we cannot control.

Sabbathing calls into question every form of exclusivity, whether sexism, racism, classism, ageism, heterosexism, ethnocentricism, or anthropocentricism. This liberating core of sabbath reflects the experience of the children of Israel being brought out of Egypt. As Old Testament scholar Brevard S. Childs puts it, "Israel observes the sabbath *in order* to remember her slavery and deliverance" (quoted by Andreasen 1978, 50). The commandment at Mount Sinai followed the deliverance from slavery. Before then Israel had been "nobody"—literally a people without an identifiable reality, "no people." Then they discovered that they were God's people, as claimed in 1 Peter (2:10)—"somebody," literally a people with a recognizable identity. Only then did they connect their present existence with universal essence. Only then did they look backward from the exodus event to the origin of creation. Only then did they find in the beginning what was present, yet unrecognized, in their midst—namely, deliverance from oppression and unconsciousness.

By remembering the Sabbath of God they recognized who they were—God's own creation. What lay within the nonconscious realm of nature was at last known. The making of meaning was lifted up into the light of consciousness. With consciousness came historical change.

Thus, the changing seasons of nature become the remembrances of generation after generation of the liberated. Judaism transformed agricultural festivals into commemorations of historical events: the spring festival turned into Passover—the Feast of Unleavened Bread—celebrating the escape from Egypt (Exod. 23:15); the end of the wheat harvest became the Feast of Weeks, celebrating "the day on which the Torah was given at Sinai" (see Exod. 23:16); an old festival of vintage became the Feast of Booths, commemorating "the dwelling of the Israelites in booths during their sojourn in the wilderness" (see Lev. 23:42–43) (Heschel [1951] 1975, 7; Rylaarsdam 1962). Instead of revelling in the cycles of nature—the phases of the moon, sunrise and sunset, planting and harvesting—people now were commanded to rejoice in remembering the liberation of creatures, great and small.

As an institution for communal continuity, the character of the Sabbath underwent change. It was a sign of the covenant between Yahweh and Israel. It was also a sign of hope for Israel's finding God's rest in the promised land. The promised land symbolized "the tangible peace from [the precariousness of] wanderings and enemies" (Andreasen 1978, 54–55). Thus, what went into its observance became more and more specific (Morgenstern 1962). In clinical language we could say the experience of liberation turned into an obsession with literal concreteness.

The early church experienced and proclaimed Jesus as Lord of the Sabbath (Mark 2:28; Luke 6:5). In doing so, they were declaring the ultimate reconciliation of all creation. Soon the Sabbath was known as the Lord's Day. By the fourth century it became, for Christians, Sunday, the eighth day. The eighth day broke the closed cycle of a seven-day week. And so the Lord's Day symbolized the eschaton, the new age of the fulfillment of time (Edwards 1982, 15–17).

Judaism gave the day a positive emphasis of worshiping Yahweh instead of merely a time of resting. The church did the same. From the time of Constantine in the fourth century to the present, Christians emphasized a "Puritan" Sabbath as disciplined in its way as the Israelite Sabbath was in its way. Puritan obedience also turned the experience of fulfillment into an obsession with specific "do's and don'ts."

The Judaic Sabbath, as the Christian Sabbath, was modified over time. In religious families, Sunday is still a day set aside for God. In the work-day world of secular society, we have gone from a six-day work week to a forty-hour work week with compulsory ten-minute breaks or "breathers" in mid-morning and afternoon. In tropical countries the siesta serves a similar purpose—a time for rest and renewal.

Whether it is a cultural break or a religious remembering of meaning, sabbath reflects a periodic recognition of a transcendent context of human origin and responsibility. More than a day for doing nothing, it is at once an eternal cycle and a historical process. In resting from labor we remember our Creator, and this remembering bestows meaning.

HOW MIGHT MEANING COME ABOUT?

I speculate that the physiological correlates of meaningful memory, or the core of our experienced self, are reflected in the three mind states of waking, sleeping, and dreaming. Understanding these mind states gives us clues to soul tending and sabbathing. These are the biorhythms that govern the state of our being.

Through the centuries people have been intrigued and dismayed by their dreams. Dreams have served as a source of revelation as well as an invasion of the demonic. In 1900, with Sigmund Freud's *The Interpretation of Dreams*, people began to investigate the significance of dreams more systematically. Yet it has only been since 1952 that the nonwaking state has been studied empirically. In that year, at the University of Chicago, dreaming moved from the bedroom into the laboratory. Physiological processes became as significant as psychological interpretation. Interest shifted from the content of dreams to the process of dreaming. As one interpreter put it: "The Impossible Dream Comes True: A Private Experience Becomes a Public Event" (Fiss 1979, 21).

An understanding of dreaming now includes not only the cognitive content and psychological dynamics of the reported dream but equally the biochemical processes of the sleep and dream states themselves (Wolman 1979). In our cycling through these mind states of waking, sleeping, and dreaming, I suggest we find a bridge between our life as human beings and our being created in the image and likeness of God.

The human sleep cycle (Arkin, Antrobus, and Ellman 1978; Drucker-Colin, Shkurovich, and Sterman 1979) has been thoroughly documented (Hobson 1988, 148). A typical night's sleep includes an initial drop into a deep phase in which we are really "out of it." That is, if wakened, we are disoriented. This is a four-stage period known as non-REM sleep. Think of it as "sleeping sleep." In the nonwaking states, deep sleep takes up about 75% of the time.

The second phase is known as REM, or rapid eye movement sleep. It takes up about 25% of the night. This stage reflects our conventional awareness of dreaming—strange and bizarre happenings, a kaleidoscopic tumbling and combining of times and places and people and objects and events. Normally we cycle through deep sleep and dream sleep on the average of 90 to 120 minutes four or five times a night (Fiss 1979, 22–26; Arkin et al. 1978; Drucker-Colin, Shkurovich, and Sterman 1979; see figure 13.1).

Sleeping and Resting: non-REM. With the invention of the microelectrode, brain scientists moved from recording large groups of nerves to recording "the electrical activity of individual nerve cells," thereby being "able to communicate directly with . . . the functional unit of the nervous system" (Hobson 1988, 160). It is now known that in the non-REM state brain activity is inhibited. The obliteration of consciousness in this state is probably due to an inhibition that blocks the transmission of information within the brain.

Both body and brain are quiet. The findings, building on the earlier work of behavioral physiologist Michel Jouvet and others (Jouvet and Moruzzi 1972; McCarley and Hobson 1979; Hobson 1988, 146–54), have led to "the theory of selective neuronal rest" of the rapidly firing smaller neurons during sleep (Hobson 1988, 167–71). The brain selectively decreases the activity of that subpopulation of "cells specifically crucial for normal waking" (Hobson 1988, 171).

It appears that the larger, slowly discharging cells maintain the continuous tonic events necessary for life. The smaller, rapidly firing cells relate to phasic events, those episodic flurries of activity that are present during waking and REM sleep (Fiss 1979, 27–28).

The effects of inhibited body-brain activity appear related to our bodies recovering their efficiency (Hauri 1979, 256). This is a physiological state of rest. It has its analogue with the Sabbath, where we are also admonished to rest.

The mind state of sleep is described by the brain state of non-REM stages 1, 2, 3, and 4 (see figure 13.1). It starts where eye movements change, going through the following stages: (1) eye movements are slow and rolling; (2) "spindles" or brief bursts of fast, low-voltage waves increase; (3) slow, high-amplitude delta waves form; and (4) eye movements cease. What has been described above is a slowing, shutting-down movement. Some people report "a steady decline in control over the course of mental activity." We become more and more drowsy and drift off into a light sleep. As we lose contact with the environment, we experience "a steady rise in the frequency of hallucinatory experience" (Vogel 1978, 97–98). Our thought "consists of fragmented images or minidramas" (Winson 1990, 86). Then we lose consciousness completely. Our entire system becomes quiet; we are at rest. Our system has entered its sabbath.

Dreaming and Synthesizing. Deep sleep is followed by REM sleep, a meaning-making process in which the body is inhibited and the brain is active. In REM sleep, although the body is resting, the brain is active. Who we are now, who we have been, and the emotional impact of what is happening—these images of ourselves and our model of self-world interaction—converge. The resulting mosaic forms a narrative of our life, no matter how illogical it seems.

Evidence suggests that

delta [deep] sleep is related to somatic recovery, while REM sleep has something to do with the recovery of higher mental functions. Blood flow measures support such a view. During delta sleep blood flow is directed mainly to the muscles, while cerebral arteries are constricted. During REM sleep cerebral blood flow increases, while blood flow to the large skeletal muscles is constricted. (Hauri 1979, 256)

The dreaming state presents a contrasting and fascinating pattern to the nondreaming state. This stage has been called *paradoxical sleep, paradoxical* because, except for the rapid movement of the eyes, it is a period of intense neuronal activity and little physical activity (Fiss 1979, 24). The psychophysiology includes three features: (1) activating the brain-mind to process information; (2) blocking sensory input, which inhibits signals coming from the outside and increases activity for messages arising from the inside; and (3) blocking motor output so we do not act on the data generated (Hobson 1988, 205–10). Even though inactive physically, we are very much "on the go." We are watching what we are doing when we are dreaming it. Perhaps this is the biochemical correlate of what Tillich (1957) spoke of as "dreaming innocence." There is potential for action without the consequences of action—the absence of actual experience, of personal responsibility, and of moral guilt (Tillich 1957, 38–41).

It is hypothesized that this activation process is a synthesizing activity. Although we fall into sleep passively, we come out actively dreaming. The brain processes information basic to both "how" we are as a physical organism and to "who" we are as an intact mammal. The function of the dreaming state is not resting from what we have been doing; it is reorganizing the meaning of what has gone on (Hobson 1988, 169, 194).

The REM state, then, is what J. Allan Hobson, professor of psychiatry at Harvard Medical School and director of the Laboratory of Neurophysiology of the Massachusetts Mental Health Center, has labeled "a *meaning-added process*" (1988, 218; italics in original). By "meaning-added," Hobson refers to residue from being awake together with persistent concerns accumulated over time (whether we are conscious of them or not). Residue from the day and concerns over time are transformed into enhanced information—that is, information weighted in the direction of what matters to us emotionally in our survival as a psychophysical mammal. Any change that carries emotional significance is likely to contribute to increased REM activity—a trip, a move, a loss, a gain, a grief, a joy.

A dramatic example of emotional survival can be found in Newton's 1970 research with 127 quadriplegic and paraplegic men (reported by Schwarz et al. 1978, 187–88). He viewed "dreaming kinesthesis as having an emergency repair function of a disrupted bodily image." On the basis of this he predicted "an increase of physical activity immediately following the disability and dropping off below normal when the new body image [became] stabilized and kinesthesis

[was] no longer necessary for its maintenance." The "emergency repair hypothesis" of dreaming was supported. "Immediately after the onset of the paralysis there was an upsurge of dreamed physical activity in excess of that of the normal controls and that with the passage of time, its level decreased and remained stable at lower than normal levels."

Similarly, a woman described taking a short trip to a distant city for a mini-vacation. A backlog of needed rest had accumulated so that she slept all the way there on the bus. As her need for intense sleep decreased, her dreaming increased (almost in superabundance), and by the end of that brief weekend, her daytime mind was on the edge of excitement: thinking up things she wanted to do, remembering ideas she had forgotten, jumping from one thought to another, "frisking about," as she put it, "like a colt let out to pasture." She felt alive again, reborn. The energy and stimulation carried over into her work week.

Dreaming and dreams are constructive processes. They take stimuli with low-recognition value and turn them into high-information narratives. Neural signals become visual imagery. Despite uncertainty about the logic of the dream, these images are "single-mindedly" woven into narratives—stories—that convey the persistent themes of our lives (Hobson 1988, 271).

REM has been found in all mammals, except the spiny anteater (echidna) (Winson 1990; [1985] 1986, 53).[1] The percentage of REM varies, making up about 25% of the sleep cycle for ourselves and cats, about 15% for rabbits, less for animals subject to predators, and more for predators with secure sleeping places (Winson [1985] 1986, 53). This evolutionary aspect of sleep may have contributed to the inclusion of "cattle" in the Sabbath commandment (Exod. 20:8). All mammals, ourselves included, need "rest" in order to "reorganize" information about themselves and their place in their environment.

REM appears in utero. It has been thought to prepare "the young organism to handle the enormous quantities of stimulation to which it is exposed during the early stages of growth" (Fiss 1979, 26). Newborns spend at least 50% of sleep in the REM state. By the age of five the percentage stabilizes at the adult level of 20% to 25%. It remains at that level until old age, when it declines to about 18% or less. Researchers (Roffwarg et al. 1966) theorize that REM is an internally generated source of stimulation that provides higher brain centers with large amounts of excitation. Such stimulation appears crucial for the maturation and maintenance of the central nervous system.

In REM we systematically process information that mixes recent events with memories. Any change is likely to activate more REM. Simply going to a

1. The spiny anteater, known as the enchida, has a large prefrontal cortex, which neuroscientist Jonathan Winson suggests enables it "to react to incoming information in an appropriate manner based on past experience and to evaluate and store new information to aid in future survival." Other mammals accomplished this storing and evaluating by REM sleep (Winson 1990, 92).

conference reorganizes neuronal information. More importantly, transitions—trips, moves, separations, losses as well as gains, whatever carries emotional significance—all contribute to enhanced REM activity.

Waking and Acting. Sleeping and dreaming are states over which we have little control. They link us with other mammals and reflect that we are "in but not of" the world. They are necessary, though not sufficient, conditions for the waking state.

When awake our brain actively responds to external input. It avoids overload by eliminating information and by organizing information according to its intention. Our sensory systems are made to reduce the amount of stimuli we take in (Ornstein [1972, 1977] 1986, 24–29). Under normal circumstances, with the observational-explanatory process, the mind constructs a stable world (Gazzaniga 1985; 1988). These left-brain processes establish the "linearity of cause-effect relations between events" (Hobson 1988, 268), what we ordinarily think of as real-world events.

THE BASIC REST-ACTIVITY CYCLE (BRAC)

In 1957 researchers William Dement and Nathaniel Kleitman reported a basic 90-to-120-minute rhythm, which they called the "basic rest-activity cycle" (the BRAC hypothesis) (Rossi 1986, 133–36; 1991). That cycle runs continuously day and night. It has been associated with endocrine metabolism and a variety of behavioral and psychological processes. These include "cycles in fantasy, hemispheric dominance, and perceptual processing. . . . Episodic hormone secretion seems to be a fundamental property of endocrine metabolism, and it is somehow related to the REM cycles" (Kripke 1982, cited by Rossi 1986, 133–34).

In other words, under normal conditions our whole life is regulated by a typical rhythm of acting and resting. The sleeping/waking cycle is known as a circadian rhythm, from the Latin words *circa* meaning "about" and *dies* meaning "a day." The cycles that come more than once a day are called ultradian rhythms, from the Latin word *ultra*, meaning "beyond," namely a frequency higher than once a day (Bloom et al. 1985, 117). Something like a REM reorganizing and synthesizing process continues day and night, year in and year out. I relate that phenomenon of biorhythms to "sabbathing" or the regular rest and renewal that goes on in our bodies round the clock.

Even though the brain-mind is active in both dreaming and waking, for some physiological reason it "lacks the capacity to test both external and internal realities" at the same time (Hobson 1988, 209). When awake, our conscious mind tests our psychic world against outer reality—how does what we feel match what we perceive? When dreaming, our unconscious brain tests the outer world against our psychic reality—how does what we sense match what matters to us?

The essence of who we are—our "biochemical individuality" (Williams 1967)—emerges out of this alternating and synthesizing of potentiality in dreaming and actuality in waking.

Recent studies (Klein and Armitage 1978) suggest that the brain's left-hemisphere and right-hemisphere activity are affected by the natural ninety-minute ultradian rhythms. These in turn "might affect psychological functioning" (Rossi 1986, 121). Each half of the brain alternates taking the lead at different times during the cycle, which suggests an alternation between the step-by-step/item-by-item analytic process of the left hemisphere and the all-at-once/leaps of imaginative holistic process of the right hemisphere (Ashbrook 1988b, 89–100, 110–17). Such rhythms appear related to the autonomic nervous system and its integrating cerebral cortical activity.

In her experimental study on cerebral hemisphere activity and autonomic nervous function as associated with alternations in the nasal breathing cycle, Debra Werntz (1981 cited by Rossi 1986, 121–22) concluded that "the whole body goes through the Rest/Activity or Parasympathetic/ Sympathetic oscillation while simultaneously going through the 'Left Body–Right Brain/Right Body–Left Brain' shift. This then produces ultradian rhythms at all levels of organization from pupil size to higher cortical functions and behavior."

In simpler language, parasympathetic/sympathetic oscillation means an alternating between relaxation and arousal in the autonomic nervous system (Bloom et al. 1985, 91–95; see figure 13.2). Our brains are made to hold together letting-go and hanging-on. These are integrated, complementary aspects of the entire neuronal system. The relaxing effects of parasympathetic activity allow for "rest and recuperation." In this state of inactivity heart rate diminishes, the pupils of the eyes constrict, and an increased blood flow to the intestines facilitates food moving through the gut. In short, the body is restored to its optimal potential.

The arousing effects of sympathetic activity ready the body for "flight or fight." In this state, heart rate picks up, the pupils widen to take in what has caught our attention, and blood flow shifts to the muscles and the brain as digestive processes slow down. In short, the body is mobilized to act.

Without most of us realizing it, the alternating rhythm of relaxing and arousing is built into our lives (Rossi 1991). In a typical work schedule a person starts at 9:00, has a break at 10:30, takes lunch at noon, returns at 1:00, breaks again at 3:00, and finishes up around 5:00. The counseling schedule is slightly less rhythmic, though it is routine: fifty-minute hours, with two back-to-back sessions constituting a normal BRAC cycle.

Most people have experiences in which they are working efficiently and suddenly realize they have let down, mentally wandered off, taken a break without knowing it. The mind goes slack; the eyes stop focusing; the body slumps. In such circumstances they have fallen into the mind state of rest, what psychotherapist Ernest L. Rossi calls "the common everyday trance" (Rossi 1986, 136; 1991). In this brain state the rapid, episodically firing neurons are inhibited. In spite of every effort to stop it, the slump is inevitable. In common parlance, people "day dream."

In these moments we disengage from what we are doing. Brain-mind activation shuts down, and the body insists that we rest. When the body takes a deep breath, then we become aware that the rest period has ended. With that we are refreshed and return to work. Oxygen is again available for sustained mental attention.

The more compulsive part of us overrides this basic rhythm. We work through the work breaks, resist the let downs, corral our wandering mind. We keep going because there is "so much to do."

Yet accumulating evidence demonstrates that by overriding and disrupting this natural cycle we set in motion the physiological activity of psychosomatic illness (Rossi 1986, 135; Borysenko 1987). Disrupting the cycle can lead to distress. Distress in turn can result in disease. When we take "breaks," we *"undercut the processes of psychosomatic illnesses at their psychophysiological source"* (Rossi 1986, 136 italics in original).

The day's ultradian cycle is the analogue of the night's circadian cycle. We fall into non-REM sleep/rest through a twilight zone of disorientation and reemerge in a REM fantasy world of kaleidoscopic possibilities. I regard this natural cycle as a mini-sabbath. In it we are gathering up and reorganizing our own mosaic of meaning.[2]

The meaning of information depends on the cumulated and consolidated input from the world and input generated from inside. When we lose sleep, especially REM sleep, we exhibit disturbed behavior (Hauri 1979; Dement 1979; Ellman et al. 1978). We become irritable, disoriented, anxious, uncertain. In extreme cases we forget who we are. Remember, for example, the experience of jet lag and the African porters who insisted on waiting for their souls to catch up with their bodies.

Apparently, REM-like mentation bridges our biological brain and our psychological mind. That combination of brain-mind activation and motor inhibition couples sensory perception with emotional state. It constitutes what is known as the limbic-frontal cortical system, the emotional core and intentional activity. In this way the brain-mind establishes the memories and connections that influence how we act (Winson [1985] 1986, 34). These ideas are

---

2. Procedures have been developed that can enhance the value of this basic activity-rest cycle. These include guided mental imagery (Shorr et al. 1980), hypnosis and self-hypnosis (Rossi 1986; Rossi and Cheek 1988), focusing (Gendlin 1978; 1980), wakeful dreaming (Smith 1989), the transcendent function (Jung 1960, 67-91), active imagination (Hannah 1981), and creative visualization (Gawain 1982), among many.

re-presented as images, which in turn are translated into memories. That bridging reality has been called the "psyche" (Winson, [1985] 1986, 6) or "the self" (Loder 1981).

This limbic-frontal cortical system works primarily on the basis of motor activity (whether actually when we are awake or imagined when we are dreaming) (Winson [1985] 1986, 217–18). We *see* and *feel* what we *do*. Because of that we "remember what we're about." In effect, we are "living forward" (Gendlin 1980, 70) toward a fuller reality.

The left hemisphere plays a primary role in creating a supposedly objective world. It organizes stimuli and interprets that organization (Gazzaniga 1988a; Laughlin et al. 1990). In parallel fashion the right hemisphere plays a primary role in creating a "subjective" world. It immerses us in a context (Ornstein [1972, 1977] 1986; Virshup and Virshup 1980).

Psychologist Paul Bakan characterizes right-hemisphere process as "raw imagery." It appears "spontaneously under certain conditions as sleep, muscular relaxation, free association, mind-wandering, and under the influence of certain drugs" (Bakan 1980, 50). The right hemisphere has been described as "regressive, primal, affective, illogical."

When the hemispheres are working together, the imagery is processed, or "cooked," by the left hemisphere. The imagery is translated into concepts and words. This allows the experience to be tested in ordinary time and space. Metaphorically speaking, the result is a meal that is both nutritious and tasty.

Rossi outlines a naturalistic approach to utilizing what he regards as the natural "ultradian healing response" (Rossi 1986, 138–40):

> first, we are to recognize when we are tired or irritable, and take a break, for those feelings are the signal of an opportunity for the healing response;

> second, we can access our inner resources by exploring where we are comfortable in our body and then by allowing that comfort to spread as we wonder how our unconscious—"all by itself"—can deal with whatever immediate problem is confronting us; and

> third, we can ratify that healing process by recognizing the comforting changes that have taken place during that period of 10 to 20 minutes in which we have lost track of time.

I speculate that the whole brain—old cortex and new—may be the most identifiable locus of the essential structuring of reality (Ashbrook 1984b; 1988b; see figure 13.3). To state the point more boldly: the brain is the main locus of sensibility or meaning (see Laughlin et al. 1990, 161).

The brain stem is the most primitive level of brain organization. It appears to be the coordinating center that controls the brain states of sleeping, dreaming, and waking (Hobson 1988, 123–33). This is an active process in which the brain creates its own energy and its own information (Hobson 1988, 15). We share these structures and functions with all reptiles. This is why the region is known as the reptilian brain or primal mind (MacLean 1970). It generates the hard-wired instinctual behavior necessary for life itself.

The limbic system is the middle level of brain organization. It processes familiar experience with new experience in an ever-reorganizing construction of what is meaningful for us in an optimal adaptation to the environment. As noted above, we share this level with all mammals, which is why the region is known as the mammalian brain or emotional mind. It contributes the emotional meaning of experience in determining how we act.

The new cortex is the most developed level of brain organization. It adds consciousness, thereby transforming all lower levels of activity into cultural expressions and evaluated experience. The region is known as the new brain or rational mind. It makes for conscious intentionality and symbolic models of reality.

In view of such data, mind states are "active central neural" processes under the control of the brain. The brain is active in and for itself. Gone is the Lockean view of the human organism as a *tabula rasa*—a blank tablet—on which the environment writes its scenario and to which we react passively. Sensory stimulation is neither sufficient cause of brain activity nor necessary for that activity. The brain controls sleeping, dreaming, and waking, with the coordinating center located "within the brain stem." In short, the brain creates its own energy and its own information (Hobson 1988, 123–33). The brain is constantly imposing "its own truth upon the external world" (Hobson 1988, 15).

It is only in the whole brain that we become "at one with our own essence" (Dourley 1975, 55). While there is no "executive neuron," no "pontifical nerve," only critical molecular processes in "constant flux," we may speak neuropsychologically of "the executive brain" (Winson [1985] 1986, 59). In similar fashion, we may speak neurotheologically of the executive brain as "the soul."

Quite simply, soul constitutes that which each of us can call our own, that which distinguishes us from everything else in creation. Further, the state of our soul is reflected in the states of our mind and their physiological correlates—namely, the states of our brain.

PARALLELS BETWEEN THE SEVENTH DAY AND THE REM-LIKE STATE

The Sabbath myth is strikingly similar to the mind states of sleeping, dreaming, and waking discussed above.

"God saw everything that he had made" (Gen. 1:31a). That sounds like the REM

process—a watching and surveying of the kaleidoscopic input that results from combining internal and external activity. In REM sleep the brain is active, engaging in all manner of busyness. Yet that activity occurs within the mythic state of dreaming innocence. All is present, all is possible. Activation of the brain-mind is not the same as activation of the body.

"... and indeed, it was very good" (Gen. 1:31b). What had been done was reorganized in such a way as to give it meaning. The reorganizing process, while under control of the active central nervous system, is something we experience more than we manage. It "happens" in us. It "happens" to us. It seems very much "other than" or "beyond" us. Such knowing-all-together is a deeply satisfying and renewing experience (see Gendlin 1962; 1978). Even though we can describe it, the synthesis remains a mystery.

"And on the seventh day God finished the work that he had done" (Gen. 2:2a). That sounds as though the surveying-reorganizing activity resulted in a closure, a tidying up, an integrating of all that had been put out. That finishing of creation was not the finality of a closed system but the fulfillment of an open system. Work was brought to a state of perfection in terms of what God had intended, an ordering of God-world interaction. And that fulfillment of the essence of creation was the groundwork, the basis of what could and would emerge in history.

"... and [God] rested on the seventh day" (Gen. 2:2b). That sounds much like the inhibition of the rapidly firing cells related to non-REM sleep. Except for the activity required to maintain biological life, the mind literally stops working. The cortical brain falls into a state of rest.

"So God blessed the seventh day and hallowed it" (Gen. 2:3a). That making whole of the meaning of creation seems very like the single-mindedness integral to the narrative-thematic—or consistency-making—process we know in dreaming. In REM-like activity we construct an inner sense of coherence and continuity. We combine what has been with what is as the basis for acting in relation to what is to come.

Here, then, is the cycle of creation-sabbath and the biorhythm of brain-mind: work, rest, reorganization, creation. The imperative to keep the Sabbath in active memory appears to be built into the biochemistry of our bodies. We find it in the cycle of sleeping, dreaming, and acting. Remembering the Sabbath is the making of soul.

When people come to us for help, at the deepest level they are seeking a center of meaning inside themselves yet beyond themselves. I understand the idea of "beyond themselves" as the rhythmicity of older brain activity. From the stand point of faith that rhythmicity is the power of God, the ultimate creating activity of the universe. It is this perspective of transcendence that frees us from bondage to space and time, from the tyranny of nonconscious existence, from exploitation by others, yes, and from consciousness itself.

Apart from that transcendent center of meaning we are limited in our ability to distinguish and decide. We are subject to conflicting and random forces inside us and around us. We exist in a vegetative state of life without living, whether as slaves of oppressive systems, as victims of a post-traumatic syndrome (Brende 1982), as workaholics of a competitive market, or as patients on life-support systems.

In reflecting on the notion of soul as meaningful memory, Chaplain Thomas Kroon[3] describes the "soul-less" lives of many of the older people with whom he ministers. He uses worship to focus on the experience of memories. The task of remembering is a vital and godly part of life. He links this with Victor Frankl's speaking about all that we have been and done as having been "safely stored in the granary of the past." For his parishioners to experience their present as meaningful—being buoyed up by their past—requires not only reconciliation and forgiveness but also "a great deal of sabbathing."

Kroon goes on to reflect on sabbath as the remembering of soul-making:

> I have understood that a potential blessing inherent in old age is living long enough to be shaped more fully into the image of God. These two notions revolve around the same point, that is, sabbathing and reflecting the imago Dei.
>
> If we could understand these "years without life" differently, as indeed one's "seventh day," then it might be possible to regain one's soul. But not without a great deal of help. So many of my folk are so frail in so many of their dimensions. But this construction [of soul making] gives me new language to talk about the nature of the "task" [of pastoral care], if one can speak of sabbathing with such a word.

Consider soul, then, as what we call our own, what distinguishes us from all others. The limbic process combines molecules of meaning and symbolic representations into a model of self-world interaction. This is not a substantial view, an immortal substance separate from a mortal substance. This is a functional view. Soul refers to the interpreting, integrating, adapting activity necessary for meaning within each of us individually and all of us as a species.

Significantly, the biorhythms of the basic rest-activity cycle "are regulated by the same hormones that modulate memory and learning" (Rossi 1986, 133). The brain changes with experience, and those changes "are influenced by hormones" modulating memory (Gold and McGaugh 1984, 65, 78–79).

Though specific brain structures and systems can be identified as loci in meaning-making, evidence suggests that "it may be unjustifiable to assume that any particular psychological concept [such as *self* or *meaning*] has a discrete . . . equivalent somewhere in the brain" (Vanderwolf and Ledung 1983, 297). Instead

3. Chaplain Thomas Kroon, personal communication, Nov. 27, 1989.

of a "static conception of individual neurons," the current model of memory is a dynamic one. "Critical molecular processes appear to be in constant flux" (Black et al. 1988, 4; see Bergland [1985] 1988). In short, memory is adaptive to an ever-changing scene.

Life is meaningful only as we can "remember." Without memory we have no meaning. And memory is synonymous with soul, that centered, whole-making activity of the brain-mind in its representation of self-world interaction. Without soul we are not ourselves. Sabbath rest and reorganization are built into our very being. The basic cycle of rest-synthesis-activity is the means we have for the making of meaning, and meaning making is the making of soul.

Jewish theologian Abraham Heschel told of a medieval sage who declared, "The world which was created in six days was a world without a soul. It was on the seventh day that the world was given a soul. This is why it is said: 'and on the seventh day [God] rested'" (Heschel [1951] 1975, 83).

In this age of scientific technology, political tyranny, and abusive relations we are in danger of losing our soul, the humanness of our humanity, the basic core of experienced reality. Only by sabbathing as God gives it and commands it can we keep body and soul together. We are to "remember the Sabbath and keep it holy." Our task as pastoral counselors is to mind the souls of those who seek our help so they, in turn, can tend their souls themselves.

CHAPTER FOURTEEN

Soul and Role

BEING A COUNSELOR AND BEING A PERSON

■ ■ ■ ■ ■

This chapter explores the specific role of the pastoral counselor as it is derived from the general role of pastor or religious authority. Both roles express the care-giving aspects of God's activity, but the specialized role takes on much of its symbolic power from expectations people have about the general role of representing God.

People in pain turn to religious authorities and pastoral counselors with high hopes and great longing for help. Their cry to the authority figure reflects their cry to God. It is at once "a cry of pain ... and a cry for help" (Boyce 1988, 22, 71), a cry of anguish and a cry for support. In its deepest sense, every cry expresses a great desire for justice, liberation, and healing.

In minding the souls of those in pain, how do pastoral counselors manage that symbolic power of representing the resources of God? How do they utilize knowledge of the psychological sciences and the dynamics of religious symbolic expectations? How do they balance the demands of their representative role and their own personal needs? How are role and soul respected, differentiated, and integrated—in the therapist as well as in the client?

BETWEEN THE PERSONAL AND THE SYMBOLIC

The following story illustrates the tension between a pastoral role and one's personal life. I take it as a paradigm of the tension between the authority of being a representative of God and the authenticity of being an individual (see Southard 1990a; Patton 1990a).

At age thirty-five and after ten years of writing daily copy for the press, Ari Goldman (Goldman 1991, 191–92) went to Harvard Divinity School to learn about religion. He was there neither as a Christian nor as a candidate for ministry. He simply was "there on an unusual leave of absence from [his] job as a religion writer for *The New York Times*."

While there Goldman seriously considered becoming a rabbi, though he eventually chose to return to reporting. But "the seed of the idea" was planted by a neighbor who lived next door, a retired army officer named Bill Doe. Doe belonged to the Roman Catholic church on the corner. He reflected how the ordinary person often regards those of us who "represent" God. One day when Ari was returning from school, Bill greeted him in a loud voice, "Hello, Rabbi!"

Every seminarian knows what that feels like. As soon as others learn that one is in seminary, that person gets labeled "Pastor." Every pastor knows what that's like. As soon as others learn that one is a minister, that person gets labeled "Reverend." Every pastoral counselor knows the shock of being perceived as a representative of God. Most of those who come for counseling expect the counselor to be a spiritual as well as a psychological resource (Henderson et al. 1992). Almost everyone hopes that their spiritual yearnings may be held together with their psychic pain (Gallup 1992; Woodruff 1992).

Goldman went over to explain that he "was not a rabbi, just a student of religion." Bill ignored the explanation and proceeded to introduce Goldman to a small man who had been long retired from the bench. "Rabbi, I would like you to meet the judge."

And so the relationship went—no longer "Ari" but "Rabbi"! Some time later Bill disappeared. Ari ran into the "judge" and asked what had happened to their neighbor Bill.

"He's at Mass General [Hospital]," the Judge told him, and added soberly, "cancer."

Goldman called the hospital and got Bill on the phone. Although he sounded tired, he was eager to hear about Ari, the family, and what else was going on in the neighborhood. When Ari asked how he was doing, Bill gave a formal report, "One operation down and one to go." Then he added that the first operation hadn't "gotten it all."

Like most of us would do, Goldman asked his friend, "Bill, tell me, is there anything I can do for you?" Without hesitating, Bill replied, "Just pray for me, Rabbi."

As a reporter Goldman had faced death when covering plane crashes and violent holdups. "But as a 'rabbi'—Bill's rabbi, anyway—I was frightened," Goldman confessed. Despite his theological studies, he had "no answers to the suffering of my friend." Even if he were to enter the ministry, Goldman believed, answers would elude him.

Then the reporter—who had gone to divinity school to acquire more knowledge about religion in order to write about it with more authority— shared "one thing [he] had learned about all religious systems. There is a point when book learning stops and faith begins. The only thing I could do was what Bill had asked. I prayed for his soul."

Reporter Ari Goldman missed part of Bill's point. Of course Bill wanted Ari's prayer as a person, as an individual, as a neighbor and friend. But Bill also was asking Ari Goldman as "Rabbi"—a *representative* of a believing community, a symbol of help and hope and God (Ashbrook 1990a). Bill had given neighbor Ari the mantle "Rabbi." In such moments titles are interchangeable—"Rabbi," "Priest," "Pastor," "Father," "Sister," "Pastoral Counselor," they all mean bearer and representative of God.

At the feeling level Goldman responded to the responsibility of bearing Bill's burden. At the same time he obscured the authority of such burden bearing—rightly and understandably so. Ari was not a rabbi or pastor or priest, not even a teacher or therapist. He was simply an ordinary person in an extraordinary situation. In response to Bill's request, he was experiencing his own limitations. He prayed for Bill's soul as a person even though he was unclear about representing a believing community and an ever-present God.

SYMBOL-BEARER OF GOD

Every pastoral counselor experiences appeals such as Bill made to Ari: "Bearer of God [Rabbi], pray for me." The request may be one of desperation or, as in Bill's case, a straightforward petition for presence in the midst of uncertainty. Unlike the case of Ari and Bill, a connection between God and an individual is most explicit for those whose role officially reflects a community of faith. Pastors and rabbis, pastoral counselors and pastoral psychotherapists do bear symbolically the meaning and power of divine presence (Ashbrook 1990a; Oates 1990). And, because men and women have chosen to identify their counseling role with "pastoral," they cannot avoid being "mana" persons.

According to the dictionary, the word *mana* refers to the impersonal supernatural power of the gods and to sacred objects in the native religions of Oceania. But pastoral theologian Urban Holmes (1978) uses the term *mana* in a way that identifies "the shamanistic roots of priesthood." A *shaman* is "one who 'bears God' to humankind . . . [a] specialist in the human soul" (Holmes 1978, 79).

While the priest plays a structured institutional role in tribal cultures, the shaman derives his or her power directly from the spirit world (see Achterberg 1990, 7–59). Holmes suggests that this differentiation between shaman and priest reflects bimodal consciousness, the receptive intuition of "antistructure" in right-brain thinking and the active rationality of "structure" in left-brain thinking (Holmes 1978, 21–34; see Turner 1969). Using the mythical language of Carl Jung, Holmes defines mana as "the divine energy from the fathomless ocean that beats upon the shores of our consciousness" (Holmes 1978, 82). This energy or power is not something that a person can claim as one's own. It is beyond our capacity to control. Yet we can mediate it in various ways. People find that power in the pastor/priest, thereby transforming an ordinary individual into a special bearer of divine presence.

In a moving way, Ari Goldman exposed the double task of being a person and bearing a role. Ari had begun to learn faith. As a person of faith, he did pray for Bill's soul. Yet no believer, no seminarian, no pastor, no therapist (even reporter Goldman) escapes the authority invested in us by others. Sometimes that authority is quite individualistic, as with Bill giving it to Ari. More typically, that authority is invested in individuals by a community, an institution, an establishment—formal, official, legitimized (Southard 1990a; Oates 1990). People are themselves yet they are other than themselves. This applies to the specialized ministry of pastoral counseling as well as to ministry in general.

The American Association of Pastoral Counselors organized in 1963 in an effort to better help pastors become competent counselors (Van Wagner 1992). One of the major issues confronting it—then and now—is the issue of role: who and what does one represent when one is a pastoral counselor? Does one need to have served as a parish pastor in order to function as a pastoral counselor? Can one engage in pastoral counseling by virtue of individual spiritual convictions? What part does a church community have in endorsing the work of a pastoral counselor?

Two other issues of role are also swirling around pastoral counselors like tornados (McHolland et al. 1993). One is third-party payments for services rendered; the other is licensing of pastoral counselors by state regulation.

Third-party payments raise the issue of the multidimensionality of people: What is physical? What is psychological? What is spiritual? What is health? What is mental health? What is spiritual health? What is wholeness? In health insurance, can the fuller dimensions of the human person be rightly included in the restricted dimension of a physical body? There is no self-evident answer to these questions, nor do I intend to address them. I allude to them here only to emphasize the unavoidable difficulty and implications of identifying role boundaries.

Licensing raises the issue of accountability to the public (see Van Wagner 1992, 92, 102). Is the practice of religion a voluntary matter and so to be protected from interference by the state? Is pastoral counseling an extension of religious practice and so independent of government regulation? Or is pastoral counseling distinguishable from an institutional base? Specifically, is pastoral counseling a profession apart from an institutional anchor, with standards subject to public monitoring? If "pastoral" is free from state regulation, should "counseling" be under state regulation? And how does one separate pastoral counseling from counseling, and counseling from psychology and social work and medicine?

No matter how these issues are resolved, pastoral counselors have to deal with the symbolic content and power carried by the adjective *pastoral*. This applies to the more generic meanings of *religious* and *spiritual*, which are also associated with pastoral counseling. By being identified with the care ministry of the community of faith, pastoral counselors are *under authority* (Wise [1966] 1989, 1–34). A pastoral counselor is *an authority* by virtue of her or his pastoral identification. Pastoral counselors *convey authority* by standing between the representative status conferred by a community of faith and those open to such identification (Patton 1990a). They are "Rabbi," "Pastor," "Priest," "Father," "Sister," "Therapist," "Teacher," "Pastoral Counselor," "Bearer of Religious Authority."

To be known as a representative of God can produce feelings of grandiosity. In the hidden recesses of our being we may find ourselves assuming we can be "Savior," "Superman" or "Superwoman," or "Wizard." The mantle or persona of the role makes us bigger than we are. Eventually—sometimes sooner, sometimes later—"Savior" gets crucified; "Superman" or "Superwoman" burns out; and "Wizard" is exposed as "The Wizard of Oz," a pudgy little person from Kansas. In the heat of everyday living the feeling that we can do anything, that we have *the* answers, that we know it all vanishes.

Regardless of how unworthy a person may feel or how inadequate one may be, once that person has been named "Pastor," "Priest," "Father," "Sister," "Rabbi," "Pastoral Counselor," "Religious Authority," he or she is a symbol-bearer of God. Pastoral counselors represent hope and help in the midst of hurt and hell. They are a reminder, to use the words of the psalmist, that "even the darkness is not dark to you [O, God]; the night is bright as the day, for darkness is as light to you" (Ps. 139:12)!

People look to pastoral counselors when life collapses. To use the powerful metaphor of Isaiah, the therapist becomes like "a great rock in a weary land" (Isa. 32:2). As I indicated earlier, this image of "a rock in a weary land" is a metaphor of caregiving in general and of pastoral counseling in particular. As a rock, a source of stability, we stop the shifting sands of life's desert and provide shade from the scorching of the day's heat, thereby allowing moisture to accumulate and new life to take root.

In the language of ritual studies, symbol-bearers are "liminal figures." They stand on the threshold between the inner life of the spirit and the outer world of society. The threshold phenomenon appears unexpectedly—in disruption, in pain, in chaos, in helplessness, in hopelessness. Life has been flowing smoothly, then suddenly everything is topsy-turvy. From a sense that life is in place, people wake up in a nightmare (at worst) or in an uncomfortable dream (at best). "Betwixt and between" (Turner 1969, 95)—an unclear place, an ambiguous state, neither all lost nor all found, a threshold place in which hearts cry out for help and hope and God—that is the symbolic role dynamic of *pastoral* counseling.

Mana figures carry the possibility of help and hope and God: new life, new reality, new being. To be in the presence of a mana person reminds people that the meaning of life involves more than the means of living. There are resources other than logical, conscious, deliberate huffing and puffing. To be in the presence of a mana person opens people to the promise of life itself—to God within.

Pastoral counselors to whom people look to be mana persons experience themselves being invested with power beyond their own. To be a mana person is to know there is more to know than people can ever master. To be a mana person is to find unsuspected promise in the least promising situations. To be a mana person is to open oneself to the mysterious receptive mode of consciousness—"the illumination of our life that comes from the symbols, metaphors, myths, and stories of our heritage that are the powerful media of God's word to us" (Holmes 1978, 95).

MANA MEN AND MANA WOMEN

Cross-cultural evidence demonstrates consistent differences in ways women and men experience religious symbols and appropriate them (Bynum et al. 1986; Bynum 1987). Different genes mean different realities (Ashbrook 1992).

As a group, female brains tend to develop and function bilaterally. Each hemisphere contributes in a similar way to information processing. There is an interweaving of the experiential and the cognitive. Further, as a group, male brains tend to develop and function asymmetrically. Each hemisphere contributes something unique to information processing. A gap exists between the experiential and the conceptual.

I have speculated (Ashbrook 1992b) that these genetic predispositions influence the ways females and males engage the world. Those differences would also be present in the ways men and women bear the symbolic role of representative of God. We can speak of "mana men" and "mana women," and the gender-sex distinction makes a difference in the process of pastoral counseling.

Women tend to perceive life in terms of connections and continuity. I believe this results in a more weblike sense of relatedness and a more experiential quality to reality (cf. Harding and Hintikka 1983; Belenky et al. 1986; Jordon 1991). The paradigm of reality is a pattern of connectedness. Men tend to perceive life in terms of polarities and otherness. I believe this is found in a more dichotomized sense of relatedness and a more objective relation to reality (cf. Harrington 1987; Smith 1989). The paradigm of reality is an association of parts and pieces.

Because who we are is influenced by genes and shaped by culture, women and men differ in how they symbolize their relation with God. Inevitably, therefore, the sexes differ in how they bear the being of God for themselves and others in a representative role such as pastoral counselor or pastor (see Corrington

1990). Both those who reject the ordination of women and those who espouse it recognize differences in the ways men and women serve as "priest" and "rabbi" and "minister." But in the final analysis, neither male nor female is the single defining attribute of the healer. Only the unique presence of each individual healer matters.

Embodied Counseling. However, all experience is "gendered," which means that all experience is shaped by the predispositions of our sex and the reinforcements of society. None of us is neuter, even a eunuch. We all are subject to the impact of society's expectations and value orientations.

In the mid-1970s, my former colleague, chaplain supervisor, and psychotherapist Maxine Glaz clarified for me different issues for women and men in ministry. She was dealing specifically with learning tasks in clinical pastoral education as well as in preparation for ministry. Women need to work on the issue of authority; men need to work on the issue of authenticity. Women struggle to exercise the power that legitimizes the responsibility they carry; men struggle to come down from an idealized pedestal and relate in mutual ways. Women need help in being assertive; men need help in being sensitive.

My experiences with family, friends, and colleagues, and my growing acquaintance with the exploding literature in women's studies have expanded and deepened that insight. As Glaz puts it, sexism is "an ugly reality" (Glaz and Moessner 1991, 52; see also Lerner 1986; Ruether 1983). Unwittingly, I have perpetuated and benefited from a male-dominant worldview. I can remember my uncomfortableness in the early 1960s with a woman student's request that I participate in her ordination. Thirty years later I wonder how I could have been so blind. I am increasingly mindful of my own active—and I would say too often "invasive" and "intrusive" (see Glaz and Moessner 1991, 23–25)—behaviors in professional as well as personal relationships. Today I wonder how can I be so insensitive. Fortunately, others help me in my struggle to be a more fully functioning human being and to be a more genuine empowerer of both women and men.

Truthfully, male and female need each other. The image and likeness of God can only be borne by the species as a whole—"male and female [God] created *them*" (Gen. 1:26–27, italics added; Bird 1981, 1987, 1988). Full knowing requires that we take account of the experience of both women and men, the experience of all peoples in all places. The world as a whole wrestles with the implications of this. For pastoral counselors, in particular, the richness of differences requires special attention.

Differences arising from the selective reinforcements of gender and from genetic predispositions inevitably must have implications for pastoral counseling. Pastoral counseling is not an abstract process. It is engaged in by individual men and women, with particular men, women, and children, who come with particular expressions of pain. Pastoral counseling is not a gender-free activity between disembodied souls. We are bodied beings, and our bodies are bearers of behavior and conveyors of meaning.

Abuse of Power. I have referred to these sex and gender differences throughout the book. Here I comment about a major feature in these differences. It involves the professional male far more than the professional female. I refer to sexuality and power, respecting boundaries between the professional task and personal relationships (Peterson 1992).

Sexual harassment, sexual abuse, and sexual exploitation are everywhere—crushing the spirit of females, distorting the experience of males, devouring the health of community. We see evidence of this in our government, in our workplaces, in our armed forces, in military academies, and in the intimacy of family life. Further, the church is not exempt. In fact, some of the most subtle and shocking expressions of the abuse of power are found among mana persons, representatives of the church's ministry (Fortune 1992; Poling 1991).

Patriarchy and sexism are cultural abominations with which everyone struggles. The abuse of power and the exploitation of sexuality are of particular concern in all helping professions, including pastoral counseling. Professional ethics committees and malpractice insurance are more entangled with these issues than almost all others combined. When power and intimacy collide, women (and children) tend to be the victims and men the violators (see Poling 1991). In both its training and its practice, pastoral counseling must deal forthrightly with the exploitative presence of male power.

Stylistic Differences. Beyond the blatant abuse of sexuality lies a vast region of subtle uncertainty yet growing consciousness of the complexity of male-female relationships and realities (Donnenwirth et al. 1983; Foy 1983; Fehlman 1990; Schuler 1990; Glaz and Moessner 1991). Differences in genetic predisposition, development (Gilligan [1982] 1983; Miller [1976] 1986; Jordon et al. 1991), cognitive laterality (Gordon 1990), response to stress (Barnett et al. 1987), psychiatric disorders (Flor-Henry 1983), communication (Tannen 1990), and supervision (Foy 1983; Jewett and Haight 1983), for instance, all compel me to be cautious about a generic approach to pastoral counseling, either in training or practice.

Such differences require our awareness of the context in which they operate (Deaux and Major 1987). Instead of compartmentalizing female and male styles, it is most fruitful to understand male and female differences as a continuum, as organizational consultants Carol Pierce and Bill Page (1988) insist and researchers Joseph Hellige (1990, 74) and Harold W. Gordon (1990, 252–54, 256–58, 260–61) describe. Recognition of differences in concrete situations is first; appreciation of differences in comparative values is second. Every style has its own integrity, its own coherence, its own competence. The issue is not being "right" or "wrong," "better" or "worse"; it is what one is doing in any particular pattern of interaction and what effects that has over time.

In supervising women counselors I have become very conscious of stylistic differences. These differences seem gender-related although not sex-specific. I tend to move in on an issue faster and more directly than women colleagues, though that is also apparent when compared with some men colleagues as well. This initiating appears to be an expression of Glaz's analysis of invasive conduct on the part of males and anxiety about intrusion on the part of females (1991, 23–25). I tend to set the pace more than allow the timing to ripen.

For instance, I might ask, "What about this response?" And the woman counselor might answer, "I noted that and put it on the back burner until the time seemed right to bring it out." Or, a woman client might be crying. I would tend to say, "You're angry. You're frustrated." And the woman counselor might inquire, "What about your tears?" Again, a male client might be crying. I would tend to say, "You're hurt. You're vulnerable." And the woman counselor might observe, "You're crying." These responses are not better or worse. They are simply different. They can be mediated in facilitative or oppressive ways. What matters is the working relationship and the integrity of the interaction.

Collegiality, collaboration, and compassion are special, though not unique, qualities of women. Because of these qualities, women are making life in general and pastoral counseling in particular more humane. I am being helped in allowing more of the rhythmic processes find their adaptive way. I find myself more hospitable, more invitational, more relational.

I am not saying that either style is better than the other. It may well be that one gender of therapist is more appropriate for some clients than for others, or at least at certain stages of therapeutic exploration. Educational psychologist and psychotherapist Janet O. Foy (1983) suggests that a woman therapist can play a more important role than a male with certain women clients. Such women struggle with issues of female sexuality, rape, hysterical personality disorders, severe disturbances, being young and uncommitted, or being lesbian. The men's movement suggests a parallel value for a male therapist to play a more important role than a female therapist with male clients.

These are issues of refinement of the therapeutic relationship. They involve discernment in psychodynamic and object relations assessment. One gender of therapist may be more desirable, though not absolutely essential, for empowering one in pain.

The Power of the Physical. Physical expressions of care and intimacy are particularly powerful, both in their healing effect and in their abusive capacity. The boundary of the personal has been violated too easily and too often by men. Yet physical contact constitutes the initial language of life and the primary language of love.

I remember one moment during one of my own experiences of psychotherapy. It came at the end of a very trying session. I had voiced many hurts and much anger. As I got up to leave, I sank back on the couch and began sobbing. At that moment my intellectualizing was gone. I simply sobbed and sobbed and sobbed.

My therapist was a reserved person by temperament. He followed proper rules of therapist-client contact, especially in those days (mid-1950s) when the analyst was to be more of a blank screen on which the patient worked out his or her transference distortions. Yet at that moment he came over and put his arm around my shoulders. He simply was with me, in a way that had been uncharacteristic of him. We said nothing, for there was nothing to be said. We stayed with the aching and sobbing until they passed. And then I left.

I would have pulled myself together whether he had come near or not. I was not coming apart at the seams even though my defenses were down. My progress in therapy would have continued without that gesture on his part. Yet, in my letting go and in his holding on, I was beginning (to use Fritz Perls' dictum) to lose my "mind" and come to my senses (Perls 1969, 50). I was experiencing a shift in my internal structure from an austere isolation to an empathic bonding (cf. Kohut 1984).

The specter of abuse creates an oversexualizing of physical contact. This is especially true in the asymmetrical relationship of a strong authority figure and a vulnerable, hurting person. Perhaps it is better to err on the side of caution. Both the seeker and the helper are at risk in violating the boundary of a professional relationship (Peterson 1992). Yet the caution can muffle connecting. Cognitive psychologist and psychotherapist Paul Gilbert reflects:

> Sexual contact, especially within therapy, is a controversial issue, and rightly so. But it is sad indeed that physical contact such as holding a patient's hand may be so feared as being construed as a sexual advance that some therapists would prefer to remain impassive behind a desk. If we are at all serious in our conditioning theories, then it would be useful to investigate just how physical contact hinders or helps on certain occasions for certain patients. This may be especially pertinent for persons with shame about the physical self. Research has suggested, for example, that a librarian who touched her customers was deemed more helpful than when she did not. On the other hand, touch can also be used as a status signal. (Gilbert 1989, 126)

Except for the suspicious person, there are few absolutes about physical contact between the caregiver and the client, explicit sexual contact being the exemption. Beyond that at moments of particular emotion it may be appropriate to hold someone's hand or to share an embrace (see Ashbrook 1971, 43–63). Caution, however, must be exercised. The counselor needs to check with the client as to the meaning a physical gesture might have for the working relationship.

MANY GATES, MANY GIFTS, MANY GRACES

I have come to reverence the way different individuals function in their professional roles. Yet finally I represent the role my way, in my person, in terms of my gifts and my graces. Others, in turn, come to the therapist role in their ways, in their persons, in terms of their gifts and their graces. These "gifts and graces," as the Methodists put it, are not better or worse. They simply are different. Different gifts, different graces; one role, many approaches.

When I forget the obvious reality of different gifts and different graces, three images in the New Testament bring me back to the reality of God. Two are from the Book of Revelation. One is that there are twelve gates into the heavenly city (21:21). Twelve is a symbolic number reflecting the twelve tribes of Israel. But the spiritual point is made—each gate differs in relation to the outside yet each gate brings us into the wholeness of the community of God. Different gates suggest different gifts, yet there is only one reality, one God.

The other image of the holy city, the new Jerusalem, is a metaphor of the many-splendored reality of our humanity. There is "no temple in the city, for its temple is the Lord God . . . And the city has no need of sun or moon to shine on it, for the glory of God is its light. . . . Its gates will never be shut by day— and there will be no night there" (Rev. 21:22–25). Because God is all-in-all, there are no special places and no special roles that are more privileged than others in bearing the presence of God. Every place and every role can be a conveyor of transformation and new life.

The third image that keeps me aware that my way is not the only way, my approach not the only approach, is found in John's Gospel: "In [God's] house there are many rooms" (John 14:2 NIV). I take that to mean "room" for everyone and "room" for me, "room" for others and "room" for ourselves. The house is God's, yet the rooms are ours. None of us can live in the whole house, even if we try. Rather, we each are to live in the room that is ours. It is our room, our place, graced with our gifts and cluttered with our "junk."

Martin Luther expressed this radical particularity in theological terms: No one can live for us, no one can die for us, no one can believe for us, no one can be baptized for us. These most personal acts are ours alone. They bear the evidence of our presence as expressions of our very being. Each of us represents— bears—the image and symbol of God in his or her own way. This does not mean we are left to our own devices. Nor does it mean that we cannot learn from each other. Pastoral counseling is never completely idiosyncratic, individualistic, and isolated. Rather, the genuineness of who we are as individuals always affects the authority with which we represent the presence of God.

Epilogue

■ ■ ■ ■ ■

I have presented pastoral counseling as a remembering of what is meaningful in life, in ourselves, in God. I have used the word *soul* to gather up that task of remembering. In remembering we are renewed for the making of more meaning for the whole of creation. To mind the soul is to cultivate who we are in ways that matter to what is genuinely human in ourselves, in those who come to us in pain, and in our communities.

Symbolically, pastoral counselors are mana people. We become keepers of the inner key of remembrance. That key opens the door to the room reserved for each of us in the dwelling place of God (John 14:2). As human beings, we remember our vulnerability—the pain of being exposed, abandoned, or excluded. At the same time we remember our vitality—the excitement of being affirmed and nurtured, the excitement of being participants. When we remember who we are for ourselves and with our clients we are on the way to making meaningful what matters in the cosmos in which we find ourselves.

Only by being faithful to the eternal cycle of working (the waking state of mind), of resting (the sleeping state of mind), and of synthesizing (the dreaming state of mind), do we share with God in the creation of soul, each person's own unique soul and our shared universal soul. God has so made us to remember the Sabbath and thereby to renew our destiny.

Too much work upsets the delicate balance of soul making. That is true whether what we do is "good" or whether what happens is traumatic. The overload disrupts the psychosystem inside us and the ecosystem around us. Too little work likewise weakens the delicate balance of soul making. That is true whether what we avoid is "bad" or whether what we do is boring. The lack of stimulation impoverishes the psychosystem inside us and the ecosystem around us.

In our role as mana persons or bearers of Being, or more simply in the reality of our being persons ourselves, we pastoral counselors are to mind the soul, attend to the task of remembering who we are. In remembering, we generate the meaning that is our origin and our destiny. To mind the soul means remembering and attending to the way life is in the universe in which we find ourselves.

Appendix

FIGURES

■ ■ ■ ■ ■

FIGURE 3.1
Basic Attitudes and Behaviors

Behavior	Attitude	Action
Withdrawn, apathetic, diffident	Active Friendliness (AF)	Initiate warm contacts
Suspicious, apprehensive	Passive Friendliness (PF)	Wait for the other's response
Manipulative, complaining, demanding	Matter-of-Fact (MF)	Set limits
Out of Control	No Demand (ND)	Eliminate demands

FIGURE 3.2
Two Interpersonal Styles

	Formal Type	**Informal Type**
Identified by	Prefers formal name, e.g., Mrs., Mr., Ms.	Prefers informal name, e.g., Helen, Hank
Basic predisposition	Feeling vulnerable	Feeling deficient
Anxiety Reaction	Fight/flight	Demanding help/ giving help
Emotional clues	Antagonism/distraction	Dependent/protective
Focus on	"What" is to be done	"Who" is to do it

Attitude Approach according to stress level

Moderate stress	Passive Friendliness	Active Friendliness
Great stress	Matter-of-Fact	Kind Firmness
Out-of-Control	No Demand	

FIGURE 3.3
Revised Interpersonal Styles and Attitudes (1983)

Indicators	Reserved-Friendly	Informal	Formal
Identified by	Initial & periodic formal name/title	Informal first name	Formal name/title
Basic predisposition	Feeling reticent	Feeling deficient (shy)	Feeling vulnerable (suspicious)
Basic emotional assumption	Responsibility	Attachment	Autonomy
Bion's groups ([1959] 1974)	(Pair)	(Depend upon leader)	(Fight-flee)
Survival behavior	Hesitate	Contact	Control
Manipulation	Constrict/wait	Connive/placate	Blame/withdraw
Focus on	"Why" it is to be done	"Who" is to do it	"What" is to be done

Attitude Approach according to stress level

Moderate stress	Respectful Friendliness	Active Friendliness	Passive Friendliness
Much stress	Explained order	Kind Firmness	Matter-of-Fact

FIGURE 4.1
Basic Assumptions in Survival and Growth

	Connectedness	Attachment	Autonomy
Developmental need	Being like the other	Being protected by the other	Having one's competence validated
Emotional predisposition	Responsible	Deficient	Vulnerable
Survival via	Reticence	Contact	Control
Manipulation	Constrict/ wait	Connive/ placate	Blame/ withdraw
Sin	Acedia (minimizing self)	Concupiscence (unlimited desiring)	Hubris (unlimited self-elevation)
Clues in the counselor	Impatient and responsible	Guilty and burdened	Angry and resentful
Theological adaptation	Companionship	Dependability	Competence
Biblical models	Friends/ wounded healer	Burden bearers/ good shepherd	One's own work/ waiting father
Strategies	"Let's put our ideas together."	"What ideas do you have?"	"How might it be done?"

Attitude Approach according to stress level

	Connectedness	Attachment	Autonomy
Moderate stress	Respectful Friendliness	Active Friendliness	Passive Friendliness
Greater stress	Explained Order	Kind Firmness	Matter-of-Fact

FIGURE 5.1
Human Brain and Lobes

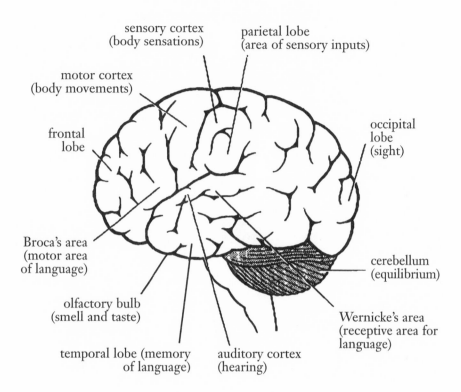

The human cortex is divided into four lobes: the frontal, parietal, temporal, and occipital, each of which is duplicated on either side of the brain. This drawing represents the left hemisphere, which in right-handed people contains regions specialized for language, including Broca's area and Wernicke's area. In addition, there are other parts of the cortex that govern specific functions, including the primary visual, auditory, sensory (tactile), and motor areas.

From: Russell, Peter. 1979. *The Brain Book.* New York: Hawthorne Books, Inc.

FIGURE 6.1
Limbic Systems

Major features of the Limbic System in the Old Mammalian Brain, a complex of curved structures appearing to nest one inside the other

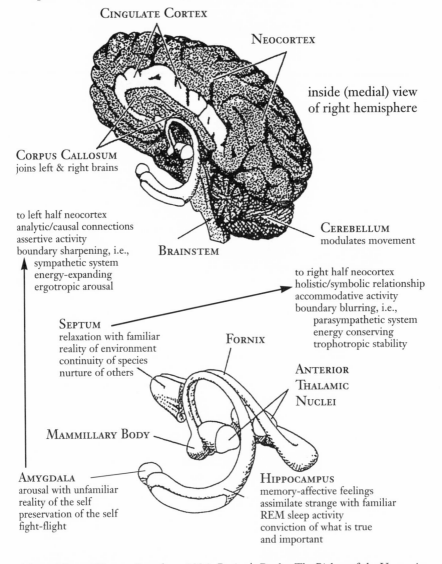

CINGULATE CORTEX

NEOCORTEX

inside (medial) view
of right hemisphere

CORPUS CALLOSUM
joins left & right brains

to left half neocortex
analytic/causal connections
assertive activity
boundary sharpening, i.e.,
   sympathetic system
   energy-expanding
   ergotropic arousal

CEREBELLUM
modulates movement

BRAINSTEM

to right half neocortex
holistic/symbolic relationship
accommodative activity
boundary blurring, i.e.,
   parasympathetic system
   energy conserving
   trophotropic stability

SEPTUM
relaxation with familiar
reality of environment
continuity of species
nurture of others

FORNIX

ANTERIOR
THALAMIC
NUCLEI

MAMMILLARY BODY

AMYGDALA
arousal with unfamiliar
reality of the self
preservation of the self
fight-flight

HIPPOCAMPUS
memory-affective feelings
assimilate strange with familiar
REM sleep activity
conviction of what is true
and important

Adapted from: Winson, Jonathan. 1986. *Brain & Psyche: The Biology of the Unconscious.* New York: Vintage Books, p. 33.

FIGURE 6.2
Uncommitted Cortex

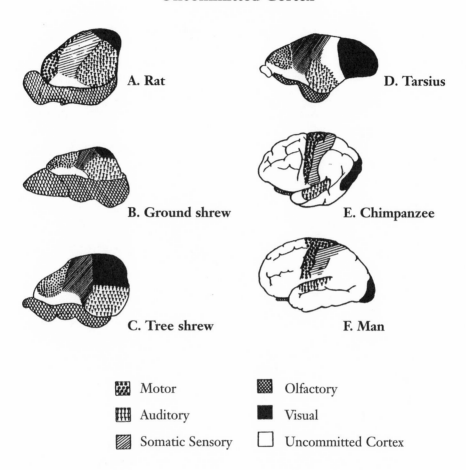

Functional diagrams of the cerebral cortex of some mammals. The blank areas suggest the approximate extent of grey matter that is not committed to motor or sensory function at birth. In man, for example, the auditory sensory-cortex has really been crowded off the external surface of the brain into the fissure of Sylvius. For this figure, I am indebted to the late Stanley Cobb.

FIGURE 6.3
Therapist Cognitive Styles Observation Checklist

Communication Style

Field Sensitive	Field Independent
____1. The therapist does more talking than the client during the session.	____1. The therapist talks less than the client during the session.
____2. The therapist personalizes communications, is self-disclosing.	____2. The therapist remains a "blank screen" for the client.
____3. The therapist uses both verbal and nonverbal modes of communication.	____3. The therapist emphasizes verbal communication.

Interpersonal Relationship Style

Field Sensitive	Field Independent
____1. The therapist is informal and establishes a close personal relationship with the client.	____1. The therapist is formal and maintains "professional" distance.
____2. The therapist focuses on the nature of the therapist-client relationship in therapy.	____2. The therapist emphasizes self-reliance and is problem-focused.

Motivational Styles

Field Sensitive	Field Independent
____1. The therapist gives social rewards to the client.	____1. The therapist emphasizes self rewards.
____2. The therapist emphasizes achievement for others as one of the goals of therapy.	____2. The therapist emphasizes achievement for self.

Therapeutic-Teaching Styles

Field Sensitive	Field Independent
____1. The therapist becomes a model for the client in teaching new behaviors, values, and perspectives.	____1. The therapist uses the discovery approach.
____2. The therapist uses direct interpretation.	____2. The therapist uses reflection, encouraging the client to arrive at his or her own interpretations.
____3. The therapist uses a deductive approach (global-to-specific) to teaching in therapy.	____3. The therapist uses an inductive (specific-to-global) approach to teaching in therapy.

From: Ramirez, Manuel, III. 1991. *Psychotherapy and Counseling with Minorities: A Cognitive Approach to Individual and Cultural Differences.* New York: Pergamon Press.

FIGURE 6.4
Cognitive Styles of the Cerebral Hemispheres

	Dominant* (Left) Brain	Nondominant (Right) Brain
General Features		
Oriented to	Concepts	Impressions
Type of thinking	Logical	Associative
Direction of attention	Narrow focus	Broad focus
Interested in	Specific & realistic	Tangible and symbolic
Takes the lead in	Rational strategy	Relational Strategy
Special Features		
Input process	Item-by-item	All-at-once
based on	Observation, i.e., detached perspective sequential & serial method	Participation, i.e., personal perspective simultaneous & parallel method
	Temporal analysis abstracts parts categorizes generalizes	Spatial synthesis attends to patterns images unifies
Output process	Step-by-step	Leaps of inference
based on	Deliberate responses slow controlled convergent a fixed structure of procedures & principles	Varied responses rapid spontaneous divergent a flexible approach of trial-and-error pragmatic
	Formal language style	Informal language style

*In most people the left hemisphere is dominant for language and related conceptual processes and the right hemisphere is not, i.e., is nondominant for these. In a small minority of the population the right hemisphere is dominant for language and so the left hemisphere is nondominant.

FIGURE 7.1
Interpersonal Maneuvers

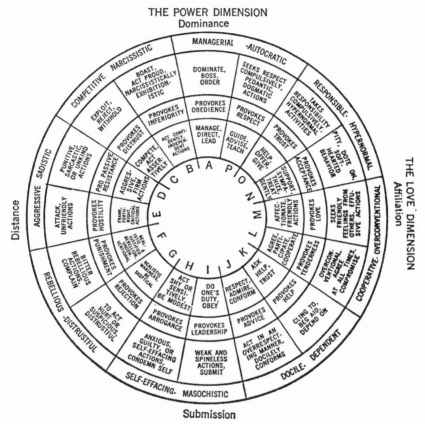

Classification of interpersonal behavior into sixteen mechanisms or reflexes. Each of the sixteen interpersonal variables is illustrated by sample behaviors. The inner circle presents illustrations of adaptive reflexes, e.g., for the variable **A, manage.** The center ring indicates the type of behavior that this interpersonal reflex tends to"pull" from the other one. Thus we see that the person who uses the reflex **A** tends to provoke others to obedience, etc. These findings involve two-way interpersonal phenomena (what the subject does and what the "Other" does back) and are therefore less reliable than the other interpersonal codes presented in this figure. The next circle illustrates extreme or rigid reflexes, e.g., dominates. The perimeter of the circle is divided into eight general categories in interpersonal diagnosis. Each category has a moderate (adaptive) and an extreme (pathological) intensity, e.g., Managerial-Autocratic.

From: Leary, Timothy. 1957. *Interpersonal Diagnosis of Personality.* New York: The Ronald Press, p. 65.

FIGURE 13.1
Stages of Sleep

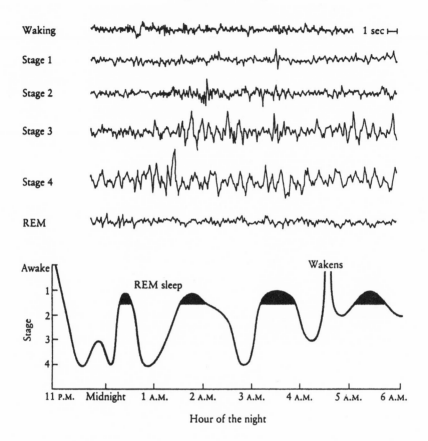

EEG patterns during REM sleep resemble those of waking EEGs (top). Sleep increases and decreases in depth, and periods of REM sleep get longer as the night progresses (above).

FIGURE 13.2
The Parasympathetic and Sympathetic Divisions of the Autonomic Nervous System

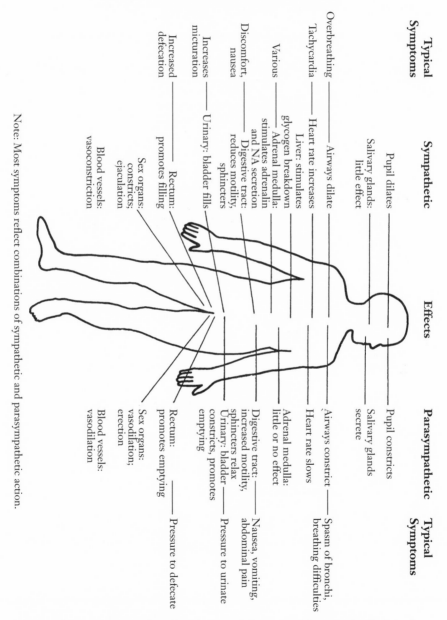

Typical Symptoms	Sympathetic Effects	Parasympathetic Effects	Typical Symptoms
Overbreathing	Pupil dilates	Pupil constricts	
	Salivary glands: little effect	Salivary glands secrete	
Tachycardia	Airways dilate	Airways constrict	Spasm of bronchi, breathing difficulties
Various	Heart rate increases	Heart rate slows	
	Liver: stimulates glycogen breakdown	Adrenal medulla: little or no effect	
Discomfort, nausea	Adrenal medulla: stimulates adrenalin and NA secretion	Digestive tract: increased motility, abdominal pain	Nausea, vomiting, abdominal pain
Increases micturition	Digestive tract: reduces motility, sphincters	Urinary: bladder constricts, promotes emptying	Pressure to urinate
Increased defecation	Urinary: bladder fills	Rectum: promotes emptying	Pressure to defecate
	Rectum: promotes filling	Sex organs: vasodilation; erection	
	Sex organs: constricts; ejaculation	Blood vessels: vasodilation	
	Blood vessels: vasoconstriction		

Note: Most symptoms reflect combinations of sympathetic and parasympathetic action.

Adapted from: Cotman and McGaugh 1980; Soloman and Davis 1983; Beck et al. 1985; thanks also to Martin Ward.

FIGURE 13.3
Levels of Brain Organization

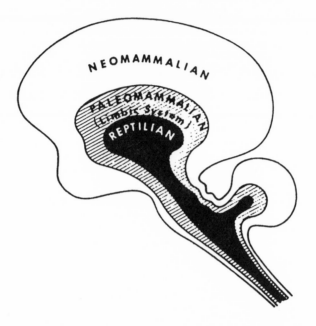

The primate forebrain. In evolution, the primate forebrain expands in hierarchic fashion along the lines of the three basic patterns that may be characterized as reptilian, paleomammalian, and neomammalian.

From: Ashbrook, James B. 1988. *The Brain and Belief: Faith in the Light of Brain Research*. Bristol, Ind.: Wyndham Hall Press.

Bibliography

■ ■ ■ ■ ■

Abbreviations
DPCC   *Dictionary of Pastoral Care and Counseling*
IDB   *The Interpreter's Dictionary of the Bible*
JPC   *The Journal of Pastoral Care*
Z*J*RS   *Zygon: Journal of Religion and Science*

References

Abba, R. 1962. "Name." In *IDB*, K–Q: 500–508.

Achterberg, Jeanne. 1985. *Imagery in Healing: Shamanism and Modern Medicine*. Boston: Shambhala/New Science Library.

_____. 1990. *Woman As Healer*. Boston: Shambhala.

Ainsworth, M. D. S. 1979. "Infant-Mother Attachment." *American Psychologist* 34:932–37.

_____. 1982. "Attachment: Retrospect and Prospect." In *The Place of Attachment in Human Behavior*, ed. Colin Murray Parkes and Joan Stevenson-Hinde, 3–30. New York: Basic Books.

_____. 1989. "Attachments Beyond Infancy." *American Psychologist* 44:704–16.

_____, M. C. Blehar, E. Waters, and S. Wall. 1978. *Patterns of Attachment: A Psychological Study of the Strange Situation*. Hillsdale, N.J.: Lawrence Erlbaum Associates.

Alter, Robert. 1981. *The Art of Biblical Narrative*. New York: Basic Books.

_____, and Frank Kermode, eds. 1987. *The Literary Guide to the Bible*. Cambridge, Mass.: The Belknap Press.

Anchin, J. C., and D. J. Kiesler, eds. 1982. *Handbook of Interpersonal Psychotherapy*. Elmsford, N.Y.: Pergamon Press.

Anderson, B. W. 1962a. "God, Names of." In *IDB*, E–J: 407–17.

———. 1962b. "Water." In *IDB*, R–Z: 806–10.

Andreasen, Nancy C. 1984. *The Broken Brain: The Biological Revolution in Psychiatry*. New York: Harper and Row.

Andreasen, Niels-Erik. 1978. *Rest and Redemption: A Study of the Biblical Sabbath*. Berrien Springs, Mich.: Andrews University Press.

Antonovsky, Aaron. 1981. *Health, Stress, and Coping*. San Francisco: Jossey-Bass.

———. 1987. *Unraveling the Mystery of Health: How People Manage Stress and Stay Well*. San Francisco: Jossey-Bass.

Arbib, Michael A., and Mary B. Hesse. 1986. *The Construction of Reality*. Cambridge: Cambridge University Press.

Arkin, Arthur M., John S. Antrobus, and Steven J. Ellman, eds. 1978. *The Mind in Sleep: Psychology and Psychophysiology*. Hillsdale, N.J.: Lawrence Erlbaum Associates.

Arndt, William, and F. Wilbur Gingrich. [1957] 1979. *A Greek-English Lexicon of the New Testament and Other Early Christian Literature*. Chicago: University of Chicago Press.

Ashbrook, James B. 1958. "The Functional Meaning of the Soul in the Christian Tradition." *JPC* 1 (Spring): 1–16.

———. 1969. "A New Day Has Taken Place: An Interpretive Case Description of the Crisis in Black-and-White." *Journal of Human Relations* 2:260–78.

———. 1970. "Counseling in a Parish Context." *Pastoral Psychology*, May, 27–38.

———. 1971. In *Human Presence-Hope: The Pastor Deals with Individual and Social Change*. Valley Forge, Pa.: Judson Press.

———. 1975. *Responding to Human Pain: For Persons Who Help*. Valley Forge, Pa.: Judson Press.

———. 1979. "The Working Brain: A New Model for Theological Exploration." *Religion in Life*, Spring, 6–16.

———. 1982. "Babel-Legion-Pentecost." *JPC* 2 (June): 118–24.

———. 1984a. "Neurotheology: The Working Brain and the Work of Theology." *ZJRS* 3 (September): 331–50.

———. 1984b. *The Human Mind and the Mind of God: Theological Promise in Brain Research*. Lanham, Md.: University Press of America.

———. 1985. "Brain, Mind and God." *The Christian Century*, March 19–26, 295–98.

———. 1986. "Quality of Life in a Home for the Elderly: A Systemic Approach." *JPC* 3 (September): 217–31.

_____, ed. 1988a. *Paul Tillich in Conversation*. Bristol, Ind.: Wyndham Hall Press.

_____. 1988b. *The Brain and Belief: Faith in the Light of Brain Research*. Bristol, Ind.: Wyndham Hall Press.

_____. 1988c. "Living With Cancer as Fantasy and Fact: First Encounter." In *Pastoral Care and Cancer*, American Cancer Society, 20–27; also in *Pastoral Psychology*, Winter, 75–84.

_____. 1989a. "The Whole Brain as the Basis for the Analogical Expression of God." *ZJRS* 1 (March): 65–81.

_____. 1989b. "The Human Brain and Human Destiny: A Pattern for Old Brain Empathy with the Emergence of Mind." *ZJRS* 3 (September): 335–56.

_____, ed. 1989c. *Faith and Ministry in Light of the Double Brain*. Bristol, Ind.: Wyndham Hall Press.

_____. 1989d. "The Complex Clarity of Pastoral Therapy: The Perspective of a Pioneer." *JPC* 4 (Winter): 363–71.

_____. 1990a. "Symbolic Dimensions of Pastoral Care Relationships." In *DPCC*, 1247–48.

_____. 1990b. "Between Broken Brains and Oppressive Beliefs: Troubled Minds." In *Religious and Ethical Factors in Psychiatric Practice*, ed. Don S. Browning, Thomas Jobe, and Ian S. Evison, 287–313. Chicago: Nelson-Hall.

_____. 1991. "Soul: Its Meaning and Its Making." *JPC* 2 (Summer): 159–68.

_____. 1992a. "Soul and Sabbath: Brain Processes and the Making of Meaning." *ZJRS* 1 (March): 31–49.

_____. 1992b. "Different Voices, Different Genes: Male and Female Created God Them." *JPC* 2 (Summer): 174–83.

_____. 1992c. "Transitional Space: The Bio-Cultural Womb of Human Development." Paper presented to the Theology and Science Section of the American Academy of Religion, San Francisco, November 1992.

_____. 1993. "From Biogenetic Structuralism to Mature Contemplation to Prophetic Consciousness." *ZJRS* 2 (June): 231–50.

_____, and Louis Charles Harvey. 1980. "Black Pastors and White Professors: A Report on Collaboration and Challenge." *Religion in Life*, Spring, 35–48.

_____, and John E. Hinkle Jr., eds. 1988. *At the Point of Need: Living Human Experience: Essays in Honor of Carroll A. Wise*. Lanham, Md.: University Press of America.

_____, and John C. Karl, 1983. "Religious Resources and Pastoral Psychotherapy: A Model for Staff Development." *Journal of Supervision and Training in Ministry*, 6:7–22.

Augsburger, David. W. 1986. *Pastoral Counseling Across Cultures.* Philadelphia: Westminster Press.

Augustine. 1873. *On The Trinity.* Vol. 7. Edited by Marcus Dods. Translated by Arthur West Hadden. Edinburgh: T. & T. Clark.

_____. 1952. *Confessions.* New York: Pocket Books.

_____. 1955. *Confessions and Enchiridion.* Edited and translated by Albert C. Outler. Philadelphia: Westminster Press.

Bailey, David H. 1992. *Alumni/AE News,* Summer. New York: Blanton-Peale Graduate Institute/The Institutes of Religion and Health.

Bakan, Paul. 1980. "Imagery, Raw and Cooked: A Hemisphere Recipe." In *Imagery: Its Many Dimensions and Applications,* ed. Joseph E. Shorr, Gail E. Sobel, Pennee Robin, and Jack A. Connella, 35–53. New York: Plenum Press.

Baldwin, James. 1961. *Nobody Knows My Name: More Notes of a Native Son.* New York: The Dial Press.

Barack, Nathan A. 1965. *A History of the Sabbath.* New York: Jonathan David.

Barclay, Craig R., and Peggy A. DeCooke. 1988. "Ordinary Everyday Memories: Some of the Things of Which Selves Are Made." In *Remembering Reconsidered: Ecological and Traditional Approaches,* ed. Ulric Neisser and Eugene Winograd, 91–125. Cambridge: Cambridge University Press.

Barnett, Rosaline C., Lois Biener, and Grace K. Baruch, eds. 1987. *Gender and Stress.* New York: The Free Press.

Barnette, H. H. 1990. "Exploitation/Oppression." In *DPCC:* 391–92.

Barrett, William. 1986. *Death of the Soul: From Descartes to the Computer.* New York: Anchor/Doubleday.

Barsalou, Lawrence W. 1988. "The Content and Organization of Autobiographical Memories." In *Remembering Reconsidered: Ecological and Traditional Approaches to the Study of Memory,* ed. Ulric Neisser and Eugene Winograd, 193–242. Cambridge: Cambridge University Press.

Basch, Michael Franz. 1988. *Understanding Psychotherapy: The Science Behind the Art.* New York: Basic Books.

Becker, Ernest. [1962] 1971. *The Birth and Death of Meaning: An Interdisciplinary Perspective on the Problem of Man.* 2nd ed. New York: The Free Press.

_____. 1973. *The Denial of Death.* Glencoe, Ill.: The Free Press.

Belenky, Mary Field, Blythe McVicker Clincky, Nancy Rule Goldberger, and Jill Mattuck Tarule. 1986. *Women's Ways of Knowing: The Development of Self, Voice, and Mind.* New York: Basic Books.

Benderly, Beryl Lieff. 1987. *The Myth of Two Minds: What Gender Means and Doesn't Mean.* New York: Doubleday.

Bennett, Lerone. 1965. *The Black Mood.* New York: Ballantine Books.

Benson, Herbert. 1975. *The Relaxation Response.* New York: William Morrow.

———. 1984. *Beyond the Relaxation Response: How to Harness the Healing Power of Your Personal Beliefs.* With William Proctor. New York: Times Books.

Bergin, A. E., and M. J. Lambert. 1978. "The Evaluation of Therapeutic Outcome." In S. L. Garfield and A. E. Bergin, eds., *Handbook of Psychotherapy and Behavior Change.* New York: Wiley.

Bergland, Richard. [1985] 1988. *The Fabric of Mind.* New York: Penguin.

Bettenson, Henry, ed. and trans. 1958. *The Early Church Fathers.* London: Oxford University Press.

Bion, Wilfred R. [1959] 1974. *Experience in Groups.* New York: Ballantine Books.

Bird, Phyllis. 1981. "'Male and Female He Created Them:' Gen. 1:27b in the Context of the Priestly Account of Creation." *Harvard Theological Review* 74:2, 129–59.

———. 1987. "Genesis 1–3 as a Source for a Contemporary Theology of Sexuality." Frederick Neumann Symposium, Princeton Theological Seminary.

———. 1995. "Sexual Differentiation and Divine Image in the Genesis Creation Texts." In *The Image of God: Gender Models in Judeo-Christian Tradition*, ed. Kari E. Børresen. Minneapolis: Fortress Press.

Black, Ira B., Joshua E. Adler, Cheryl F. Dreyfus, Wilma F. Freidman, Edmund F. LaGamma, and Arthur H. Roach. 1988. "Experience and the Biochemistry of Information Storage in the Nervous System." In *Perspectives in Memory Research*, ed. Michael S. Gazzaniga, 3–22. Cambridge: MIT Press.

Bleier, Ruth, ed. 1986. *Feminist Approaches to Science.* New York: Pergamon Press.

Bloom, Floyd E., Arlyne Lazerson, and Laura Hofstadter. 1985. *Brain, Mind, and Behavior.* New York: W. H. Freeman and Company.

Bogen, Joseph. 1973. "The Other Side of the Brain: An Appositional Mind." In *The Nature of Human Consciousness: A Book of Readings*, ed. Robert E. Ornstein, 101–25. Reprinted from the *Bulletin of the Los Angeles Neurologi-*

cal Societies 3 (July 1969): 135–62. San Francisco: W. H. Freeman and Company.

_____. 1990. "Partial Hemispheric Independence with the Neocommissures Intact." In *Brain Circuits and Functions of the Mind: Essays in Honor of Roger W. Sperry*, ed. Colwyn Trevarthen, 211–30. Cambridge: Cambridge University Press.

Boisen, Anton. 1936. *Exploration of the Inner World*. New York: Willett, Clark & Co.

_____. 1960. *Out of the Depths*. New York: Harper and Brothers.

Bollas, Christopher. 1987. *The Shadow of the Object: Psychoanalysis of the Unknown Thought*. New York: Columbia University Press.

Bonhoeffer, Dietrich. (1953) 1956. *Letters and Papers from Prison*. Edited by Eberhard Bethge and translated by Reginald H. Fuller. London: SCM Press.

Borysenko, Joan, with Larry Rothstein. 1987. *Minding the Body, Mending the Mind*. Reading, Mass.: Addison-Wesley Publishing Company.

Bowlby, John. 1969; 1973; 1980. *Attachment; Separation: Anxiety and Anger; Loss: Sadness and Depression*. New York: Basic Books.

Boyce, Richard Nelson. 1988. *The Cry to God in the Old Testament*. Atlanta, Ga.: Scholars Press (Dissertation series/Society of Biblical Literature; No. 103).

Brende, Joel Osler. 1982. "Electrodermal Responses in Post-traumatic Syndromes: A Pilot Study of Cerebral Hemisphere Functioning in Vietnam Veterans." *The Journal of Nervous and Mental Disease* 6:352–61.

_____. 1984. "The Psychophysiologic Manifestations of Dissociation: Electrodermal Responses in a Multiple Personality Patient." *Psychiatric Clinics of North America* 1 (March): 41–50.

_____. 1987. "Dissociative Disorders in Vietnam Combat Veterans." *Journal of Contemporary Psychotherapy* 2 (Summer): 77–86.

_____, and I. L. McCann. 1984. "Regressive Experiences in Vietnam Veterans: Their Relationship to War, Post-traumatic Symptoms and Recovery." *Journal of Contemporary Psychotherapy* 1 (Spring/Summer): 57–75.

_____, and Erwin Randolph Parson. 1985. *Vietnam Veterans: The Road to Recovery*. New York: Plenum Press.

Brewer, Earl D. C., ed. 1975. *Transcendence and Mystery*. New York: IDOC/North America.

Bridgman, P. W. 1959. *The Way Things Are*. Cambridge: Harvard University Press.

Brodsky, Annette M., and Rachel Hare-Mustin, eds. 1980. *Women and Psychotherapy: An Assessment of Research and Practice*. New York: The Guilford Press.

_____. 1980. "Psychotherapy and Women: Priorities for Research." In *Women and Psychotherapy: An Assessment of Research and Practice*, ed. Annette M. Brodsky and Rachel Hare-Mustin, 385–409. New York: The Guilford Press.

Browning, Don S. 1976. *The Moral Context of Pastoral Counseling*. Philadelphia: Westminster Press.

_____. 1983. *Religious Ethics and Pastoral Care*. Philadelphia: Fortress Press.

_____. 1987. *Religious Thought and the Modern Psychologies: A Critical Conversation in the Theology of Culture*. Philadelphia: Fortress Press.

_____, Thomas Jobe, and Ian S. Evison, eds. 1990. *Religious and Ethical Factors in Psychiatric Practice*. Chicago: Nelson Hall.

Buber, Martin. 1937. *I and Thou*. Translated by Ronald Gregor Smith. Edinburgh: T. & T. Clark.

Burhoe, Ralph Wendell. 1973. "The Concepts of God and Soul in a Scientific View of Human Purpose." *ZJRS* 5, 3–4 (September-December): 412–42.

_____. 1981. *Toward A Scientific Theology*. Belfast: Christian Journals Limited.

Buttrick, George A., gen. ed. 1962. *The Interpreter's Dictionary of the Bible*. 4 vols. New York: Abingdon Press.

Bynum, Caroline Walker. 1987. *Holy Feast and Holy Fast: The Religious Significance of Food to Medieval Women*. Berkeley, Calif.: University of California Press.

_____, Stevan Harrell, and Paula Richman, eds. 1986. *Gender and Religion: On the Complexity of Symbols*. Boston: Beacon Press.

Capps, Donald. 1979. *Pastoral Care: A Thematic Approach*. Philadelphia: Westminster Press.

_____. 1983. *Life Cycle Theory and Pastoral Care*. Philadelphia: Fortess Press.

_____. 1984. *Pastoral Care and Hermeneutics*. Philadelphia: Fortess Press.

_____. 1990. *Reframing: A New Method in Pastoral Care*. Philadelphia: Fortress Press.

Carkhuff, Robert R. 1969. *Helping and Human Relations*. 2 vols. Amherst, Mass.: Human Resources Development Press.

Carpenter, Malcolm B. [1943] 1976. *Human Neuroanatomy*. 7th ed. Baltimore: The Williams & Wilkins Company.

Carson, Robert C. 1969. *Interaction Concepts of Personality*. Chicago: Aldine-Atherton.

Cassirer, Ernst. 1946. *Language and Myth*. Translated by Susanne K. Langer. New York: Dover Publications.

Chodorow, Nancy. [1978] 1979. *The Reproduction of Mothering: Psychoanalysis and the Sociology of Gender*. Berkeley: University of California Press.

Chopp, Rebecca S. 1986. *The Praxis of Suffering: An Interpretation of Liberation and Political Theologies*. Maryknoll, N.Y.: Orbis Books.

Ciaccia, Cecilia, R. N. 1984. History of Dr. James B. Ashbrook's Consultation at St. Ann's Home/The Heritage, Rochester, NY: St. Ann's Home (an internal memographed report, Aug. 3).

Cirlot, J. E. [1967, 1971] 1974. *A Dictionary of Symbols*. 2nd edition. Translated by Jack Sage. New York: Philosophical Library.

Cleaver, Eldrige. 1968. *Soul on Ice*. New York: Delta Publishing Company.

Clinebell, Howard. [1966] 1984. *Basic Types of Pastoral Care and Counseling*. Rev. and enlarged. Nashville, TN: Abingdon Press.

Cobb, John. 1977. *Theology and Pastoral Care*. Philadelphia: Fortress Press.

Collins, William J. 1982. "The Pastoral Counselor's Countertransference as a Therapeutic Tool." *JPC* 2 (June): 125–35.

Colman, Arthur D., and W. Harold Bexton, eds. 1975. *Group Relations Reader: An A. K. Rice Institute Series*. Sausalito, Calif.: GREX.

————, and Marvin H. Geller, eds. 1985. *Group Relations Reader 2: An A. K. Rice Institute Series*. Washington, D.C.: A. K. Rice Institute.

Cone, James. 1970. *A Black Theology of Liberation*. Philadelphia: J. B. Lipincott.

Coren, Stanley. 1992. *The Left-Hander Syndrome: The Causes & Consequences of Left-Handedness*. New York: The Free Press.

Corrington, G. P. 1990. "Women in Pastoral Ministries, History of." In *DPCC*, 1334–36.

Courtois, Christine A. 1988. *Healing the Incest Wound: Adult Survivors in Therapy*. New York: W. W. Norton.

Couture, P. 1990. "Ritual and Pastoral Care." In *DPCC*, 1088–90.

d'Aquili, Eugene G. 1983. "The Myth-Ritual Complex: A Biogenetic Structural Analysis." *ZJRS* 3 (September): 247–69.

Davies, G. Henton. 1962. "Memorial, Memory." In *IDB*, K–Q: 344–46.

Davies, W. D. 1962. "Law in the NT." In *IDB*, K–Q: 95–102.

Davis, Madeleine, and David Wallbridge. 1981. *Boundary & Space: An Introduction to the Work of D. W. Winnicott*. New York: Brunner/Mazel Publishers.

Dawson, John L. M. Binnie. 1977. "An Anthropological Perspective on the Evolution and Lateralization of the Brain." In *Evolution and Lateralization of the Brain*, ed. Stuart J. Dimond and David A. Blizard, 424–47. New York: Annals of The New York Academy of Sciences, vol. 299.

Deaux, Kay, and Brenda Major. 1987. "Putting Gender into Context: An Interactive Model of Gender-Related Behavior," *Psychological Review* 3:39–89.

Dement, William D. 1979. "The Relevance of Sleep Pathologies to the Function of Sleep." In *The Functions of Sleep*, ed. Rene Drucker-Colin, Mario Shkurovich, and M. B. Sterman, 273–93. New York: Academic Press.

Diamond, Adele. 1991. "Frontal Lobe Involvement in Cognitive Changes During the First Year of Life." In *Brain Maturation and Cognitive Development: Comparative and Cross-Cultural Perspectives*, ed. Kathleen R. Gibson and Anne C. Petersen, 127–80. New York: Aldine DeGruyter.

Diamond, Marian Cleeves. 1984. "Age, Sex, and Environmental Influences." In *Cerebral Dominance: The Biological Foundations*, ed. Norman Geschwind and Albert M. Galabura, 134–46. Cambridge, Mass.: Harvard University Press.

———, 1988. *Enriching Heredity: The Impact of the Environment on the Anatomy of the Brain*. New York: Free Press/A Division of Macmillan, Inc.

Donnenwirth, Richard A., Georgann Hilbert, and Barbara Sheehan. 1983. "CPE Training Module on Gender, Sexuality and Collegiality." *Journal of Supervision and Training* 6:141–52.

Dourley, John P. 1975. *Paul Tillich and Bonaventure: An Evaluation of Paul Tillich's Claim to Stand in the Augustinian-Franciscan Tradition*. Leiden: E. J. Brill.

Downing, Nancy E., and Kristin L. Rousch. 1985. "From Passive-Acceptance to Active Commitment: A Model of Feminist Identity Development for Women." *The Counseling Psychologist* 4 (October): 695–709.

Drucker-Colin, Rene, Mario Shkurovich, and M. B. Sterman, eds. 1979. *The Functions of Sleep*. New York: Academic Press.

DuBois, W. E. Burghardt. [1953, 1961] 1968. *The Souls of Black Folk: Essays and Sketches*. New York: Fawcett Publishers.

Eccles, John C. 1983. Foreword. In *Neurobiology of the Hippocampus*, ed. W. Seifert, xiii–xvi. London: Academic Press.

———. 1989. *Evolution of the Brain: Creation of the Self*. London and New York: Routledge.

Edwards, Tilden. 1982. *Sabbath Time: Understanding and Practice for Contemporary Christians*. New York: Seabury Press.

Egan, Gerald. 1982. *The Skilled Helper.* 2nd ed. Monterey, Calif.: Brooks/Cole.

Eigen, Michael. 1991. "Winnicott's Area of Freedom: The Uncompromisable." In *Liminality and Transitional Phenomena*, ed. Nathan Schwartz-Salant and Murray Stein, 67–88. Wilmette Ill.: Chiron Publications.

Eliade, Mircea. 1959a. *The Sacred and the Profane.* Translated by Willard R. Trask. New York: Harcourt Brace Jovanovich.

_____. 1959b. *Cosmos and History: The Myth of the Eternal Return.* Translated by Willard R. Trask. New York: Harper and Row.

_____. [1951] 1964. *Shamanism: Archaic Techniques of Ecstasy.* Revised from original French version. New York: Pantheon Books, Bollingen Foundation.

_____, gen. ed. 1987. *The Encyclopedia of Religion.* New York: Macmillan.

Ellen, C. 1990. "Sexism." In *DPCC*, 1143–45.

Ellison, Ralph. 1952. *The Invisible Man.* New York: Random House.

Erikson, Eric. 1968. *Identity: Youth and Crisis.* New York: W. W. Norton.

Fairbairn, W. R. D. 1952. *An Object-Relations Theory of the Personality.* New York: Basic Books.

Fairweather, Eugene R., ed. and trans. 1970. *A Scholastic Miscellany: Anselm to Ockham.* The Library of Christian Classics, Vol. 10 (Westminster Press). New York: Macmillan.

Fehlman, F. Y. 1990. "Sexuality, Biological and Psychosocial Theory of." In *DPCC*, 1151–54.

Fiss, Harry. 1979. "Current Dream Research: A Psychobiological Perspective." In *Handbook of Dreams: Research, Theories and Applications*, ed. Benjamin B. Wolman, 20–75. New York: Van Nostrand Reinhold Company.

Flor-Henry, Pierre. 1983. *Cerebral Bases of Psychopathology.* Boston, Mass.: John Wright-PSE, Inc.

Folsom, James C. 1965. "Treatment Team, Tuscaloosa Veterans Administration Hospital, Attitude Therapy and the Team Approach." *Mental Hospitals*, November, 307–20.

_____. 1968. "Reality Orientation for the Elderly Mental Patient." *Journal of Geriatric Psychiatry* Vol. 1 (Spring): 291–307.

Fortune, Marie. 1992. "How the Church Should Imitate the Navy." *The Christian Century*, August 26–September 2, 756–66.

Fowler, James W. 1987. *Faith Development and Pastoral Care*. Philadelphia: Fortress Press.

Fox, Robin. 1986. "The Passionate Mind: Brain, Dreams, Memory, and Social Categories." *ZJRS* 21 (March): 31–46.

Foy, Janet O. 1983. "Women in Pastoral Counseling: The Clients, the Therapists and the Supervisors." *Journal of Supervision and Training in Ministry* 6:175–86.

Frackre, Gabriel. 1978. *The Christian Story*. Grand Rapids: Wm. B. Eerdmans Publishing Company.

Frank, Jerome D. 1973. *Persuasion and Healing: A Comparative Study of Psychotherapy*, rev. ed. Baltimore: Johns Hopkins University Press.

Frankl, Victor E. 1978. *The Unheard Cry for Meaning: Psychotherapy and Humanism*. New York: Simon and Schuster.

Freedman, D. N. 1962. "Pentateuch." In *IDB*, K–Q: 727.

Freire, Paulo. 1970. *Pedagogy of the Oppressed*. New York: Herder & Herder.

Freud, Sigmund. [1923] 1962. *The Ego and the Id*. Translated by Joan Riviere. Revised and newly edited by James Strachey. New York: W. W. Norton.

_____. [1937] 1964. *Analysis Terminable and Interminable*. Standard ed., 23:7–137. London: Hogarth Press.

Friedman, Edwin H. 1985. *Generation to Generation: Family Process in Church and Synagogue*. New York: The Guilford Press.

Gallup Organization, The. 1992. Research: The Samaritan Institute/The American Association of Pastoral Counselors. January. Denver, Colo./Fairfax, Va.

Gardner, Howard. 1985. *The Mind's New Science: A History of the Cognitive Revolution*. New York: Basic Books.

Gawain, S. 1982. *Creative Visualization*. New York: Bantam Books.

Gazzaniga, Michael S. 1985. *The Social Brain: Discovering the Networks of the Mind*. New York: Basic Books.

_____. 1988a. *Mind Matters: How Mind and Brain Interact to Create Our Conscious Lives*. Boston: Houghton Mifflin.

_____, ed. 1988b. *Perspectives in Memory Research*. Cambridge, Mass.: A Bradford Book/The MIT Press.

Gendlin, Eugene T. 1962. *Experiencing and the Creation of Meaning.* New York: Macmillan.

_____. 1978. *Focusing.* New York: Everest House.

_____. 1980. "Imagery Is More Powerful with Focusing: Theory and Practice." In *Imagery: Its Many Dimensions and Applications,* ed. Joseph E. Shorr, Gail E. Sobel, Pennee Robin, and Jack A. Connella, 65–73. New York: Plenum Press.

Gerkin, Charles V. 1984. *The Living Human Document: Re-Visioning Pastoral Counseling in a Hermeneutical Mode.* Nashville: Abingdon Press.

_____. 1986. *Widening the Horizons: Pastoral Responses to a Fragmented Society.* Philadelphia: Westminster Press.

_____. 1990a. "Crisis Ministry." In *DPCC,* 246–48.

_____. 1990b. "Interpretation and Hermeneutics, Pastoral." In *DPCC,* 591–93.

Geschwind, Norman. 1972. "Language and the Brain." *Scientific American,* April, 76–83.

_____, and Albert M. Galaburda, eds. 1984. *Cerebral Dominance: The Biological Foundations.* Cambridge, Mass.: Harvard University Press.

Gibson, Kathleen, and Anne C. Petersen, eds. 1991. *Maturation and Cognitive Development: Comparative and Cross-Cultural Perspectives.* New York: Aldine De Gruyter.

Gilbert, Lucia Albino. 1980. "Feminist Therapy." In *Women and Psychotherapy: An Assessment of Research Practice,* ed. Annette M. Brodsky and Rachel Hare-Mustin, 245–65. New York: The Guilford Press.

Gilbert, Paul. 1989. *Human Nature and Suffering.* Hillsdale, N.J.: Lawrence Erlbaum Associates.

Gilligan, Carol. [1982] 1983. *In a Different Voice: Psychological Theory and Women's Development.* Cambridge, Mass.: Harvard University Press.

_____, Janie Victoria Ward, Jill McLean Taylor, with Betty Bardige. 1988. *Mapping the Moral Domain: A Contribution of Women's Thinking to Psychological Theory and Education.* Cambridge, Mass.: Center for the Study of Gender, Education and Human Development. Harvard University Graduate School of Education.

Glaz, Maxine, and Joan Moessner. 1991. *Women in Travail and Transition.* Philadelphia: Fortress Press.

Gold, Paul E., and James L. McGaugh. 1984. "Endogenous Processes in Memory Consolidation." In *Memory Consolidation: Psychology of Cognition,* ed. Herbert Weingartner and Elizabeth S. Parker, 65–83. Hillsdale, N.J.: Lawrence Erlbaum Associates.

Goldberg, Michael. 1981 and 1982. *Theology and Narrative: A Critical Introduction*. Nashville: Abingdon Press.

Goldman, Ari. 1991. *The Search for God at Harvard*. New York: Times Books/Random House.

Gooden, W. E. 1990. "Soul (Black Church)." In *DPCC*, 1203.

Gordon, Harold W. 1990. "The Neurobiological Basis of Hemisphericity." In *Brain Circuits and Functions of the Mind: Essays in Honor of Roger W. Sperry*, ed. Colwyn Trevarthen, 249–65. Cambridge: Cambridge University Press.

Graber, Julia A., and Anne C. Petersen. 1991. "Cognitive Changes at Adolescence: Biological Perspectives." In *Brain Maturation and Cognitive Development: Comparative and Cross Cultural Perspectives*, ed. Kathleen R. Gibson and Anne C. Petersen, 253–79. New York: Aldine De Gruyter.

Graham, L. K. 1990. "Touching/Physical Support." In *DPCC*, 1279.

Greenberg, Jay R., and Stepehen A. Mitchell. 1983. *Object Relations in Psychoanalytic Theory*. Cambridge, Mass.: Harvard University Press.

Grier, William H., and Price M. Cobbs, 1968. *Black Rage*. New York: Basic Books.

Grinberg, Leon, Dario Sor, and Elizabeth Tabak de Bianchedi. 1977. *Introduction to the Work of Bion: Groups, Knowledge, Psychosis, Thought, Transformations, Psychoanalytic Practice*. Translated from the Spanish by Alberto Hahn. New York: Jason Aronson.

Grobel, K. 1962. "Gospels." In *IDB*, E–J: 449.

Grolnick, Simon A. 1990. *The Work and Play of Winnicott*. Northvale, N.J.: Jason Aronson.

Groome, Thomas H. 1980. *Christian Education: Sharing Our Story and Vision*. San Francisco: Harper and Row.

Gurman, Alan S., and David P. Kniskern, eds. 1981. *Handbook of Family Therapy*. New York: Brunner/Mazel.

Gustafson, James Paul. 1986. *The Complex Secret of Brief Psychotherapy*. New York: W. W. Norton & Company.

Hackney, R., A. Ivey, and E. Oetting. 1970. "Attending, Island, and Hiatus Behavior: A Process Conception of Counselor and Client Interaction." *Journal of Counseling Psychology* 17:342–46.

Hampden-Turner, Charles. 1981. *Maps of the Mind: Charts and Concepts of the Mind and Its Labyrinths*. New York: Collier Books/Macmillan.

Hannah, Barbara. 1981. *Encounters with the Soul: Active Imagination as Developed by C. G. Jung*. Santa Monica, Calif.: Sigo Press.

Harding, Sandra, and Merrill Hintikka, eds. 1983. *Discovering Reality: Feminist Perspectives on Epistemology, Metaphysics, Methodology, and Philosophy of Science*. London: D. Reidel Publishing Company.

Harrelson, W. J. 1962. "Law in the O.T." In *IDB*, K–Q: 77–89.

Harrington, Anne. 1987. *Medicine, Mind, and the Double Brain: A Study in Nineteenth Century Thought*. Princeton: Princeton University Press.

Harwood, Alan, ed. 1981. *Ethnicity & Medical Care*. Cambridge: A Commonwealth Fund Book/Harvard University Press.

Hauri, Peter. 1979. "What Can Insomniacs Teach Us about the Functions of Sleep?" In *The Functions of Sleep*, ed. Rene Drucker-Colin, Mario Shkurovich, and M. B. Sterman, 251–71. New York: Academic Press.

Heilbrun, Carolyn G. 1988. *Writing a Woman's Life*. New York: W. W. Norton.

Heilman, Kenneth M. 1977. "Language and the Brain: Relationship of Localization of Language Function to the Acquisition and Loss of Various Aspects of Language." In *Education and the Brain: The 77th Yearbook of the National Society for the Study of Education*, Part 1, 143–68. Chicago: University of Chicago Press.

Hellige, Joseph B. 1990. "Hemispheric Asymmetry." In *Annual Review of Psychology*, vol. 41, ed. Mark R. Rosenzweig and Lyman W. Porter, 55–80. Palo Alto, Calif.: Annual Reviews, Inc.

Henderson, Daniel C., John D. Gartner, Joanne Marie G. Greer, and Barry K. Estadt. 1992. "Who Sees a Pastoral Counselor? An Empirical Study of Client Characteristics." *JPC* 2 (Summer): 210–17.

Heschel, Abraham Joshua. [1951] 1975. *The Sabbath: Its Meaning for Modern Man*. New York: Farrar, Straus.

Hewstone, Miles, ed. 1983. *Attribution Theory: Social and Functional Extensions*. Oxford: Basil Blackwell.

Hillman, James. 1975. *Re-Visioning Psychology*. New York: Harper and Row.

Hiltner, Seward. 1958. *Preface to Pastoral Theology*. New York: Abingdon Press.

_____. 1967. *Theological Dynamics*. Nashville: Abingdon Press.

_____, and Lowell Colston. 1961. *The Context of Pastoral Counseling*. Nashville: Abingdon Press.

Hinkle, John E., Jr. 1988. "The Living Human Experience Across Cultures." In *At the Point of Need: Living Human Experience*. Essays in Honor of Carroll A. Wise, ed. James B. Ashbrook and John E. Hinkle Jr., 185–99. Lanham, Md.: University Press of America.

_____. 1989. "Care and Culture." In *The Meaning of Pastoral Care* by Carroll A. Wise, with revisions and additions by John E. Hinkle Jr., 141–70. Bloomington, Ind.: Meyer-Stone.

_____, and Gregory A. Hinkle. 1992. "Surrendering the Self: Pastoral Counseling at the Limits of Culture and Psychotherapy." *JPC* 2 (Summer): 103–16.

Hippocrates. 1923. *Hippocrates.* With an English translation by W. H. S. Jones. Vol. 2. New York: G. P. Putnam's Sons.

Hobson, J. Allan. 1988. *The Dreaming Brain.* New York: Basic Books.

Holifield, E. Brooks. 1983. *A History of Pastoral Care in America, From Salvation to Self-Realization.* Nashville: Abingdon Press.

Holmes, Urban T., III. 1978. *The Priest in Community: Exploring the Roots of Ministry.* New York: Seabury Press.

Holstein, K. A. 1990. "Personality Development, Biological and Socializing Influence In." In *DPCC:* 899–901.

Hooper, Judith, and Dick Teresi. 1986. *The Three-Pound Universe: The Brain— From the Chemistry of the Mind to the New Frontiers of the Soul.* New York: Laurel.

Horton, Paul C., Herbert Gerwirtz, and Karole J. Kreutter, eds. 1988. *The Solace Paradigm: An Eclectic Search for Psychological Immunity.* Madison, Conn.: International Universities.

Howard, George S. 1991. "Cultural Tales: A Narrative Approach to Thinking, Cross-Cultural Psychology and Psychotherapy." *American Psychologist* 3 (March): 187–97.

Howard, K. I., D. E. Orlinsky, and J. A. Hill, 1969. "The Therapist's Feelings in the Psychotherapeutic Process." *Journal of Clinical Psychology* 25: 83–93.

Hunter, Rodney J., gen. ed. 1990a. *Dictionary of Pastoral Care and Counseling.* Nashville: Abingdon Press.

_____. 1990b. "Human Condition/Predicament." In *DPCC:* 541.

Ivy, A. 1971. *Microcounseling.* Springfield, Ill.: Thomas.

Jackson, Gordon E. 1981. *Pastoral Care and Process Theology.* Lanham, Md.: University Press of America.

_____. 1990. "Process Theology and Pastoral Care." In *DCPC:* 956–959.

Jacobs, Louis. 1987. "Shabbat." In *The Encyclopedia of Religion*, vol. 13, gen. ed. Mircea Eliade. New York: Macmillan.

Jewett, Julia, and Emily Haight. 1983. "The Emergence of Feminine Consciousness in Supervision." *Journal of Supervision and Training in Ministry* 6:164–74.

Johnson, Mark. 1987. *The Body in the Mind: The Bodily Basis of Meaning, Imagination, and Reason*. Chicago: University of Chicago Press.

Jones, Alan W. 1985. *Soul-Making: The Desert Way of Spirituality*. San Francisco: Harper and Row.

Jones, James W. 1991. *Contemporary Psychoanalysis & Religion: Transference and Transcendence*. New Haven: Yale University Press.

Jordon, Judith V., Alexandra G. Kaplan, Jean Baker Miller, Irene P. Stiver, and Janet L. Surrey. 1991. *Women's Growth in Connection: Writings from the Stone Center*. New York: The Guilford Press.

Jouvet, Michel, and Giusseppe Moruzzi. 1972. *Neurophysiology and Neurochemistry in Sleep*. Heidelberg: Springer-Verlag Berlin.

Jud, Gerald J. 1975. "Shalom Retreats: An Experience in Transcendence." In *Transcendence and Mystery*, ed. Earl D. C. Brewer, 134–49. New York: IDOC/North America.

Julian of Norwich. [1966] 1976. *Revelations of Divine Love*. Translated into Modern English and with an introduction by Clifton Walters. Baltimore: Penguin Books.

Jung, C. G. [1926] 1971. *Psychological Types*. A revision by R. F. C. Hull of the translation by H. G. Baynes. Bollingen Series 20. Vol. 6. *The Collected Works of C. G. Jung*. Princeton: Princeton University Press.

———. 1960. *The Structure and Dynamics of the Psyche*. Vol. 8. *The Collected Works of Carl G. Jung*. Translated by R. F. C. Hull. Princeton: Princeton University Press.

Karl, John C. 1989. "Conversation in Many Tongues: Pastoral Consultation." In *Faith and Ministry in Light of the Double Brain*, ed. James B. Ashbrook, 137–76. Bristol, Ind.: Wyndham Hall Press.

———, and James B. Ashbrook. 1983. "Religious Resources in Pastoral Therapy: A Model for Staff Development." *Journal of Supervision and Training in Ministry* 6:7–22.

Keen, Sam, and Anne Valley Fox. 1973. *Telling Your Story: A Guide to Who You Are and Who You Can Be*. Garden City, N.Y.: Doubleday & Company.

Kegan, Robert. 1982. *The Evolving Self: Problem and Process in Human Development*. Cambridge, Mass.: Harvard University Press.

Keith-Lucas, Alan. 1972. *Giving and Taking Help*. Chapel Hill: University of North Carolina Press, 1972.

Kelly, George A. 1955. *The Psychology of Personal Constructs*. New York: W. W. Norton.

Kierkegaard, Søren. (1944) 1957. *The Concept of Dread*. Translated with introduction and notes by Walter Lowrie. Princeton: Princeton University Press.

Kiesler, Donald J. 1988. *Therapeutic Metacommunication: Therapist Impact Disclosure as Feedback in Psychotherapy.* Palo Alto, Calif.: Consulting Psychologists Press.

Kimura, Doreen. 1985. "Male Brain, Female Brain: The Hidden Difference." *Psychology Today* 19 (November): 50–58.

Kittel, Gerhard, ed. 1964. *Theological Dictionary of the New Testament.* Grand Rapids: Wm. B. Eerdmans Publishing Company.

Klein, R., and R. Armitage. 1978. "Rhythms in Human Performance: One-and-Half-Hour Oscillations in Cognitive Style." *Science* 204:1326–28.

Kohut, Heinz. 1971. *The Analysis of the Self.* New York: International Universities Press.

———. 1977. *The Restoration of the Self.* New York: International Universities Press.

———. 1984. *How Does Analysis Cure?* Chicago: University of Chicago Press.

Kolb, Bryan, and Ian Q. Whishaw. [1980] 1985. *Fundamentals of Human Neuropsychology.* 2nd ed. New York: W. H. Freeman and Company.

Kolb, D. A. 1976. *LSI: Learning Style Inventory: Technical Manual.* Boston: McBer and Company.

———, I. M. Rubin, and J. M. McIntyre, eds. 1974. *Organizational Psychology: A Book of Readings.* 2nd ed. Englewood Cliffs, N.J.: Prentice-Hall.

———. 1979. *Organizational Psychology: An Experiential Approach.* 3rd ed. Englewood Cliffs, N.J.: Prentice-Hall.

Konner, Melvin. [1982] 1983. *The Tangled Wing: Biological Constraints on the Human Spirit.* New York: Harper Colophon Book.

———. 1991. "Universals of Behavioral Development in Relation to Brain Myelination." In *Brain Maturation and Cognitive Development: Comparative and Cross-Cultural Perspectives,* ed. Kathleen R. Gibson and Anne C. Petersen, 181–223. New York: Aldine De Gruyter.

Kripke, D. 1982. "Ultradian Rhythms in Behavior and Physiology." In *Rhythmic Aspects of Behavior,* ed. F. Brown and R. Graeber, 313–44. Hillsdale, N.J.: Lawrence Erlbaum Associates.

Kubie, J. L., and J. B. Ranch Jr. 1983. "Sensory-Behavioral Correlates in Individual Hippocampus Neurons in Three Situations: Space and Context." In *Neurobiology of the Hippocampus,* ed. W. Seifert, 433–47. London: Academic Press.

Lakoff, George. 1987. *Women, Fire, and Dangerous Things: What Categories Reveal About the Mind.* Chicago: University of Chicago Press.

_____, and Mark Johnson. 1980. *Metaphors We Live By*. Chicago: University of Chicago Press.

Lancaster, Brian. 1991. *Mind, Brain, and Human Potential: The Quest for an Understanding of Self*. Rockport, MA: Element.

Larsen, Stephen. [1976] 1988. *The Shaman's Doorway: Opening Imagination to Power and Myth*. Barrytown, N.Y.: Station Hill Press.

Laughlin, Charles D., Jr., John McManus, and Eugene G. d'Aquili. 1990. *Brain, Symbol & Experience: Toward a Neurophenomenology of Human Consciousness*. Boston: New Science Library/Shambhala.

Leary, Timothy. 1957. *Interpersonal Diagnosis of Personality*. New York: The Ronald Press Company.

LeFevre, Perry D. 1956. *The Prayers of Kierkegaard*. Chicago: University of Chicago Press.

Leff, Gordon. 1958. *Medieval Thought: St. Augustine to Ockham*. Baltimore: Penguin Books.

Lerner, Gerda. 1986. *The Creation of Patriarchy*. New York: Oxford University Press.

Levy, Jerre. 1980. "Varieties of Human Brain Organization and the Human Social System." *ZJRS* 4 (December): 351–75.

_____. 1985. "Interhemispheric Collaboration: Single-Mindedness in the Asymmetrical Brain." In *Hemisphere Function and Collaboration in the Child*, ed. Catherine T. Best, 11–29. Orlando, Fla.: Academic Press.

Lewis, C. S. 1955. *Surprised By Joy: The Shape of My Early Life*. London: G. Blers.

Libet, Benjamin G. 1985. "Unconscious Cerebral Initiative and the Role of Conscious Will in Voluntary Action." *The Behavioral and Brain Sciences*, 8:529–66.

_____, Curtis A. Gleason, Elwood W. Wright, and Dennis K. Pearl. 1983. "Time of Conscious Intention to Act in Relation to Onset of Cerebral Activity (Readiness-Potential): The Unconscious Initiation of a Freely Voluntary Act." *Brain* 106:623–42.

Lieberman, Morton A. 1972. "Behavior and Impact of Leaders." In *New Perspectives on Encounter Groups*, ed. Lawrence N. Solomon and Betty Berzon, 135-70. San Francisco: Jossey-Bass.

_____, Irvin D. Yalom, and Matthew B. Miles. 1973. *Encounter Groups: First Facts*. New York: Basic Books.

Lifton, Robert Jay. 1979. *The Broken Connection: On Death and the Continuity of Life*. New York: Simon and Schuster.

_____. 1990. "Adult Dreaming: Frontiers of Form." In *New Dimensions in Adult Development*, ed. Robert A. Nemiroff and Calvin A. Colasrusso, 419–41. New York: Basic Books.

Loder, James E. 1981. *The Transforming Moment: Understanding Convictional Experience.* San Francisco: Harper and Row.

Loftus, Elizabeth F., and John C. Yuille. 1984. "Departures from Reality in Human Perception and Memory." In *Memory Consolidation: Psychobiology of Cognition*, ed. Herbert Weingartner and Elizabeth S. Parker, 163–83. Hillsdale, N.J.: Lawrence Erlbaum Associates.

London, Perry. 1964. *The Modes and Morals of Psychotherapy.* New York: Holt, Rinehart, and Winston.

Lynch, Gary, and Michel Baudry. 1988. "Structure-Function Relationships in the Organization of Memory." In *Perspectives in Memory Research*, ed. Michael S. Gazzaniga, 23–91. Cambridge: MIT Press.

MacLean, Paul D. 1970. "The Triune Brain, Emotion, and Scientific Bias." In *The Neurosciences: Second Study Program*, editor-in-chief F. O. Schmitt, 336–49. New York: The Rockefeller University Press.

_____. 1977. "A Mind of Three Minds: Educating the Triune Brain." In *Education and the Brain: The 77th Yearbook of the National Society for the Study of Education*. Part 2, ed. Jeanne S. Chall and Allan F. Mirsky, 308–42. Chicago: University of Chicago Press.

_____. 1985. "Brain Evolution Relating to Family, Play, and the Separation Call." *Archives of General Psychiatry* 42 (April): 405–17.

_____. 1990a. *The Triune Brain in Evolution: Role in Paleocerebral Functions.* New York: Plenum Press.

_____. 1990b. "Obtaining Knowledge of the Subjective Brain ('Epistemics')." In *So Human a Brain: Knowledge and Values in the Neurosciences*, ed. Anne Harrington. Boston: Birkhauser, 1992, 57–70. Prepublication paper for An Interdisciplinary Workshop sponsored by the Dibner Religion 4 (Winter): 710–14. Institute for the History of Science and Technology, August 2–5, 1990.

Mahoney, Michael J. 1991. *Human Change Processes: The Scientific Foundation of Psychotherapy.* New York: Basic Books.

Malcolm X. 1964. *The Autobiography of Malcolm X.* New York: Grove Press.

Malony, H. Newton, John E. Hinkle, Jr., Richard A. Hunt. 1990. *Clergy Assessment and Career Development.* Nashville: Abingdon Press/General Board of Higher Education and Ministry. United Methodist Church.

Marecek, Jeanne, and Marilyn Johnson. 1980. "Gender and the Process of Therapy." In *Women and Psychotherapy: An Assessment of Research and Practice*, ed. Annette M. Brodsky and Rachel Hare-Mustin, 67–93. New York: The Guilford Press.

Maxmen, Jerold S. 1985. *The New Psychiatry*. New York: New American Library.

May, Robert. 1980. *Sex and Fantasy: Patterns of Male and Female Development*. New York: W. W. Norton.

May, Rollo. 1950. *The Meaning of Anxiety*. New York: The Ronald Press.

_____. 1951. "Psychotherapy, Religion, and the Achievement of Selfhood." In *Liberal Learning and Religion*, ed. A. N. Wilder, 296–323. New York: Harper.

Mbiti, John S. [1969] 1970. *African Religions and Philosophy*. Garden City, N.Y.: Anchor Books.

McAdams, Dan P. 1985. *Power, Intimacy, & the Life Story: Personological Inquiries into Identity*. Homewood, Ill.: The Dorsey Press.

McCarley, Robert W., and J. Allan Hobson. 1979. "The Form of Dreams and the Biology of Sleep." In *Handbook of Dreams*, ed. Benjamin B. Wolman, Montague Ullman, and Wilse B. Webb, 76–130. New York: Van Nostrand Reinhold.

McFague, Sallie. 1982. *Metaphorical Theology: Models of God in Religious Language*. Philadelphia: Fortress Press.

_____. 1987. *Models of God: Theology for an Ecological, Nuclear Age*. Philadelphia: Fortress Press.

McGlone, Jeannette. 1980. "Sex Differences in Human Brain Asymmetry: A Critical Survey." *The Behavioral and Brain Sciences* 3:215–63.

McGoldrick, Monica, John K. Pearce, and Joseph Giordano. 1982. *Ethnicity and Family Therapy*. New York: The Guilford Press.

McHolland, James, ed. 1992. *The Future of Pastoral Counseling*. Fairfax, Va.: The American Association of Pastoral Counselors.

Miles, Margaret R. 1990. "Infancy, Parenting, and Nourishment in Augustine's *Confessions*." In *The Hunger of the Heart: Reflections on the "Confessions" of Augustine*, ed. Donald Capps and James E. Dittes, 219–35. West Lafayette, Ind.: Society for the Scientific Study of Religion, Monograph Series, no. 8.

Miller, George A. 1956. "The Magical Number Seven: Plus or Minus Two. Some Limits on Our Capacity for Processing Information." *Psychological Review* 9:81–97.

_____, E. Galanter, and K. H. Pribram. 1960. *Plans and the Structure of Behavior*. New York: Holt, Rinehart and Winston.

Miller, Jean Baker. [1976] 1986. *A New Psychology of Women*. Boston: Beacon Press.

_____. 1991. "The Development of Women's Sense of Self." In Judith V. Jordon, Alexandra G. Kaplan, Jean Baker Miller, Irene P. Stiver, and Janet L. Surrey, *Women's Growth in Connection: Writings from the Stone Center*, 11–26. New York: The Guilford Press.

Mills, L. O. 1990. "Pastoral Care (History, Traditions, and Definitions)." In *DPCC*, 836–44.

Mishkin, Mortimer, and Tim Appenzeller. 1987. "The Anatomy of Memory," *Scientific American* (special report), 1–12.

Mitchell, Kenneth R., and Herbert Anderson. 1983. *All Our Losses, All Our Griefs: Resources for Pastoral Care*. Philadelphia: Westminster Press.

Mitchell, Stephen A. 1988. *Relational Concepts in Psychoanalysis: An Integration*. Cambridge, Mass.: Harvard University Press.

Moltmann, J. 1967. *Theology of Hope: On the Ground and the Implications of Christian Eschatology*. New York: Harper and Row.

_____. 1990. "Eschatology and Pastoral Care." In *DPCC*, 360–62.

Morgan, James. 1932. *The Psychological Teaching of St. Augustine*. London: Elliot Stock.

Morgenstern, J. 1962. "Sabbath." In *IDB*, R–Z: 135–41.

Morton, Nelle. 1987. *The Journey Is Home*. Boston: Beacon Press.

Natterson, Joseph. 1991. *Beyond Counter-Transference: The Therapist's Subjectivity in the Therapeutic Process*. Northvale, N.J.: Jason Aronson.

Neisser, Ulric. 1988. "What Is Ordinary Memory the Memory Of?" In *Remembering Reconsidered: Ecological and Traditional Approaches to the Study of Memory*, ed. Ulric Neisser and Eugene Winograd, 356–73. Cambridge: Cambridge University Press.

Nelson, Katherine. 1988. "The Ontogeny of Memory for Real Events." In *Remembering Reconsidered: Ecological and Traditional Approaches to the Study of Memory*, ed. Ulric Neisser and Eugene Winograd, 244–76. Cambridge: Cambridge University Press.

Nelson, William. 1987. *Ministry Formation for Effective Leadership*. Nashville: Abingdon Press.

Neuger, Christie Cozad. [1991] 1992. "Feminist Pastoral Theology and Pastoral Counseling: A Work in Process." *Journal of Pastoral Theology* 2:35–57.

Niebuhr, Reinhold. 1951. *The Nature and Destiny of Man*. Vols. 1 and 2. New York: Charles Scribner's Sons.

Nouwen, Henri. 1972. *Wounded Healer: Healing Ministry in Contemporary Society*. Garden City, N.Y.: Doubleday.

Oates, W. E. 1990. "Pastoral Care (Contemporary Methods, Perspectives, and Issues)." In *DPCC*, 832–36.

Oates, Whitney J., ed. 1948. *The Basic Writings of St. Augustine: On the Trinity.* New York: Random House.

Oglesby, William B., Jr. 1980. *Biblical Themes for Pastoral Care.* Nashville: Abingdon Press.

Olton, D. S. 1983. "Memory Functions and the Hippocampus." In *Neurobiology of the Hippocampus*, ed. W. Seifert, 335–73. London: Academic Press.

Orlinsky, David E., and Kenneth I. Howard. 1980. "Gender and Psychotherapeutic Outcome." In *Women and Psychotherapy: An Assessment of Research and Practice*, ed. Annette M. Brodsky and Rachel Hare-Mustin, 3–34. New York: The Guilford Press.

Ornstein, Robert E. [1972, 1977] 1986. *The Psychology of Consciousness.* Revised and updated. New York: Penguin Books.

Orr, Judith L. 1991. "Ministry with Working-Class Women." *JPC* 4 (Winter): 343–53.

Oswald, Roy, and Otto Kroeger. 1988. *Personality Types and Religious Leadership.* Washington, D.C.: Alban Institute.

Pannell, W. 1990. "Racism." In *DPCC*, 1035–38.

Parkes, Colin Murray, and Joan Stevenson-Hinde, eds. 1982. *The Place of Attachment in Human Behavior.* New York: Basic Books.

Pasteur, Alfred B., and Ivory T. Toldson. 1982. *Roots of Soul: The Psychology of Black Expressiveness.* Garden City, N.Y.: Anchor Press/Doubleday.

Paterson, Randolph J., and Greg Moran. 1988. "Attachment Theory, Personality Development, and Psychotherapy." *Clinical Psychology Review* 8:611–36.

Pattison, E. M. 1990. "Defense and Coping Theory." In *DPCC*, 267–69.

Patton, John. 1983. *Pastoral Counseling: A Ministry of the Church.* Nashville: Abingdon Press.

———. 1990a. "Authority Issues in Pastoral Care." In *DPCC*, 62–63.

———. 1990b. "Emergency, Psychology of Pastor in." In *DPCC*, 349–50.

———. 1990c. "Pastoral Counseling." In *DPCC*, 849–54.

———. 1990d. "Personal Story, Symbol, and Myth in Pastoral Care." In *DPCC*, 893–94.

———. 1990e. "Rage and Hostility." In *DPCC*, 1038–39.

———. 1990f. "Sexual Issues in Pastoral Care." In *DPCC*, 1148–49.

_____. and Brian H. Childs. 1988. *Christian Marriage & Family: Caring for Our Generations*. Nashville: Abingdon Press.

Pavelsky, R. L. 1990. "Crisis Intervention Theory." In *DPCC*, 245–46.

Penfield, Wilder. 1975. *The Mystery of the Mind: A Critical Study of Consciousness*. Princeton, N.J.: Princeton University Press.

Perecman, Ellen, ed. 1984. *Cognitive Processing in the Right Hemisphere*. New York: Academic Press.

Perls, Frederick S., Ralph F. Hefferline, and Paul Goodman. 1951. *Gestalt Therapy: Excitement and Growth in the Human Personality*. New York: Julian Press.

_____. 1969. *Gestalt Therapy Verbatim*. Compiled and edited by John O. Stevens. Lafayette, Calif.: Real People Press.

Peterson, Marilyn R. 1992. *At Personal Risk: Boundary Violations in Professional-Client Relationships*. New York: W. W. Norton.

Pierce, Carol, and Bill Page. 1988. *A Male/Female Continuum: Paths to Colleagueship*. Laconia, N.H.: A New Dynamics Publication.

Pierce, James David. 1986. *A Multidimensional Scaling of the Cognitive Dimensions Used by Seminary Students in Their Perception of Biblical Material*. Unpublished doctoral dissertation. Evanston, Ill.: Northwestern University. See *Faith and Ministry in Light of the Double Brain*, ed. James B. Ashbrook, 243–61. Bristol, Ind.: Wyndham Hall Press, 1988.

Pine, Fred. 1985. *Developmental Theory and Clinical Process*. New Haven: Yale University Press.

Poling, James Newton. 1991. *The Abuse of Power: A Theological Problem*. Nashville: Abingdon Press.

Popov, N., and H. Matthies. 1983. "Changes in Hippocampal Glycoproteins During Learning and Memory Processing." In *Neurobiology of the Hippocampus*, ed. W. Seifert, 473–87. London: Academic Press.

Progoff, Ira. 1975. *At a Journal Workshop: The Basic Text and Guide for Using the Intensive Journal*. New York: Dialogue House Library.

_____. 1980. *The Practice of Process Meditation: The Intensive Journey Way to Spiritual Experience*. New York: Dialogue House Library.

Pruyser, Paul W. 1976. *The Minister as Diagnostician: Personal Problems in Pastoral Perspective*. Philadelphia: Westminster Press.

Ramirez, Manuel, III. 1991. *Psychotherapy and Counseling with Minorities: A Cognitive Approach to Individual and Cultural Differences*. New York: Pergamon Press.

Ramshaw, Elaine. 1987. *Ritual and Pastoral Care*. Philadelphia: Fortress Press.

Reed, Bruce. 1978. *The Dynamics of Religion: Process and Movement in Christian Churches*. London: Darton, Longman & Todd.

Reyes-Netto, Benoni. 1985. "Hidden Agenda in Cross-Cultural Pastoral Counseling." *JPC* 4 (December): 342–48. (See also Silva-Netto.)

Rhodes, Lynn N. 1987. *Co-Creating: A Feminist Vision of Ministry*. Philadelphia: Westminster Press.

Richardson, Alan, and John Bowden, eds. 1983. *The Westminster Dictionary of Christian Theology*. Philadelphia: Westminster Press.

Ricoeur, Paul. 1967. *The Symbolism of Evil*. Translated by Emerson Buchanan. Boston: Beacon Press.

_____. 1974a. *The Conflict of Interpretations: Essays in Hermeneutics*. Evanston: Northwestern University Press.

_____. 1974b. *Interpretation Theory: Discourse and the Surplus of Meaning*. Fort Worth: Texas Christian University Press.

_____. 1980. *Essays on Biblical Interpretation*. Edited with an introduction by Lewis S. Mudge. Philadelphia: Fortress Press.

Rizzuto, Ana-Maria. 1979. *The Birth of the Living God: A Psychoanalytic Study*. Chicago: University of Chicago Press.

Roffwarg, Howard, Joseph N. Muzio, and William Dement. 1966. "Ontogenetic Development of the Human Sleep Cycle." *Science* 152:604–19.

Rogers, Carl. 1951. *Client-Centered Therapy*. Boston: Houghton Mifflin.

_____. 1961. *On Becoming a Person: A Therapist's View of Psychotherapy*. Boston: Houghton Mifflin.

Rolston, Holmes, III. 1987. *Science and Religion: A Critical Survey*. New York: Random House.

Rosch, Eleanor, and Barbara B. Lloyd, eds. 1978. *Cognition and Categorization*. Hillsdale, N.J.: Lawrence Erlbaum Associates.

Rosenstock-Huessy, Eugen. 1946. *The Christian Future or The Modern Mind Outrun*. New York: Charles Scribner's Sons.

Rossi, Ernest Lawrence. [1986] 1993. *The Psychobiology of Mind-Body Healing: New Concepts of Therapeutic Hypnosis*. Rev. and englarged. New York: W. W. Norton.

_____. 1991. *The 20-Minute Break: Using the New Science of Ultradian Rhythms*. With David Nimmons. Los Angeles: Jeremy P. Tarcher.

_____, and David B. Cheek. 1988. *Body-Mind Therapy: Methods of Ideodynamic Healing in Hypnosis*. New York: W. W. Norton.

Roth, Gilbert. 1989. *The Professional Development of a Pastoral Counselor: A Comparative Study of Two Models of Case Presentation.* Unpublished D.Min. thesis, Garrett-Evangelical Theological Seminary, Evanston, Ill.

Ruether, Rosemary Radford. 1983. *Sexisim and God-Talk: Toward a Feminist Theology.* Boston: Beacon Press.

Rumelhart, David, James L. McClelland, and the PDP Research Group. [1986] 1987. *Explorations in the Microstructure of Cognition. Computational Models of Cognition and Perception.* Vol. 1, Foundations; Vol. 2, Psychological and Biological Models. Cambridge, Mass.: MIT Press. A Bradford Book.

Russell, Letty M. 1979. *The Future of Partnership.* Philadelphia: Westminster Press.

————. 1981. *Growth in Partnership.* Philadelphia: Westminster Press.

Rylaarsdam, J. C. 1962. "Feasts and Fasts." In *IDB*, E–J: 260–64.

Sanders, James A. 1987. "The Challenge of Fundamentalism: One God and World Peace." Mimeographed lecture.

Sartre, Jean-Paul. [1946, 1948, 1949] 1956. *No Exit and Three Other Plays.* New York: Vintage Books.

Saussy, Carroll. 1991. *God Images and Self-Esteem: Empowering Women in a Patriarchal Society.* Louisville, Ky.: Westminster/John Knox Press.

Savage, John. 1987. "Story-Telling and Story-Listening." Reynoldsberg, Ohio: L.E.A.D. Consultants. A video presentation.

Schofield, William. 1964. *Psychotherapy: The Purchase of Friendship.* Englewood Cliffs, N.J.: Prentice-Hall.

Schon, Donald A. 1983. *The Reflective Practitioner: How Professionals Think in Action.* New York: Basic Books.

Schuler, C. E. 1990. "Women, Psychology of." In *DPCC*, 1331–34.

Schwarz, David G., Lissa N. Weinstein, and Arthur M. Arkin. 1978. "Qualitative Aspects of Sleep Mentation." In *The Mind in Sleep: Psychology and Psychophysiology*, ed. Arthur M. Arkin, John S. Antrobus, and Steven Ellman, 143–241. Hillsdale, N.J.: Lawrence Erlbaum Associates.

Scoville, B., and B. Milner. 1957. "Loss of Recent Memory After Bilateral Hippocampal Lesions." *Journal of Neurological Neurosurgical Psychiatry* 20:11–21.

Seifert, W., ed. 1983. *Neurobiology of the Hippocampus.* London: Academic Press.

Shah, Idries. [1966] 1972. *The Exploits of the Incomparable Mulla Nasrudin.* Drawings by Richard Williams. New York: E. P. Dutton.

————. (1964) 1971. *The Sufis.* London: Jonathan Cape.

Sherrill, Lewis J. 1951. *The Struggle of the Soul.* New York: Macmillan.

Sherrington, Charles S. 1941. *Man on His Nature.* Gifford Lectures. New York: The Macmillan Company.

Shorr, Joseph E., Gail E. Sobel, Pennee Robin, and Jack A. Connelia. 1980. *Imagery: Its Many Dimensions and Applications.* New York: Plenum Press.

Siegel, Bernie S. 1986. *Love, Medicine and Miracles.* New York: Harper and Row.

Silva-Netto, Benoni. 1992. "Pastoral Counseling in Multi-Cultural Context." *JPC* 2 (Summer): 131–39. (See also Reyes-Netto.)

Smith, Archie, Jr. 1982. *The Relational Self: An African-American Perspective.* Nashville: Abingdon Press.

Smith, Charlotte. 1989. "The Investigation of Brain Wave Symmetry: An EEG Imaging Study Based on the Wakeful Dreaming Process." Unpublished doctoral dissertation, Northwestern University, Evanston, Ill.

Smith, George Adam. 1908. *The Book of Isaiah. Vol. 1. 1–39.* New York: A. C. Armstrong and Son.

Smith, Hewstone, ed. 1983. *Attribution Theory: Social and Function Extensions.* Oxford: Basil Blackwell.

Southard, S. 1990a. "Authority, Pastoral Care." In *DPCC*, 61–62.

_____. 1990b. "Religious Language in Pastoral Care." In *DPCC*, 1068.

Spence, Donald P. 1982. *Narrative Truth and Historical Truth: Meaning and Interpretation in Psychoanalysis.* New York: W. W. Norton Company.

Sperry, Roger W. 1990. "Forebrain Commissurotomy and Conscious Awareness." In *Circuits and Function of the Mind: Essays in Honor of Roger W. Sperry,* ed. Colwyn Trevarthen, 371–88. Cambridge: Cambridge University Press.

_____. 1991. "Search for Beliefs to Live By Consistent with Science." *ZJRS* 26 (June): 237–58.

Spilka, Bernard. 1990. "God, Ideas and Images of." In *DPCC*, 465–66.

_____. R. W. Hood, Jr., and R. L. Gorsuch. 1985. *The Psychology of Religion: An Empirical Approach.* Englewood Cliffs, N.J.: Prentice-Hall.

Springer, Sally P., and Georg Deutsch. [1981, 1985] 1989. *Left Brain, Right Brain.* 3rd ed. New York: W. H. Freeman and Company.

Squire, L. R. 1983. "The Hippocampus and the Neuropsychology of Memory." In *Neurobiology of the Hippocampus,* ed. W. Seifert, 491–511. London: Academic Press.

_____. 1987. *Memory and Brain.* New York: Oxford University Press.

_____, Neal J. Cohen, and Lynn Nadel. 1984. "The Medial Temporal Region and Memory Consolidation: A New Hypothesis." In *Memory Consolidation: Psychobiology of Cognition*, ed. Herbert Weingartner and Elizabeth S. Parker, 185–210. Hillsdale, N.J.: Lawrence Erlbaum Associates.

Stern, David. 1985. *The Interpersonal World of the Infant: A View from Psychoanalysis and Developmental Psychology*. New York: Basic Books.

Stokes, Allison. 1985. *Ministry after Freud*. New York: Pilgrim.

Strunk, O., Jr., 1990. "Counseling and Psychotherapy." In *DPCC*, 236–37, 238.

Sullender, R. S. 1990. "Dependence/Independence." In *DPCC*, 273–74.

Sullivan, Harry Stack. 1953. *The Interpersonal Theory of Psychiatry*. New York: W. W. Norton.

Sunbeck, Deborah. 1991. *Infinity Walk: Preparing Your Mind to Learn*. Rochester, N.Y.: Infinity Press.

Super, Charles M. 1991. "Developmental Transitions of Cognitive Functioning in Rural Kenya and Metropolitan America." In *Brain Maturation and Cognitive Development: Comparative and Cross-Cultural Perspectives*, edited by Kathleen R. Gibson and Anne C. Petersen, 225–51. New York: Aldine De Gruyter.

Tannen, Deborah. 1990. *You Just Don't Understand: Women and Men in Conversation*. New York: William Morrow.

Tavris, Carol. 1992. *The Mismeasurement of Woman*. New York: Simon and Schuster.

Taylor, Charles W. 1991. *The Skilled Pastor: Counseling as the Practice of Theology*. Minneapolis: Fortress Press.

TenHouten, Warren D. 1985. "Cerebral-Lateralization Theory and the Sociology of Knowledge." In *The Dual Brain: Hemispheric Specialization in Humans*, ed. Eran Zaidel, 341–58. New York: The Guilford Press.

Theissen, Gerd. 1987. *Psychological Aspects of Pauline Theology*. Translated by John P. Galvin. Philadelphia: Fortress Press.

Tillich, Paul. 1947. *The Protestant Era*. Chicago: University of Chicago Press.

_____. 1948. *The Shaking of the Foundations*. New York: Charles Scribner's Sons.

_____. 1951; 1957; 1963. *Systematic Theology*. Vols. 1, 2, and 3. Chicago: University of Chicago Press.

_____. 1952. *The Courage to Be*. New Haven: Yale University Press.

_____. 1955. *The New Being*. New York: Charles Scribner's Sons.

_____. 1959. *Theology of Culture*, ed. Robert C. Kimball. New York: Oxford University Press.

Tracy, David. 1975. *Blessed Rage for Order: The New Pluralism in Theology*. Minneapolis, Minn.: The Winston Seabury Press.

_____. 1981. *The Analogical Imagination: Christian Theology and the Cultural of Pluralism*. Chicago: University of Chicago Press.

_____. 1987. *Plurality and Ambiguity: Hermeneutics, Religion, Hope*. San Francisco: Harper and Row.

Trevarthen, Colwyn. 1986. "Brain Sciences and the Human Spirit." *ZJRS* 21 (June): 161–200.

_____. 1990. "Growth and Education in the Hemispheres." In *Brain Circuits and Functions of the Mind: Essays in Honor of Roger W. Sperry*, ed. Colwyn Trevarthen, 334–63. Cambridge: Cambridge University Press.

Trible, Phyllis. [1978] 1985. *God and the Rhetoric of Sexuality*. Philadelphia: Fortress Press.

Truax, Charles B., and Robert R. Carkhuff. 1967. *Toward Effective Counseling and Psychotherapy: Training and Practice*. Chicago: Aldine-Atherton.

Turkington, Carol. 1990. "Hormones and Behavior: A Stronger Link Suggested." *APA Monitor*, January.

Turner, Victor W. 1969. *The Ritual Process: Structure and Anti-Structure*. Chicago: Aldine Press.

Tutu, Desmond M. 1979. "Black Theology/African Theology—Soul Mates or Antagonists?" In *Black Theology: A Documentary History, 1966–1979*, ed. Gayraud S. Wilmore and James H. Cone, 483–91. Maryknoll, N.Y.: Orbis Books.

Tyler, Leona, E. 1961. *The Work of the Counselor*. 2nd ed. Englewood Cliffs, N.J.: Prentice-Hall.

Vanderwolf, C. H., and L. W. S. Ledung. 1983. "Hippocampal Rhythmical Slow Activity: A Brief History and Effects of Entorhinal Lesions and Phencyclidine." In *Neurobiology of the Hippocampus*, ed. W. Seifert, 275–302. London: Academic Press.

Van Wagner, Charles A., II. 1992. *The AAPC: A History of the American Association of Pastoral Counselors (1963–1991)*. Abridged and edited by Allison Stokes. Fairfax, Va.: American Association of Pastoral Counselors.

Virshup, Evelyn, and Bernard Virshup. 1980. "Visual Imagery: The Language of the Right Brain." In *Imagery: Its Many Dimensions and Applications*, ed. Joseph E. Shorr, Gail E. Sobel, Denee Robin, and Jack A. Connella, 107–12. New York: Plenum Press.

Vogel, Gerald W. 1978. "Sleep-Onset Mentation." In *The Mind in Sleep: Psychology and Psychophysiology*, ed. Arthur M. Arkin, John S. Antrobus, Steven J. Ellman, 97–110. Hillsdale, N.J.: Lawrence Erlbaum Associates.

Waber, D. P. 1976. "Sex Differences in Cognition: A Function of Maturation Rate?" *Science*, May, 572–73.

———. 1979. "Cognitive Abilities and Sex-related Variations." In *Sex-related Differences in Cognitive Functioning: Developmental Issues*, ed. H. A. Wittig and A. C. Petersen. San Francisco: Academic Press.

Wada, John A. 1977. "Pre-Language and Fundamental Asymmetry of the Infant Brain." In *Evolution and Lateralization of the Brain*, vol. 299, ed. Stuart J. Dimon and David A. Blizard, 370–79. New York: Annals of the New York Academy of Sciences.

Walaskay, Paul W. 1977. "The Mystic Experience of the Apostle Paul: Recovery of a Model for Christian Living." In *Christianity for Pious Skeptics*, ed. James B. Ashbrook and Paul W. Walaskay, 15–88. Nashville: Abingdon Press.

Walker, James Lynwood. 1971. *Body and Soul: Gestalt Therapy and Religious Experience*. Nashville: Abingdon Press.

Warrington, E. K., and M. James. 1967. "An Experimental Investigation of Facial Recognition in Patients with Unilateral Cerebral Lesions." *Cortex* 3:317–26.

Watzlawick, P., J. H. Beavin, and D. D. Jackson. 1967. *Pragmatics of Human Communication*. New York: W. W. Norton.

Weingartner, Herbert, and Elizabeth S. Parker, eds. 1984. *Memory Consolidation: Psychobiology of Cognition*. Hillsdale, N.J.: Lawrence Erlbaum Associates.

Werntz, Debra. 1981. "Cerebral Hemisphere Activity and Autonomic Nervous Function." Unpublished doctoral dissertation, University of California, San Diego.

White, Michael, and David Epston. 1990. *Narrative Means to Therapeutic Ends*. New York: W. W. Norton.

Wiley, Christine Y. 1991. "Ministry of Empowerment: A Holistic Model of Pastoral Counseling in the African-American Community." *JPC* 4 (Winter): 355–64.

Will, James E. 1994. *The Universal God: Justice, Love, and Peace in the Global Village*. Louisville, KY: Westminister John Knox Press.

Williams, Charles. 1939. *The Descent of the Dove: A Short History of the Holy Spirit in the Church*. London: The Fontana Library.

Williams, Daniel Day. 1961. *The Minister and the Care of Souls*. New York: Harper and Brothers.

Williams, Roger John. 1967. *You Are Extraordinary*. New York: Random House.

Wilmore, Gayraud S., and James H. Cone, eds. 1980. *Black Theology: A Documentary History, 1966–1979*. Maryknoll, N.Y.: Orbis Books.

Winnicott, D. W. 1965. *The Maturational Processes and the Facilitating Environment*. New York: International Universities Press.

———. 1971. *Playing and Reality*. New York: Basic Books.

Winograd, Eugene. 1988. "Continuities Between Ecological and Laboratory Approaches to Memory." In *Remembering Reconsidered: Ecological and Traditional Approaches to the Study of Memory*, ed. Ulric Neisser and Eugene Winograd, 11–20. Cambridge: Cambridge University Press.

Winson, Jonathan. [1985] 1986. *The Brain & Psyche: The Biology of the Unconscious*. New York: Vintage Books.

———. 1990. "The Meaning of Dreams." *Scientific American*, November, 86–96.

Wise, Carroll A. [1966] 1989. *The Meaning of Pastoral Care*. With revisions and additions by John E. Hinkle, Jr. Bloomington, Ind.: Meyer, Stone, and Company.

Wolf, Ernest S. 1988. *Treating the Self: Elements of Clinical Self Psychology*. New York: The Guilford Press.

Wolman, Benjamin B., ed. 1979. *Handbook of Dreams: Research, Theories and Applications*. New York: Van Nostrand Reinhold Company.

Woodruff, C. Roy. 1992. "Director's Dialogue." *APC Newsletter* 3 (Summer): 3, 26–27.

Wright, Kenneth. 1991. *Vision and Separation: Between Mother and Baby*. Northvale, N.J.: Jason Aronson.

Young-Eisendrath, Polly, and Florence Wiedemann. 1987. *Female Authority: Empowering Women Through Psychotherapy*. New York: The Guilford Press.

Zaidel, Dahlia W. 1991. "Long-term Semantic Memory in the Two Cerebral Hemispheres." In *Brain Circuits and Functions of the Mind: Essays in Honor of Roger W. Sperry*, ed. Colwyn Trevarthen, 266–80. Cambridge: Cambridge University Press.

Index

■ ■ ■ ■ ■